Assessment Matters in Higher Education

SRHE and Open University Press Imprint
General Editor: Heather Eggins

Assessment Matters in Higher Education

Choosing and Using
Diverse Approaches

Edited by
Sally Brown and
Angela Glasner

The Society for Research into Higher Education
& Open University Press

Published by SRHE and
Open University Press
Celtic Court
22 Ballmoor
Buckingham
MK18 1XW

email: enquiries@openup.co.uk
world wide web: http://www.openup.co.uk

and 325 Chestnut Street
Philadelphia, PA 19106, USA

First published 1999

A catalogue record of this book is available from the British Library

ISBN 0 335 20242 X (pb)   0 335 20243 8 (hb)

Library of Congress Cataloging-in-Publication Data

Assessment matters in higher education: choosing and using diverse
    approaches / edited by Sally Brown and Angela Glasner.
        p.   cm.
    Includes bibliographical references and index.
    ISBN 0-335-20243-8 (hardcover). – ISBN 0-335-20242-X (pbk.)
    1. Universities and colleges–Examinations.   2. College students–
Rating of.   3. College teaching–Evaluation.   4. Education, Higher–
Evaluation.   5. Educational tests and measurements.   I. Brown,
Sally.   II. Glasner, Angela, 1947– .
LB2366.A77   1998
378.1'662–dc21
                                                                98–20742
                                                                    CIP

Typeset by Graphicraft Limited, Hong Kong
Printed in Great Britain by St Edmundsbury Press Ltd,
Bury St Edmunds, Suffolk

Contents

Preface

Assessment matters: that is the premise on which this book is based. It matters to students, the tutors who assess them, the institutions in which they are assessed, the parents, partners and carers who support them, it matters to the employers who would like to offer them jobs on graduation and to the funders and who pay for higher education and want to see the maintenance of standards and value for money.

Throughout the world, it is apparent that the subject of assessment is becoming more and more central to the whole process of higher education, as we seek to find ways to assure and enhance the quality of educational provision, with a changed focus on outcomes rather than on input. If we want to know what students have learned and how effective the learning process has been, the evidence we primarily turn to is student work and how it has been assessed. For example, both the New Zealand Qualifications Authority (NZQA) and the Quality Assurance Agency for Higher Education in the UK are demonstrating a deepening interest in identifying threshold standards and benchmarks and, in order to have the information we need to enable these processes to be achieved, we need to focus ever more closely on assessment strategies, practices and evaluation. We need to be absolutely confident about the ways in which we assess students.

This book contains four parts: in Part 1: Systems Approaches to Assessment, we explore strategies which are used institutionally to manage and change the ways in which students are assessed. In Part 2: Exploring the Effectiveness of Innovative Assessment, we look at diversified and novel approaches that enable assessment to be truly part of learning and which offer opportunities to satisfy more of the demands we make on the process than may be possible with conventional assessment. In Part 3: Assessing Practice, we concentrate on assessing what students can do, which is an area that more and more higher education practitioners are keen to undertake, not only in vocational degrees but also in those subjects where we are keen to develop transferability of intellectual attributes. Part 4: Towards Autonomous Assessment centres on ways of involving students themselves as we believe this is enormously valuable in helping students to develop the self-evaluative capacities that are essential for life-long learning.

The nature of assessment is that it is a dynamic developmental process which develops and changes as the needs arise and as understanding of the process improves. This book aims to provide a snapshot of current thinking and to look forward to future developments pragmatically and with optimism.

Sally Brown and
Angela Glasner

Notes on Contributors

Angela Brew works in the Centre for Teaching and Learning at the University of Sydney. She has worked in the area of academic development for over 20 years and has researched in the area of teaching and learning in higher education and related fields in the UK and in Australia. Her published work includes *Directions in Staff Development*, published by the Open University Press.

Sally Brown is Head of the Quality Enhancement Unit and the University of Northumbria at Newcastle. She is an experienced educational developer and consultant on matters of teaching, learning and especially assessment, and publishes widely in these areas. She was co-chair of the Staff and Educational Development Association (SEDA) and is their events coordinator.

T. Dary Erwin is Professor of Psychology and Director of the Centre for Assessment Research and Studies at James Madison University in Virginia, USA. His current projects include initiation of a doctoral programme in Assessment and Measurement and utilization of computer-based assessment.

Neil D. Fleming is a freelance education consultant after retiring in 1998 as Director, Education Centre, Lincoln University, New Zealand, where he was responsible for the staff development programme. His current research is into modal preferences for improved learning and teaching. His overseas consultancy clients are principally in the South Pacific and South East Asia.

Graham Gibbs is Co-Director of the Centre for Higher Education Practice at the Open University, UK, and Convenor of the International Consortium for Educational Development in Higher Education. He was previously Professor and Head of the Oxford Centre for Staff Development at Oxford Brookes University. He is the author of *Assessing Student Centred Courses* and other books on assessment.

Angela Glasner is Pro-Vice-Chancellor (Academic) at the University of Portsmouth. She has overall responsibility for a wide portfolio of teaching and learning agendas and for the development of the University's strategies in this area. She joined the University of Portsmouth from the Higher Education Funding Council for England (HEFCE) where she had occupied a number of posts including Regional Consultant for the East Midlands and the West Midlands, and Associate Director in the Quality Assessment Division. In the latter role, her portfolio included the development of an equal opportunities policy and its associated practices, the co-ordination of research, and the evaluation of the assessment method. Her earlier academic career spanned a number of years in universities in England and Australia, culminating as Head of the School of Social Sciences at Oxford Brookes University. Her recent research and writing includes a review of the position of women in Europe as well as a number of analyses of the operation of the quality assessment method.

Mike Heathfield is a tutor in the Community and Youth Studies team at the University College of St Martin, Lancaster. His current research interest is how professional practice can be 'captured' and measured using assessed and graded fieldwork experiences.

Shirley Jordan is Senior Lecturer in French at Oxford Brookes University. Her research into pedagogic issues concerns the application of ethnographic approaches to the period of residence abroad for language learners in higher education.

Gordon Joughin is an education consultant at the Queensland University of Technology, Brisbane, Australia and Managing Director of Training Strategies Pty Ltd. His background includes social work and adult education, academic staff development, and the strategic use of technology to support flexible learning. His current research at the Griffith Institute for Higher Education focuses on students' experience of oral assessment.

Andy Lapham is currently Head of Academic Programmes in the University Centre for Complementary Learning at Thames Valley University, London. His teaching background is in information systems and he has research interests in the use of communications and information technology to facilitate the learning process. He is currently completing a PhD in educational research at Lancaster University.

Liz McDowell is Director of Research and Evaluation and is Senior Lecturer in the Centre for Advances in Higher Education at the University of Northumbria at Newcastle, UK. She has been involved in a number of educational research and evaluation projects and also worked jointly on the Impact of Assessment project together with Sally Brown.

Phil Race is Programme Director of the University of Durham Certificate in Teaching in Higher Education and writes on issues of teaching, learning, assessment and study skills.

Garth Rhodes is Accreditation Adviser at the University of Northumbria. His primary role is centred around the strategic development and implementation of initiatives to provide an infrastructure for the delivery and integration of competence and work-based learning activities within the academic curriculum. He has worked in the field of Vocational Education and Training for over 20 years, and was first involved in the development of key skills (then core skills) programmes in the early 1980s, during his time as Training Coordinator for the Northumberland County Council's Youth and Adult Training Scheme.

Paul Roach was awarded a PhD in Geometric Modelling at the University of Wales, College of Cardiff in 1992, and is currently a lecturer in the Division of Mathematics and Computing, School of Accounting and Mathematics, at the University of Glamorgan. He is managing research projects in the application of artificial intelligence to maritime cargo transport, and an EU-funded project in the development of pedagogical tools for raising awareness of the challenges of the 'Information Society' among young Europeans.

Kay Sambell is a Research Associate in the Centre for Advances in Higher Education. She is particularly interested in student perspectives on alternative assessment.

Freda Tallantyre is Pro-Vice Chancellor of Client Services at the University of Derby. She was formerly Regional Consultant for Yorkshire and Humberside with the Higher Education Funding Council for England (HEFCE), and before that worked for 11 years at the University of Northumbria at Newcastle (UNN). Her interest and experience in the field of Key Skills was derived first from acting as Director of the Enterprise in Higher Education programme at UNN, where she subsequently developed an institution-wide framework for integrating Key Skills into the curriculum. She was a founder member of the Ability-Based Curriculum national network, and was engaged as a consultant to the HEFCE's Fund for the Development of Teaching and Learning projects, particularly to support those concerned with Key skills in the curriculum.

Ray Webster is currently a Senior Lecturer in Information Systems in the Centre for Information Management at Thames Valley University. His main areas of interest include the design of agents for information retrieval and human–computer interaction issues in education. His current work involves the effect of cognitive styles on interface design.

Gill Young is Reader in Educational Development and the Manager of the Research Unit in the Centre for Teaching and Learning at the Wolfson Institute of Health Sciences, Thames Valley University, London. She is currently researching a practice-based education project. Her main fields of interest are the assessment of theoretical and practice learning, and open and distance education. She is an Academic Coordinator for Nursing and Health programmes at the Open Learning Foundation.

Part 1

Systems Approaches to Assessment

What are the factors which enable and encourage change in assessment, and what are those which inhibit change? The four chapters in Part 1 are concerned to explore the context within which assessment operates in higher education, and each in turn argues for a critical scrutiny of current assessment practices and an awareness of the opportunities for innovation.

In Chapter 1 (Institutional Strategies for Assessment) Sally Brown argues that assessment is an integral part of learning. It is an essential element in the learning process and must not be treated as a bolt-on extra at the end of the teaching and learning process. Moreover, academic staff are in a unique position to influence this element of the higher education process by choosing to develop 'fit for purpose' assessment strategies. Sally Brown then provides us with a menu which enables effective choices to be made. We are not required to innovate, but working through the choices enables active decisions to be made to ensure that assessment is integrated with the learning process, is dynamic, and does satisfy the requirements of all the stakeholders to the educational process.

In Chapter 2 (Innovations in Student Assessment: A System-wide Perspective) Angela Glasner presents a summary of the main forms of assessment in the UK, identified by subject peers. She paints a very general picture of the form which assessment takes across a number of subject areas. While the emphasis varies in different subject areas, there is much commonality of practice, with exams and written coursework essays predominating across most subjects. Not surprisingly, reviewers seem generally to endorse the methods used by their colleagues although in a number of subject areas they are critical of over-reliance on single methods and of poor articulation between the assessment methods and the range of skills increasingly being developed in the curriculum. A number of factors are examined to account for the persistence of traditional methods of assessment and the absence of widespread innovation. There are long traditions to assessment, especially in the older, long-established universities and in the traditional subject areas, traditions often fiercely preserved by the external examiner systems and the straitjackets of assessment regulations. However, as the case study of Environmental Studies seeks to show, even in subject areas which lack a long tradition, innovation does not predominate, and there are grounds for reviewing the balance and rigour of assessment.

Dary Erwin urges action now in Chapter 3 (Assessment and Evaluation: A Systems Approach for their Utilization). The place of higher education is changing: in the UK and the USA, tuition costs raise the question of the value of university education. The mode of delivery is changing, with increasing opportunities for distance delivery methods, and increased fragmentation of long course programmes through semesterization and modularization. No longer is it sufficient to satisfy those within the system of higher education itself that assessment is robust: accountability and validity extend beyond the institution today. Dary Erwin urges colleagues collectively and systematically, in ways that reflect and emphasize the values of academia, to address the questions and concerns which are increasingly being raised about the outputs of our university system before others do so.

Graham Gibbs encourages innovation in Chapter 4 (Using Assessment Strategically to Change the Way Students Learn). He echoes Dary Erwin in seeing assessment as the most powerful lever which teachers have to influence the way students respond to courses and behave as learners. If assessment is as important and critical to students' learning as he suggests, then we cannot afford to ignore its evolution. Using case studies to illustrate his argument, Graham Gibbs suggests that a systematic and planned approach to innovation is not only possible but also to be encouraged. Assessment changes have consequences, so we should think strategically to maximize and focus the impact in ways which are intentional rather than accidental.

1

Institutional Strategies for Assessment

Sally Brown

A nightmare

'I am going to be assessed tomorrow. I know where I have got to go
and what time. I know the format of the assessment. What I don't know
is what they want. I've never had any kind of human response to anything I've done so far working on this course. I'm not sure to what
extent I am required to remember things and how much I am supposed to put it into my own words. They keep saying "You need to
demonstrate you have understood the material" but I don't know how
to do this. I don't know who to ask for help, as the tutors are all so
busy. It's not like the assignments we had at school. I've never done
anything like this before. It's making me nervous and I feel ill. I don't
know what will happen to me if I miss it. Will it matter if I don't write
very fast?'

Assessment for learning

This nightmare is a reality for many students. The ways in which universities
assess students' achievements are often a mystery to them. And it's often
not a lot better for the academics who frequently regard assessment as very
separate from the teaching and learning process, something to think about
once the curriculum has been devised and plans for delivery finalized.

Here I will argue that assessment is far more important than this and
should be an integral part of learning and therefore something institutions
tackle strategically. It must not be an optional extra, a bolt-on, an after-
thought. Instead the assessment strategies we use must be a result of conscious decisions based on informed choice. When assessment is at its best, it
can be motivating and productive for students, helping them know how well
they are doing and what else they need to do. It lets staff know how they
and their students are doing and it gives them the performance indicators

that they need. Poor assessment works in the opposite direction: at its worst, it is tedious, meaningless, gruelling and counterproductive.

It can be argued that the single most useful thing we as teachers can do to influence positively the processes of teaching and learning is to make the right choices in designing a 'fit-for-purpose' assessment strategy. As David Boud suggests: 'students can escape bad teaching: they can't avoid bad assessment' (Boud 1994).

Why might universities want to change the way we assess?

Good assessment of students' knowledge, skills and abilities is absolutely crucial to the process of learning, I would argue. Everyone concerned needs to have faith in a system, which must therefore be, and be seen to be just, even-handed, appropriate and manageable. I believe that if we get the processes and practice of assessment right, then learning of the appropriate type will ensue.

Boud again suggests:

> assessment methods and requirements probably have a greater influence on how and what students learn than any other single factor. This influence may well be of greater importance than the impact of teaching materials.
>
> (Boud 1988)

Here I argue that the conventional ways by which we choose how to assess our students are just not good enough to achieve what we want, so we need to radically review our assessment strategies to cope with changing conditions we have to face in higher education internationally.

Firstly, I will list some of the factors which might encourage a desire to change the assessment methods and media. Major changes have resulted from the introduction of modularization or unitization of curriculum delivery into institutions. This has often resulted in a whole range of problems such as unequal demands on students' time, overassessment, reduced time available for teaching, 'cantonization' of the curriculum, increased workloads, more complex assessment regulations, and so on (Brown and Saunders 1995). At the same time, increasing student numbers have made traditional forms of assessment seem less appropriate as the numbers of assignments handed in increases, the proportion of time necessary for assessing work grows and the pressure on staff to give meaningful feedback in a relatively short amount of time develops (Gibbs *et al.* 1992). We are also seeing a greater diversity of students presenting themselves in our classes, with non-traditional entrance qualifications, varied backgrounds, unequal prior knowledge and experience and different learning styles (Brown *et al.* 1994).

Alongside this, many lecturers are becoming aware that a very wide range of methods exists, many of which are underused, either due to ignorance or fear about their use. As we focus more and more on the generic skills that constitute the 'graduateness' of a graduate, many academics are coming to perceive the need for different types of assessment. These will need to be able to test a whole range of key skills and abilities which will be useful to students in their studying and in their working lives in addition to testing the traditional knowledge base we expect our graduates to possess (Brown *et al.* 1995). Assessment of these skills is an integral part of competence-based assessment programmes.

A further stimulus to improving our assessment practices is provided in the UK by the Quality Assurance Agency's guidelines on subject review in our institutions of higher education. The *Subject Review Handbook* for the English system requires those who visit subject departments to evaluate the contribution that assessment makes to student learning, based on sampling student work. Reviews also sample the quality of assessment design and feedback to students (QAAHE 1997). They are interested in sampling:

- the quality of feedback to students
- the match of methods of assessment to the intended learning outcomes
- the appropriateness to the student profile, level and mode of study
- students' understanding of assessment methods and criteria.

These appear to me to be eminently sensible guidelines and lecturers in UK universities are usually keen to satisfy such requirements. At the same time, they often have intrinsic reasons to improve assessment practices, evidenced by their desire to find innovatory approaches to promote more effective learning:

> The possibility that innovative assessment encourages students to take a deep approach to their learning and foster intrinsic interest in their studies is widely welcomed.
>
> (McDowell 1996)

We recognize also a desire to make assessment an integral part of the learning process that can actually shape the process in productive ways (Knight 1995).

What makes assessment innovatory?

It is easier to say what is not innovatory than what is, since what will seem new to an individual, a course, a discipline or an institution may well have been known and used widely in other contexts. As I am using it here, the term is used to describe methods and media that are chosen for specialized and context-specific pedagogic reasons to replace what have historically been the prime instruments of assessment (often the three-hour unseen exam):

> It is not the actual methods or tools of assessing which we believe should be changed in many cases, rather the underlying philosophy and the aims of their use and application.
>
> (Harris and Bell 1990)

Choosing and using 'fit-for-purpose' assessment

To get a system of assessment that is fit for purpose, it is helpful to ask ourselves the following (interrelated) questions:

- Why are we assessing?
- What are we assessing?
- How are we assessing?
- Who is best placed to assess?
- When should we assess?

These questions are useful in themselves, but also provide us with a helpful agenda so that we choose assessment systems that work. We therefore need to adopt an integrative approach to the answers that we get, so that we can make sense of it all. Hence I will consider here each of these crucial questions in turn.

Choosing the reasons for assessment

Elsewhere I have argued that a wide range of reasons exist why we assess students (Brown and Knight 1994), and that the choices we make in designing assessment instruments will be affected by the particular purposes on any individual occasion. To summarize, among other things we may wish to assess students in order to:

- provide feedback to students so they can learn from mistakes and build on achievements
- classify or grade student achievement
- enable students to correct errors and remedy deficiencies
- motivate students and focus their sense of achievement
- consolidate student learning
- help students to apply abstract principles to practical contexts
- estimate students' potential to progress to other levels or courses
- guide selection or option choice
- give us feedback on how effective we are being at promoting learning
- provide statistics for internal and external agencies.

Formative and summative assessment
Assessment is often described as being either formative or summative. These are often presented as opposites, whereas I see them as ends of the same continuum. However, while formative assessment is primarily characterized by being continuous, involving mainly words and with the prime purpose of helping students improve, summative assessment instead tends to be end point, largely numerical and concerned mainly with making evaluative judgements. A pre-submission critique of work in progress is a typical example of formative assessment, whereas an end-of-programme exam exemplifies summative assessment.

Inevitably, no form of assessment is purely summative or formative. For example, a summative final-year exam result gives students realistic feedback about their likelihood of getting funding for a higher degree and formative feedback usually contains language of judgement ('good', 'lacking in depth', 'untidy', 'inadequately referenced', 'exceptionally detailed', etc.).

Nevertheless, if students in the early stages of a course are needing preliminary guidance on how they are doing, a formal written exam, providing no guidance on what went right and wrong other than raw numbers, may well be counterproductive. Similarly, if the prime purpose of an assignment is to provide a mark which will determine the degree classification awarded, then formative assessment is probably less useful at this stage than a percentage mark.

Choosing what we assess

Frequently, in institutions of higher education, we assess a very limited range of students' skills, knowledge and ability. We provide in our documentation the demonstration of a demanding and worthy list of learning outcomes or objectives, many of which bear little relationship to what we actually assess in practice. We give them the same old types of activity to do again and again, testing knowledge to the cost of ability, product to the cost of process and a limited range of skills, knowledge and abilities that students and employers tell us are hopelessly restricted in the outside world, rather than what will really be useful to them. Obviously, we need to achieve a balance of these things that is appropriate to the level and context of the curriculum, but often the scales fall all too heavily on one side.

If we reward, through our marking, information recall and repetition of what has been taught (as much traditional assessment does), then this is what students will think we want and perform accordingly. If we wish to encourage the higher-level skills such as the application of theoretical knowledge to a given context, analysis and synthesis of new components of their learning and sensitive evaluation of how students themselves and their peers have achieved, then we need to look at new ways of assessment.

Good assessment is about *description*, so that tutors and students recognise what is under discussion, *evaluation*, so that value judgements can be available and meaningful to all concerned and *remediation*, so that improvements can be made in performance where there are errors and deficiencies. Traditional assessment is usually good at only the second of these, and often misses out on the kind of advice and support that students need to make the most of their studies.

For students to maximize the learning benefit they can achieve, they need to be able to look with new eyes at the work they have undertaken, to understand the reasons by which assessment decisions have been made and to look to ways of remedying defects and supplying omissions. The description phase is often the most valuable, when the assessor describes what has been presented so that judgements made can be based on concrete examples.

We need to ensure that we make it clear to students that we are not just assessing what is easy to assess. The choices we make concerning assessment should be valid in that we assess what we teach and what students learn. If the relevant skill is unicycling, we should not be asking the students to write a history of the unicycle or to describe the parts of a unicycle or indeed give instructions on how to mount a unicycle: instead we should assess them on doing it!

Choosing how we assess

Looking at courses in universities and colleges internationally, I notice that the range of ways in which students are assessed is extremely limited, with around 80 per cent of assessments being in the form of exams, essays and reports of some kind. I am making a distinction here between the approaches used for assessment and the methods, that is, the techniques and tools used for assessment. By approaches, I mean the following:

- *Self-assessment,* which involves students in the 'processes of determining what is good work in any given situation' (Boud 1995) and can help students to become more effective learners as they build up personal evaluative skills.
- *Peer assessment,* by which students are involved in assessing other students, providing feedback opportunities for their colleagues and the development of comparative evaluative facilities for themselves (Brown and Dove 1990).
- *Group-based assessment,* which helps students to develop transferable interpersonal skills and may help to save staff time (Brown *et al.* 1994).
- Approaches involving *negotiated learning programmes,* particularly through learning contracts by which students can negotiate how they progress through the stages of entry profile, needs analysis, action planning, tasks and evaluation according to their own needs and prior experience so that they can ultimately demonstrate that they have achieved the required learning outcomes.
- *Computer-based assessment,* wherein, for example, students can get rapid feedback on their keyed-in responses to your questions, with screens full of text giving them reasons why their answers were right or wrong (Brown *et al.* 1996).
- *Workplace-based assessment* by supervisors or line managers for part-timers or students on placement, who are usually best placed to assess student achievement in off-campus locations (Brown and Knight 1994).

The kinds of approach we are using will influence our choice of the methods or techniques we plan to use.

Choosing assessment methods
Methods of assessment available are too numerous to detail here but have been described elsewhere (Brown and Knight 1994; Brown *et al.* 1997). These

include memorandum reports, exhibitions, learning packages, creative productions, annotated bibliographies, reviews, live critiques, journalistic pieces, vivas, assessed seminars, memorandum reports, records of achievement, profiles, multiple-choice questions (paper or computer-based), and a whole range of methods of assessing practice that are described in Chapter 8.

Selecting the right method of assessment is really important: if we want students to read widely, we could ask them to produce annotated bibliographies or individual mind-maps exploring a topic, for example, rather than write yet another lengthy essay which may or may not have required extensive research. If we want them to demonstrate an understanding of audience, we could ask them to write journalistic pieces or a project file to be used for resource-based learning by high school students.

Assignments that can be marked in class by peers and tutors like poster displays and presentations can also be valuable. If we want them to reflect on their own practice, we could perhaps ask them to keep a log or a reflective diary. Alternatively, they could be asked to produce a critical incident account in which they unpack not only what happened in a specific context, but also the theory that underpins their interpretation of the events, as well as suggestions about how they might act on future occasions. Too often, students are often offered a very restrictive diet of assessment methods which do not enable them to demonstrate the range of their abilities. We need to ensure that we choose the most appropriate methods to test what we really want students to demonstrate.

Alternative exams
Exams can be a useful element of a mixed diet of assessment, so we do not want to throw the baby away with the bathwater. Traditional examinations in universities are often three hours' long (in some countries six or nine hours is not unknown). They often comprise only unseen questions, sometimes involving a small element of choice, with students frequently (in non-mathematical subjects) being asked to write three or more essays in continuous prose. We often tend to forget that, in addition to traditional exams, there are a variety of kinds of examination that can be chosen to supplement or substitute for them.

Different formats we can choose from include:

- Open-book exams, which reduce the reliance of students on rote learning, and test instead what students can do with the information.
- Take-away papers, which diminish the dangers of strictly time-constrained tests and allow students to produce more thoughtful and polished work.
- Case studies, where the exam questions are based on case materials provided before or during the exam, enabling synthesis, analysis and evaluation to be tested.
- Objective structured clinical examinations (OSCEs) which use a number of assessment stations within a room, with students being tested typically on ten or more different learning objectives for about ten minutes each.

- Simulations, often nowadays on computers, in which students are required to work in realistic environments to demonstrate skills and abilities.
- In-tray exercises, where students are provided with a dossier of papers to work on, with a variety of tasks being given throughout the duration of the exam, in a way that simulates real practice where unknown elements and red herrings sometimes are encountered.
- Exams that use an element of multiple-choice questions or short answers, so that students are not always trying to write essays and can demonstrate understanding of a wide range of topics.

Choosing who is best placed to assess

In higher education internationally, the person doing the assessment is usually the tutor. However, as indicated above, this may not always be the best one for the job. Below I list the agents I think are available to participate in the assessment process and some indicators which may help colleagues make appropriate choices about who to get to do what.

- *Tutors* are good at assessing work when it is imperative that their subject expertise or evaluative judgement plays a part in the assessment process. This is rarer than we often assume. Contexts where tutors are probably best include final-year dissertations, closed-book exams and higher degree theses.
- *Self-assessment* is inevitable when students are reviewing their own development and performance, when there is a reflective component, when critical incident accounts are used, and anywhere where progression and added value are discussed.
- *Peer assessment* is really helpful in providing students formative feedback, perhaps at interim submission stage or when students are undertaking tasks without marks that count. It can also be useful for summative assessment. Within this approach, *interpeer assessment*, where students assess other students, can be valuable when individuals and groups are assessing the products or performances of each other, for example, when they listen to presentations, view posters and exhibitions or read each other's handouts or reviews. *Intrapeer assessment*, where students assess other students with whom they have been working, is especially useful in group work to allow tutors access to areas they would not normally reach, particularly associated with the process of learning rather than just the outcome.
- *Employers, practice tutors and line managers* are often best placed to assess learning undertaken outside the institution of higher education and have done so for many years for placement students, day-release students and students on sandwich courses.
- *Clients* can also assess students when they have been on the receiving end of students, for example, patients in hospitals being cared for by students in training, clients of the law clinics within legal practice courses where

students offer legal advice, supervised by trained solicitors, or the recipients of support provided by trainee careers officers.

In all cases, the twin pillars that support assessment are *criteria* and *evidence*. If appropriate judgements are to be made, then the criteria by which this occurs need to be explicit, available, open to interrogation and shared. This is important to ensure intertutor reliability, just as much as it is for effective self-assessment and peer assessment. If confidence is to be maintained, then the satisfaction of criteria should not be a matter of mere assertion. The tutor needs to ask where the evidence can be found of the achievements on which a student assessing herself claims a merit for her contribution to the group project. What did she do? Where are the logs of the group meetings? The notes from the brainstorms? The project file which attributes different areas of achievement to different students? The peer evaluations that support her assertions?

We must not forget also that if any new people (students, clients, employers or others) are to assess student work, these will need practice, support, briefing, rehearsal, opportunities to ask questions, perhaps mentor support, and always a person to contact if they are worried or need advice.

Choosing when we should assess

Unsurprisingly, I would argue against the 'sudden death' approach to assessment. Indeed I am against surprises of all kinds in assessment. If a student is staggered by the mark given to a piece of work, and cannot understand how it was achieved, then we have fallen down somewhere.

Assessment needs to be incremental, since if it is all left to a single episode of assessment right at the end of a course or unit, students have no time to put right the problems and avert tragedies. Too often we assess when it is convenient for our systems rather than when it is helpful to students' further development. In some institutions it is already possible for students to indicate when they feel ready to be assessed, rather than waiting or rushing to be prepared for predetermined occasions. If we are to provide genuine flexible learning systems, then our assessments need to be more flexible too.

We need to explore every avenue to find ways that assessment can be staged and remediable, hence my suggestion that the students themselves and other people might have a role to play here.

I argue we should allow students to be assessed, a bit at a time, and be allowed to get it wrong at rehearsal stage. This is where we might consider using technology. Can we use computer-based packages to help students check how much they have learned at regular intervals? Can we use computer-generated questions as well as means of checking answers? Is it possible to incorporate multiple-choice questions (MCQs) in our assessment strategy? MCQs are much more sophisticated than many of us once believed (look at the UK Open University for examples of best practice here) and do not always have to be self-generated. Innumerable packages (admittedly of variable quality) exist and can be used 'off the peg'. At the same time, software like Questionmark is available to enable computer-based assessment to be designed readily by those without specialist programming expertise. It is also becoming increasingly possible to use optical mark scanners, which 'read' marks on preprinted forms, or optical character recognition software to take some of the drudgery out of checking results.

If we wish to avoid the nightmare described at the beginning of this chapter and choose and use assessment strategies to promote learning, then we need to think through what we are doing and to have a clear rationale for each of the decisions we make. We need to be sure that assessment for learning can do the following:

- Enable individual differences between students to be celebrated rather than be regarded as problematic, and be accommodated in ways that ensure equivalence if not identicality of experience.
- Clearly explain the purposes of the assessment to all stakeholders so that the process is open, transparent and sound.
- Provide students with meaningful and useful feedback that can help them to enhance their performance and learn at a deep level by reflecting on their performance.
- Provide institutions with the data they require for the certification of achievement.
- Enable the articulation of awards with the requirements of professional bodies.
- Be an integral part of curriculum design, so that meaningful choices are made about all five of the key factors described above.
- Involve criteria that are clear, explicit and public, so that students and staff know what constitute threshold and higher standards for achievement.
- Be of an appropriate amount to be manageable for staff and students, without stretching either group beyond the bounds of reason.
- Be demonstrably valid, reliable and consistent.

The choices we make will be instrumental in determining whether assessment is fit for our purposes, whether it becomes genuinely a part of the learning process or whether it becomes an increasingly meaningless and bureaucratic task. The challenge remains for us all in our own institutions to ensure that assessment strategies are designed to satisfy the requirements of all stakeholders, while at the same time being a truly dynamic and educational process.

References

Boud, D. (1988) *Developing Student Autonomy in Learning.* London: Kogan Page.
Boud, D. (1994) Keynote speech at SEDA Conference on Assessment, Telford, May 1994.

Brown, G., Bull, J. and Pendlebury, M. (1997) *Assessing Student Learning in Higher Education.* London: Routledge.

Brown, S. and Dove, P. (eds) (1990) *Self and peer assessment,* SEDA Paper 63. Birmingham: SEDA.

Brown, S. and Knight, P. (1994) *Assessing Learners in Higher Education.* London: Kogan Page.

Brown, S. and Saunders, D. (1995) 'The challenges of modularisation'. *Innovations in Education and Training,* 32(2), pp. 96–105.

Brown, S., Rust, C. and Gibbs, G. (1994) *Strategies for Diversifying Assessment in Higher Education.* Oxford: Oxford Centre for Staff Development.

Brown, S., Race, P. and Rust, C. (1995) 'Using and experiencing assessment' in P. Knight (ed.) *Assessment for Learning in Higher Education.* London: Kogan Page.

Brown, S., Race, P. and Smith, B. (1996) *500 Tips on Assessment.* London: Kogan Page.

Gibbs, G., Jenkins, A. and Wisker, G. (1992) *Assessing More Students.* Oxford: Oxford Centre for Staff Development.

Harris, D. and Bell, C. (1990) *Evaluating and Assessing for Learning.* London: Kogan Page.

McDowell, L. (1996) 'Enabling student learning through innovative assessment' in G. Wisker and S. Brown (eds) *Enabling Student Learning: Systems and Strategies.* London: Kogan Page, SEDA.

Knight, P. (ed.) (1995) *Assessment for Learning in Higher Education.* London: Kogan Page.

Quality Assurance Agency for Higher Education (1997) *Subject Review Handbook,* October 1998–2000. Bristol: QAA.

2

Innovations in Student Assessment: A System-wide Perspective

Angela Glasner

Beyond our own experiences as teachers and learners, and sometimes as external examiners, how are we as individuals able to gain a picture of current assessment practice? We can, for example, attend conferences or seminars in our own subject or of a more thematic nature across several disciplines, we can share experiences and we can read widely. In general, however, it has been difficult to locate our own practices and experience in a wider context or indeed readily to summarize assessment practice nationally. There is talk of the need for change, of centres of excellence in innovation, but getting the broader picture is difficult. This chapter draws upon the experience of assessment of quality in UK universities since 1993 by the Higher Education Funding Council for England (HEFCE), and from this, a broad overview can be derived.

One of the purposes of subject review, introduced to UK higher education in 1993 as quality assessment, is to encourage improvements in the quality of education: assessors are asked to identify good practice during their assessment of a particular institution's programmes in a specific subject, including that relating to the assessment methods and awareness. The quality assessment process was introduced to UK higher education under section 70 of the Further and Higher Education Act 1992 and implemented in 1993. The early rounds of assessment conducted between Summer 1993 and Spring 1995 operated with a three-point assessment scale of 'excellent', 'satisfactory' and 'unsatisfactory'. Since April 1995, the method has assessed the quality of education against six aspects and generated a graded profile and a threshold judgement. Both methods were designed to enable recognition of, and response to, diversity of mission, intake and intention across the higher education sector and provided for a subject peer-based judgement of the effectiveness of the provision in delivering to the specific aims and objectives set. In October 1997, the work of quality assessment was transferred to the new Quality Assurance Agency for Higher Education

(QAA) under a contract for service. The method as defined by HEFCE continues to be delivered. From October 1998 to the summer of 2000, the method is to be known as subject review.

In undertaking quality assessment and subject review, reviewers are directed as part of their evaluation of teaching, learning and assessment to: consider whether the assessment methods are clear, explicit and consistent, at the appropriate level; and effective in assessing achievement of the subject aims and objectives. *The Assessors' Handbook* currently being used (HEFCE 1995) provides a set of notes in the form of an *aide-mémoire* which gives a clearer breakdown of how reviewers should evaluate assessment. It does not draw attention explicitly to innovation, but it does allow and encourage assessors to note innovation when they come across it.

In providing a systems overview in this chapter, I will review the discussion of subject-specific patterns from the overviews of those subjects which have been assessed to date, and try to draw out some common themes and some differences. This discussion points to some variables which may impact upon the opportunities for successful innovation in student assessment. I later focus on environmental studies as a case study of a subject which might be regarded as having a greater potential for innovation than many more established disciplines.

The extent of innovation in subjects assessed between 1993 and 1995

The clearest overall picture of the extent to which effectiveness and innovation characterized the provision in the fifteen subjects assessed between 1993 and 1995 is provided in the overview reports which are published at the end of each assessment round. These assessment rounds included subjects broadly representative of the range of higher education: professionally accredited courses (law, mechanical engineering, applied social work, architecture), science subjects (chemistry, computer studies, geology, and the more interdisciplinary environmental studies), humanities/social sciences (history, social policy and administration, anthropology, geography, business studies) and arts subjects (English, music).

For most courses in law, assessment included examination and coursework in varying combinations. Coursework mainly took the form of essays, projects, dissertations and assessed presentations. Dissertations and projects were used to encourage students to pursue scholarly work and independent research. Where coursework contributed to the overall assessment, it was particularly challenging and did not overlap with the examination papers set. In some courses, the trend was to reduce examinations and place increased emphasis on coursework. In one college, various methods were used with increased weight given to coursework as the degree progressed. Innovative systems of assessment included group projects which had to be submitted as a written report and an audio-visual presentation. It was also the case that suitable and challenging assessments enabled students to explore and to develop their skills.

In architecture, assessment procedures were generally appropriate and matched to the needs of the curriculum and the students. The assessment of studio project work was often used to measure the level of students' knowledge in other aspects of architecture courses, this practice reflecting the emphasis given to the synthesis of elements within the design process.

Project work is a feature of many subject areas. In mechanical engineering, the positive influence of staff scholarship, research and industrial consultancy on laboratory and project work was particularly noteworthy, generating student motivation and a sense of relevance, particularly in sessions with properly trained research students assisting in the teaching process. Publication of the results of student work was seen, in one instance, to be a motivating factor and, in another, the most successful final-year projects led to postgraduate research projects for industry. In several institutions, projects undertaken by final-year undergraduates and postgraduate students were of direct benefit to sponsoring organizations.

In chemistry, projects and dissertations were important vehicles for learning, giving students the opportunity to study specialist topics in depth. Most projects scrutinized by assessors were competently conducted and written up, although a minority were insufficiently open-ended and presented little challenge. In many universities, students were expected to give oral presentations on their projects which can make a contribution to the overall mark. Significant benefits accrued to student learning where peer groups were able to contribute to the assessment of oral presentations. Several innovations under the Enterprise in Higher Education initiative were noted by assessors, including one where students were given a business project to manufacture, analyse, market and sell a chemical product. Most chemistry courses include continuous assessment of practical performance as a matter of routine, but staff, particularly in the former Universities Funding Council (UFC) (pre-1992 university) institutions, were more reluctant to accept that a significant contribution to overall performance could be derived from continuous assessment of theoretical material. Nevertheless, some institutions had recognized that there was scope for the introduction of assessment techniques which allowed all candidates the opportunity to display their talents.

Excellent practice was seen in chemistry when written examinations were combined with continuous assessment, timed assignments, oral presentations subjected to peer and self-assessment, dissertations or extended essays, and research projects, all of which made a numerical contribution to the final assessment. Some institutions were also experimenting successfully with group projects and with mid-sessional multiple-choice tests designed to check on student progress and understanding, particularly in the early stages of their courses. There was, however, a danger of overassessment, particularly in modularized or unitized courses where course organizers were often urged to take greater care to monitor overall assessment loads and to prevent the bunching of assignments. The assessment of industrial placements presented further difficulties; most institutions did not incorporate the sandwich year into the final assessment, although an increasing number recognized successful completion by means of a 'Diploma of Industrial Studies' or similar award.

In computer studies, all institutions assessed student progress by means of written examinations supported by coursework of various types, including both practical and written work. The contribution made by each component to the overall assessment varied according to level of course and type of institution, but practical assessment was usually a significant feature. Former UFC institutions tended to rely more heavily on written examinations, which can be marked with reasonable precision and provide external examiners with evidence of course content and level, while it was not uncommon to find some modules in subdegree courses assessed entirely by coursework. In honours' degree and postgraduate courses, a final-year project was a universal requirement which typically contributed 20–25 per cent to the overall mark achieved for the year. Both projects and written examinations were subject to double marking, involving at least two members of staff; a few institutions had introduced anonymous marking of examinations.

In environmental studies, the methods of assessment were generally found to be appropriate, suitably varied and clear to students. All the institutions used written examinations supported by coursework of various types, including written work, practical work and fieldwork. The contributions made by each component to the overall assessment varied according to level of course and type of institution, but practical exercises and fieldwork were usually a significant feature. In the final assessment, coursework varied between a minimum of 20 per cent of the overall marks, which attracted criticism from the assessors, to a maximum of 50 per cent. Some of the more innovative methods of assessment in environmental studies, which usually made a small contribution to the overall marks for any given year because of their experimental nature, included group projects, individual oral presentations marked by staff and by peer groups, video-taped presentations and poster papers. 'Open note' and 'seen' papers provided variety in the format of examinations and, in one course, an integrative final examination paper asked students to assess a key objective of the course. In another, candidates were given 36 hours to prepare an environmental impact assessment for one of the final-year examination papers – this being trialed as external examiners had expressed some reservations.

All geology providers used a range of assessment methods, commonly based on a combination of continuous coursework assessment and end-of-year or end-of-module examinations. The range of methods used to assess the development of transferable skills included oral and poster presentations. Often the assessors found assessments to be well matched to subject aims and objectives and expected learning outcomes. In other cases, a review of the assessment strategy was recommended to ensure appropriate testing of a range of general and transferable skills. A few providers had introduced an element of self-assessment and peer-group assessment. Feedback to students on their performance ranged from detailed written evaluations to informal, orally transmitted comments from tutors. In a few instances, the assessors recommended the introduction of more formal feedback mechanisms. In some cases, there was scope for a closer alignment of assessment methods and the stated learning objectives.

The main methods of assessing student attainment in geography were unseen examinations, coursework essays and reports, projects, fieldwork reports and seminar presentations. There was a growing diversity of assessment methods, with some departments introducing means for assessing transferable skills including, for example, group working and oral presentations. Nevertheless, in about 30 per cent of departments the assessors considered the assessment regime to be too dependent upon unseen examinations and essays. In almost every case, these departments were in the former UFC sector. Best practice was judged to occur where there was a close match between the intended learning outcomes and the assessment methods used, and where students were given full details of assessment criteria and procedures. One department had a commendably open policy of giving students full feedback of all marks and discussion of examiners' comments on assessed scripts. In another case, MSc students had produced group project work based on real problems for external clients. Another model of good practice incorporated detailed and constructive written feedback, double-blind and anonymous marking of examination scripts, marking moderated between tutors and options, and annual publication of marks associated with each course.

A range of assessment methods was used in history programmes. Approximately 75 per cent of programmes included an element of continuous or selected coursework assessment alongside written examinations. In some cases, a particular mode of assessment was used to test specific outcomes, as for example when a compulsory dissertation was identified as a summative assessment of independent learning. However, the assessment methods chosen sometimes failed to cover the full range of learning outcomes described. For example, the assessment of certain transferable skills at undergraduate level was not always evident, particularly where assessment was based largely on written examinations. In contrast, in other cases, these skills were tested, with students being required to word-process assignments, or being assessed on seminar contributions and group projects.

Despite the range and variety of teaching and learning methods noted in Social Policy and Administration, there was a lack of corresponding variety in approaches to assessment. Written work in the form of essays and examination scripts was by far the most widely used method of assessment and was used exclusively in over 60 per cent of cases. In very few instances were seminar or other forms of oral presentation formally assessed. Despite the many examples of cooperative group work, project work, report writing and case study analysis, only very rarely were students given any assessment credit for the hard work and enthusiasm displayed in these sessions. The development of general transferable skills was rarely measured or assessed.

A variety of assessment methods based on examinations and coursework was used in different forms and varying combinations on most courses and programmes in business and management studies. Reviewers commented on some instances of best practice where the teaching, learning and assessment methods complemented one another and where the strategies used were well understood by students. However, not all assessment regimes were robust, and there was evidence of increased pressure on staff of marking larger batches of written work within reasonable timescales. A frequent consequence was lack of individual feedback.

The content of applied social work courses was largely prescribed by the Central Council for Education and Training in Social Work (CCETSW) which clearly stated the essential competencies and knowledge required by a newly qualified social worker. Consequently, competency-based outcomes largely shape the curricula, and there was an emphasis upon skill development for practice across a range of settings in the courses visited. Assessment methods were varied. They included individual and group presentations, orals, essays, observation records and videotaped sessions. In comparison with other discipline areas, the range of assessment methods used was extensive and often innovative, but reviewers were critical of the implementation of these methods. They commented on instances of slow turnaround of students' work, poor feedback and carelessness in marking.

A wide range of assessment methods was employed in anthropology. These methods included seen and unseen timed examinations, coursework, dissertations, practical notebooks, presentations and video and film material. In most cases, the methods of assessment were well matched to the objectives of courses. Assessment tools were generally well designed to enable students to demonstrate the full extent of their knowledge and understanding. Examples of good practice included the preparation of periodic reports on progress for discussion with the student and the use of peer assessment and team performance grades explicitly related to the particular characteristics of a mature student intake.

In English, much care was taken to ensure that methods of assessment were effective, fair and appropriate to aims and objectives. Within these parameters, there were many examples of willingness to experiment both with innovative methods of assessment and with the weighting between unseen examination and coursework, though excessive reliance on either method elicited critical comments from the assessors. Some methods reported as highly effective when they match the expressed educational objectives included: setting challenging examination questions requiring careful research and analysis; dissertations; projects; portfolios of work; presentations; independent study and self-directed work; oral examinations; original writing; book and drama reviews; drama production plans; bibliographic exercises; and video production. In contrast, a number of providers were criticized for: an overdependence on traditional written examinations that neglected the assessment of student achievement of some stated objectives related to skills in, for example, creative writing or the use of IT; uncertainty about marking criteria; and the absence of double marking to confirm attainment. Overall, the evidence indicated that while there was much that was lively and innovative in the assessment of English, there was a need to develop a closer match between modes of assessment and the stated objectives, building upon the instances of good practice.

For music students, in addition to formal examinations, aural tests and the submission of essays and dissertations, a variety of methods was used in the assessment of compositions, recitals and recordings. While general assessment procedures were usually well understood by students and staff, detailed assessment criteria were not always available and, where they did exist, might not be provided for students. There were particular issues for the assessment of musical performance, for example, a lack of guidance for performance teachers on marking criteria and attainment levels expected, the way in which such teachers were involved in the allocation of final marks and an absence of formal mechanisms for keeping records of students' achievements. Some institutions had responded to such concerns by publishing a carefully considered guidance manual, in which students and instrument and voice teachers were given the agreed syllabus for performance, showing levels and progression, commitment of time and arrangements and expectations in respect of assessment. In order to develop students' critical judgement and awareness of quality, some institutions involved students in peer-group assessment of performance, working to a detailed set of criteria. In general, assessment methods in music were varied and usually well matched to curriculum content and delivery. However, there was a need in many institutions for the development of explicit assessment criteria, published for students and staff.

Evidence of innovation

In general, across all subjects, methods for assessing students did not depart significantly from the conventional form of examination, coursework essays and very limited use of practical work, although there are different emphases as shown in Table 2.1. In large part, these differences arise from the nature of the subjects in which the student assessment takes place, and it is clearly true that curricula do dictate different learning contexts. The constraints which operate on some subjects, such as the requirements for professional accreditation of competence as practitioner in turn have implications for assessment. However, the truism of subject difference may be more apparent than real. While, in general, the methods were regarded by subject peers as appropriate to the learning objectives, there were weaknesses in the extent to which assessment methods and strategies adequately provided opportunities for students to demonstrate and be appraised against the full range of knowledge and skills which form the learning objectives set.

Table 2.1 Emphasis on subject areas

Subject area	Particular features of assessment	Innovation identified by peers
Law	Exams and coursework	Group projects, audio-visual presentations
Chemistry	Projects and dissertations, oral presentations, continuous assessment of practicals	Peer-group assessment, assessment of oral presentation, Enterprise in Higher Education initiatives, e.g. business projects, mid-season multiple-choice test of progress and standing
History	Continuous or selected coursework assessment	Use of dissertation as summative assessment of independent learning
Mechanical engineering	Labs and project work	
Architecture	Assessed student project work	
Business and management studies	Exams and coursework	
Social work	Individual and group presentations, essays, orals, video sessions, records of observations	
Computer studies	Exams supported by coursework, final-year project	
Social and public administration	Exams and essays	
Environmental studies	Written exams supported by coursework (written work, practical work, field work)	Groups projects, poster papers, oral presentations, peer assessment, video-taped presentations, environmental impact assessment
Geography	Unseen exams, coursework, essays, reports	Groupwork, oral presentations
English	Exam and coursework	Challenging exams, portfolios of work, original writing, book and drama reviews

Table 2.1   (Con't)

Subject area	Particular features of assessment	Innovation identified by peers
Anthropology	Seen and unseen timed exams, coursework and dissertation, practical notebooks, presentations, video and film material	Peer assessment, team performance grading
Geology	Continuous coursework and exams, oral and poster presentations	Self- and peer assessment
Music	Formal exams, aural tests, essay and dissertations	Peer-group assessment of performance, development of guidance manual

Several of the overview reports identify different patterns across the two former sectors, with a greater tendency to use formal, end-of-session, closed-book examinations in the former 'old' university sector, and greater exploration and use of coursework methods in the former polytechnic sector (the 'new' universities and colleges). In part, this may be a reflection of the different academic structures of the two broad categories of institutions, with a greater tendency for new discipline areas, including interdisciplinary and applied subjects to have developed within the former polytechnic sector, and for long-established, traditional subjects with long convention of examination as the sole method of assessment in the former 'old' university sector. However, there are also correlations between the type of institution and the type and diversity of the student population.

Across all institution types, there are factors which tend to inhibit innovation: university regulations circumscribe what is possible in many institutions, often prescribing a particular balance between formal examinations and written work and the form which the latter, in particular, may take. The external examiner system currently tends to encourage replication rather than innovation. Increased pressures generated by the massification of higher education and the declining unit of resource encourage the retention of assessment systems which are economical on staff time and which reduce the need for marking time and iterative feedback on their performance with students. There are concerns about student assessment overload and about the ability to determine authorship and to inhibit plagiarism. Nevertheless, some innovation does occur, and the pattern of assessment experienced by today's undergraduate and postgraduate appears to be more likely to involve a variety of coursework components as well as examinations than that of students of even a decade ago.

Assessment in subjects reviewed since 1995

A further eight subjects were assessed during the period 1995–6. They were: chemical engineering; linguistics; sociology; French; German; Italian; Iberian languages and studies; and Russian and Eastern European languages and studies. Overall, the reviewers indicated a need for the use of a greater range of techniques and methods in the assessment of students' work. In the modern languages, there was a need to ensure that the period abroad – typically the third year in a four-year programme of study – was more effectively integrated into the curriculum, including through assessment and monitoring of the learning experience. Across all the subject areas, reviewers urged that attention should be paid to the provision of better feedback on student work.

In chemical engineering, the use of the design project in undergraduate programmes was highlighted as a particularly successful learning experience – promoting integration of the different strands of the subjects as well as the development of transferable skills – in 40 per cent of the provision reported on. There were variations in the way in which the project was designed in different courses, but in general it enabled the assessment of small team group working through a joint report, often compiled in stages. A small number of providers were introducing peer assessment as one dimension of the overall assessment process. However, the reviewers were critical of the extent to which students understood assessment schemes, despite generally conscientiously set out and clearly documented procedures.

In sociology, assessment methods were found to be varied and to reflect the diversity of the provision which covered a wide range of specialisms across the social sciences, cultural studies, women's studies, ethnic and development studies. The range included exams, essays, project and practical work, and individual research dissertations. In a number of courses, the reviewers observed innovative uses of assessment, usually contributing only a small proportion of the overall assessment, which included group projects, video-taped presentations and poster papers. However, innovative approaches were found in only half the providers, and in the remainder the reviewers comment on the predominance of a narrower range of assessment methods with written essays and exams forming the main elements.

Assessment in linguistics was deemed to be effective in 60 per cent of programmes. The strengths included: a range of methods well matched to the curricula; a structure for assessment that reflected the objectives including knowledge and skills; and processes that were fair and consistent. In one institution, the practice of requiring students to reflect regularly on their achievements through self-assessment, was particularly commended. However, in 40 per cent of programmes, the quality of the assessment procedure did not match fully the high quality of the teaching: students experienced a limited range of methods, typically based on time-limited written exams, and in some cases it was not clear to what extent practical or laboratory work was assessed, or how it was assessed.

Many of the same themes cut across the different languages assessed during this period. In French, assessment practice was patchy: while in 30 per cent of cases it was varied and well matched to teaching and learning objectives, in more than one-fifth of cases the range of methods was considered too narrow. Innovation was identified to include the production of portfolios of independent work, dossiers of achievement of various kinds, and group projects, sometimes involving the imaginative use of technology. Areas of concern for the reviewers were the inconsistency and inadequacy of feedback, found in 20 per cent of cases, and lack of clarity or inconsistency of application of criteria, especially in relation to the assessment of language competence.

In German, the reviewers also found a significant level of lack of clarity, with 20 per cent of programmes being characterized by absence or mismatch of the assessment methods to the teaching and learning strategy. With the exception of moves away from the three-hour exam and greater use of assessed essays and dissertations, there was little innovation. In a small minority of cases, there was a sense of shared ownership of assessment, with self-assessment playing a significant part. Most significantly, there was little evidence in most institutions that the period spent abroad contributed significantly to the student's degree classification, although an increasing number of programmes were introducing some form of credit rating. However, this raised concerns about comparability, and was often the focus for specific recommendations.

Spanish and Portuguese (Iberian languages and studies) courses were generally regarded as having assessment procedures which were appropriately varied and well matched to the teaching and learning needs of the students. However, the reviewers felt that some programmes could give more attention to the integration and assessment of the year abroad, and to formulating and disseminating consistent marking criteria. In Italian courses, the variety of assessment methods was found to have increased substantially over the recent years, and most students were assessed using a combination of exams, oral and aural testing, essays, tutorial presentations, group work and dissertation. While in general the combination of methods was well matched to the objectives, in some institutions there was an overreliance on formal exams which meant that not all learning outcomes were fully tested. Again, assessors found that students were not always given adequate information about the assessment diet, nor about the marking criteria. Feedback on students' work was very variable, in some instances not existing at all.

Learning in Russian and Eastern European languages was encouraged through a varied range of assignments. Oral work, essays and report writing were commonplace, although the balance between these forms of assessment varied from provider to provider. A minority of the courses encouraged students to acquire a wider range of transferable skills through the use of peer assessment and self-assessment. Many courses had developed clear, structured criteria to assess the acquisition of language skills, but some still relied on the unseen exam as the main method of assessment, and the reviewers questioned the effectiveness of this approach in testing the full range of knowledge and skills which underpinned the programmes.

Overall, the evidence from the assessments of the period from Autumn 1995 suggests that there is an increasing range of methods being used, but the familiar exam and coursework essay still predominate. It is too early to draw conclusions from the first few reports published in relation to the subjects assessed since 1996, but this set of subjects (agriculture and forestry; food science; town and country planning and landscape; land and property management; civil engineering; building; electrical and electronic engineering; mechanical, aeronautical and manufacturing engineering; materials technology; general engineering; American studies; Middle Eastern and African studies; East and South Asian studies; history or art, architecture and design; communication and media studies; dance, drama and cinematics) will provide an interesting set of comparators for the professional and applied studies in the earlier rounds. An analysis of the reports on these subject reviews will provide an opportunity to reflect on the extent to which more systematic integration of assessment with teaching and learning has been achieved.

Is innovation easier in new subjects?

On embarking on this part of the chapter, I can be little more than speculative: the early round of assessment visits were selective: HEFCE did not visit all institutions. Moreover, the early rounds encompassed only one-quarter of the entire range of subject areas. Here, I will look at one subject area, environmental studies, which I have chosen for a number of reasons which might suggest a greater propensity to innovation. It is a relatively new subject, uninhibited by traditional practices. It tends to interdisciplinary, which might encourage innovative cross-fertilization in so far as there are significant differences between subject areas. Finally, it is free of the constraints of a professional or statutory body accrediting context. The discussion below is based upon a review of all of the individual quality assessment reports.

In only three institutions were assessment-related practices the focus of specific commendation. In one case, there were well-developed procedures for managing students' dissertations, including prior preparation, supervision and assessment. In another case, the use of a wide range of assessment methods relevant to the specific modules and to the overall programme of study was commended. In the third case, well-organized and effective group work, and clear guidance given to students on the methods and criteria of assessment were the focus of commendation. While not the focus of specific commendation, some innovative features were noted in other institutions: group work where individual contributions were taken into account and staff took steps to minimize the potential for plagiarism in coursework; assessment of mock public enquiries and other oral contributions; and Higher National Diploma (HND) placement experience integrated into coursework. However, not all innovations were successful: it was the view of the peer assessors that some assessments, particularly those based on posters, may not have sufficiently tested students' critical faculties or challenged their skills, and project work was not always being used sufficiently formatively.

Much good practice was evident, and some of it would have been innovative in other subject areas or other contexts. Field reports, in themselves well organized, were associated with verbal and written reports which were effectively assessed. The wide range of assessment methods used included oral and video presentation, projects and laboratory assessment, as well as more traditional essays and examinations. In several instances, there was effective use of group work and presentation of written assignments and seminars.

In a number of institutions, however, specific recommendations were made which related to assessment, itself evidence that fellow environmental scientists regarded there being grounds for more systematic, if not innovative, practice. Individual institutions were encouraged to provide more opportunities to students to demonstrate their ability to synthesize material, to provide an appropriate range of assessment activities which would give sufficiently challenging assignments and to consider how external examiners could obtain an overview of students' performance. There was some sense in a number of institutions that the balance of assessment was not quite right, as judged by the peers, and in one case, a greater need for rigour was urged. In one case, a claim for 'deep learning' was judged not to have been realized: rather the coursework design was seen to encourage superficiality and an uncritical approach to the material. Elsewhere, the recommendations were associated with the quality and speed of feedback to students.

Thus while in a relatively new and, as yet, not rigidly formed subject area some innovation was apparent, it was by no means dominant, and indeed there remained scope for improvement in the application and interpretation of conventional examination and coursework methods.

Conclusions

Freeman (1987), writing in a rather different context, suggests (if I paraphrase him rather substantially) that we need a taxonomy of innovations which distinguishes between incremental change, radical new ideas which are successfully implemented and major new paradigm shifts. The evidence from the quality-assessment process in England and Northern Ireland suggests that much incremental change is taking place: for example, the wholesale reliance upon formal end-of-session examinations as the sole mode of assessing students for the award of their degrees has effectively disappeared. Coursework is a component of student assessment in the majority of subject areas as shown in Table 2.1. Project work seems to have been increasingly introduced into the sciences and applied subject areas, and presentations have become a phenomenon of the assessment diet in a smaller number of subject areas.

Some significant radical approaches – as defined by the subject peers who reviewed the different courses – can be found, but they are not yet firmly grounded in practice. Some of these more innovative practices were seen to be grappling with the difficult areas of assessing group working skills. Others were harnessing the opportunities provided by new technologies to enable presentation skills to be more explicitly assessed, with video-taping which was previously found in anthropology being used in law and environmental studies. As well as group-work assessment, peer assessment was being used innovatively in a number of subjects. The challenges associated with innovation in these modes of assessment are discussed elsewhere in this book. What the discussions illustrate clearly is that innovation is itself a continuous process of incremental change once the innovation is embarked upon. Continuous refinement is needed to secure the optimal effectiveness of the innovation.

In my judgement, and in the context of the data revealed by the quality-assessment process, we have not yet experienced in the UK a major paradigm shift. The impetus for paradigm shifts does not necessarily come from within. It is conceivable that the combined forces of a more consumer-oriented student population with the perspective of the fee-paying client, a standards-defining academia keen to promote the excellence and uniqueness of its provision, and the language of competence and skills, will combine to provide the revolutionary context in which assessment will be viewed as inextricably linked to learning in higher education of the twenty-first century. There are certainly a number of academics and students keen to see a shift from the traditional focus on assessment as a summative statement of specific knowledges, for what many would argue are excellent reasons.

References

Freeman, C. (1987) 'The case for technological determinism' in R. Finnegan *et al.* (eds) *Information Technology: Social Issues.* Milton Keynes: The Open University.

HEFCE (1993) *The Assessors' Handbook* (October 1993). Bristol: HEFCE. [Covers the first 15 subjects]

HEFCE (1995) *The Assessors' Handbook* (October 1995). Bristol: HEFCE. [Covers revised methods for the eight subjects reviewed between April 1995 and September 1996]

HEFCE (1996) *The Assessors' Handbook* (October 1996). Bristol: HEFCE. [Covers the 16 subjects being reviewed October 1996 to September 1998]

QAA (1997) *The Subject Review Handbook* (December 1997). [Covers review of subject provision October 1998 to 2000]

3

Assessment and Evaluation: A Systems Approach for their Utilization

T. Dary Erwin

The future of higher education depends on our action now. It depends in part upon our explanations about the purposes and value of college and upon our ability to document the effectiveness of the programmes and services our institutions provide for students. How do we represent our purposes of higher education? How do we utilize or establish systems of programme assessment that are credible to our constituents and meaningful to ourselves? This chapter will describe some of the public policy issues confronting higher education and address some of the ways educators can respond through assessment practice.

The increasing press for accountability

One of the most influential US governors in education, Roy Romer, recently wrote:

> Yet, I continue to be amazed at the resistance I encounter to examining whether we can measure and report on effective learning at individual institutions and provide good information to inform consumers about their choices. I also continue to be amazed at the inability of policy-makers and public leaders to create meaningful and useful account-ability systems for higher education. Finally, I am amazed at how many people are content to rest on the laurels of the past and insist that our higher education institutions need not change because they are the best in the world.
>
> (Romer 1995)

In the USA, Romer's comments capture the sentiment of many persons outside of higher education who occupy some role of governance or influence over higher education.

Recent decades in US higher education may be characterized by rising tides of accountability (Lenning 1977; Ewell 1984; Erwin 1991; Knight 1995). In the USA, the 1980s were characterized by government officials primarily requesting institutional information to understand better what a college degree means and where public money goes. Linking budgets with student performance indicators was relatively isolated in very few states such as Tennessee. In the early 1990s, stronger links are being made between re-source allocations and state priorities. In the absence of quality measures of student learning and development, states are substituting outputs such as retention rates and graduation rates or measures of resources such as per-centage of budget towards direct instruction for performance indicators. As academics are aware, these outputs and resource measures unfortunately do not reflect what happens in the classroom or any aspect of student learn-ing on campus.

Now, and continuing into the next century, external constituents are questioning the role of traditionally delivered instruction, often calling for technology in lieu of a teacher for greater cost efficiency and access. More about this last issue will be discussed later. Why are the demands for accountability increasing? Terenzini (1997) and Candy (1997) list some insti-tutional pressures for these demands:

- spiralling costs of attendance and operation
- accrediting agency requirements to assess student learning outcomes and to incorporate the findings in operational and programmatic planning and decision-making
- corporate and government leaders' alarm about economic competitive-ness in a global market
- writers both inside the academy (e.g. Smith 1990; Anderson 1992; Huber 1992) and out (e.g. Sykes 1988; Perelman 1992) who have attacked col-leges' and universities' reward structures and current directions
- employers' increasing dissatisfaction with the skills their new employees bring to the workplace from their baccalaureate programmes (Candy 1997: 170; Terenzini, 1997: 1–2).

The proportion of US state budgets allocated to higher education has been in steady decline for over 12 years, while tuition increases have exceeded the US consumer price index (Baumol and Blackman 1995). Left just to economic reasoning, the value of a US college degree is questionable when college costs are compared to median incomes of college graduates or median incomes of households (Institute for Research on Higher Education 1997b). Sharply escalating college tuition becomes more than an economic issue; elected officials have adopted it as a political issue. A recent *Newsweek* magazine (Princeton Survey Research Associates 1997) poll in the USA asked parents of young children about their goals and worries. The second most frequent concern was, 'You won't be able to afford his/her college costs'. This was ahead of other worries about their children's health and general concerns about their upbringing.

College administrators' responses have not satisfied anyone:

Unable to be precise about how their institutions add value to either their students or their communities, campus leaders fall back on tried and true statements about quality and excellence, about the beauty of learning and the dedication of faculty, students, staff, alumni, trustees, neighbours . . . [reviewers] exasperated to the point of irreverence, shout 'What's the message?'

(Institute for Research on Higher Education 1997a: 6)

Faculty and administrators who once conceived of assessment for account-ability as a local occurrence now find demands for accountability through-out the Western world (Mahony 1990; Brown and Knight 1994; Desruisseaux 1994; Westerheijden and van Vught 1995; Brown 1997). Colleges and uni-versities in the USA have replied in a timid and unorganized way, and government-elected officials and the public are becoming increasingly impatient (Ehrenfeld 1996). Part of the strategy to rectify this situation is to define clear educational purposes including 'candid accounting of academic strengths and weaknesses and an analysis of markets to be served' (Institute for Research on Higher Education 1997a: 6). No longer can assessment as pro-gramme evaluation be deemed a passing fad. No longer should we dream of a return to the old days of assumed goodwill and continued financial sup-port without a more coherent response about the effectiveness of college.

Alternatives to traditionally delivered instruction

In their frustration about lack of change in higher education, USA govern-ment leaders (e.g. Blumenstyk 1995) are finding alternatives to traditional lecture-based universities. The greater use of technology to deliver instruc-tion heads the lists of reforms (Erwin and Rieppi, in press). Use of the web and other online instruction is touted as the new reality (Sanchez 1997). Eleven governors in the western USA have begun a 'virtual university' formerly called the Western Governors University as a perceived cost-effective alter-native to handle the increasing population growth in the western USA. (For example, see the University of Colorado's site http://www.cuonline.edu/) The governors' reasoning lies with the belief that similar learning can be transmitted via the web thus eliminating the need for buildings and full-time staff. Indeed, companies are being formed to handle collegiate instruction over the web. (For example http://www.real.com/products/ realvideo/indes.htm) Certainly the evolution of The Open University (http:/ /www.open.ac.uk/ou/ou.html) from audio-tape to video-tape to web is a prime example of successful use of technology in higher education. More-over, the movement to modularization in the UK, similar to semesters in the USA, makes delivery of collegiate content more convenient as separate units, technologically delivered or not.

In addition to emerging technological innovations within higher educa-tion, other non-traditional alternatives are rising outside the traditional college and university structure. Business and corporate companies are expanding their role in training and education:

A multi-billion dollar knowledge industry has developed outside established educational institutions, responding in more direct, and usually more effective ways, to the needs of the industry and the labor market. This is leading to the erosion of the monopoly the universities have enjoyed in providing training and granting educational credentials with good currency in the private sector.

(Davis and Botkin 1994: 76)

Motorola University and Hamburger University of McDonald's begin to blur the distinction between training and education as they expand their scope. Some upwardly mobile business employees wonder which is better: a certificate in advanced networking from Novell Technologies or a Master of Business Administration? The greater presence of for-profit institutions such as the University of Phoenix is nudging cross-town rivals for students and often succeeding in meeting needs (Strosnider 1997).

What is the common theme among these alternatives to traditional delivery of instruction? A competitive spirit that claims similar quality for lower cost and greater flexibility is one common denominator. Such alternative delivery systems are no longer conceived as radical (Candy 1997); however, their effectiveness is not yet demonstrated (Erwin and Rieppi, in press; McAleese 1997). This lack of meaningful feedback is not deterring states and institutions from moving ahead or making claims. Admittedly, it is a paradox that lack of effectiveness information is characteristic of both paradigms, yet the desire to change seems to win favour with government leaders willing to reward innovation. Nevertheless, issues of accountability do not fade but loom even larger the tighter the resources. The next section outlines some action that institutions can take when responding about the value of higher education.

Activating an assessment programme

Having discussed the need for institutions to respond to external calls for accountability, what steps might be undertaken? This section outlines an assessment process for institutional improvement and external accountability. What evidences of student learning can an institution furnish according to its various programmes or services?

Assessment, or programme evaluation in this context, is the 'process of defining, selecting, designing, collecting, analyzing, interpreting, and using information to increase students' learning and development' (Erwin 1991: 15). Assessment information may still be used as feedback to individuals, but the primary purpose of assessment information, as described in this chapter, points towards aggregate, programme impact. Moreover, it is necessary to consider that assessment information will be reported and used by multiple audiences. Assessment data might be used by departmental colleagues, departmental chairpersons, deans, vice presidents and presidents, institutional oversight boards, system oversight boards, government officials and the public. The language of the reports might be adjusted accordingly.

The quality of the assessment methods requires serious attention, especially to external audiences. Often, educators may conduct informal, unstructured student interviews as viable sources; however, these informal interviews may not be deemed credible to external audiences who are already sceptical about our self-procedures.

What should be the scope of an institutional assessment programme? It is typically advantageous to focus efforts initially around major or discipline-based programmes. Usually an organization supports this approach because departments are natural intact units, and many professional associations already devote part of their annual meetings to assessing learning in its discipline.

The scope of assessment also broadens to areas in basic skills and general education or 'graduateness' (Pearce 1997). These areas have been more commonplace in the USA and are emerging within the UK. Basic skills, or the collegiate skills such as reading, writing and mathematics, are expected of students' college matriculation. As the admission process is opened (greater numbers of students with less abilities), identification and remediation of basic skills through assessment assumes a greater place. The Organization for Economic Cooperation and Development has predicted this problem already in its review planning for the future of higher education by member countries.

The other major area for assessment encompasses general education or graduateness as the Higher Education Quality Council (Pearce 1997) defined. Both in the USA and UK, business and the public are stressing the importance of general education/graduateness or the knowledge, skills, personal characteristics a college graduate possesses regardless of major field of study (Pearce 1997). While US universities devote about one-third of their undergraduate curriculum, many UK universities have conceived 'graduateness' as key skills and knowledge largely obtained prior to university. In spite of this viewpoint, UK universities are attempting to further define 'skills across the major curricula' such as communication and critical thinking skills. Unfortunately, many disciplines apply different definitions of these skills thus prohibiting common definitions. To further illustrate the assessment process through example, two sub-areas of Technology and Aesthetic Development/Fine Arts, will be illustrated. The choice of these two areas does not imply that each collegiate institution should adopt these too, but to provide realistic examples.

Defining educational purposes

Establishing or defining educational objectives or purposes is the first step in the assessment process. One must know what to assess before attempting to assess it. Sample objectives for technology or information seeking skills might include the following statements.

- Formulate and conduct an effective information search strategy that includes a variety of reference sources, such as encyclopaedias, library catalogues, indexes, bibliographies, statistics sources, government publications and resources available on the Internet.
- Evaluate information sources in terms of accuracy, authority, bias and relevance.
- Use information effectively by adapting it to a purpose, organizing it, and acknowledging and properly documenting sources.
- Use electronic publishing to create a document that contains textual, tabular, graphical and pictorial elements.
- Use multiple computing environments to communicate interactively both locally and globally.
- Demonstrate public speaking using presentation software and projection technology.

Note the action-oriented verbs that provide expectation of what these students should know and be able to do as a function of the educational experience. Use of precise and specific language is paramount; vague and general wording confuses the entire process of instructional delivery and assessment and can suggest lack of focus or lack of ability of the teaching staff as perceived by external audiences. Sometimes skills are easier to articulate so another example in the fine arts from my institution is described below.

Learning in the fine arts is stated as part of general education at my institution. But how is fine arts defined? What should be taught? Sample objectives in the fine arts might include the following statements:

- Identify and analyse the aesthetic, emotive, persuasive and informative content of artistic and literary works. In writing and speaking, use appropriate vocabulary (defined in a separate document for the descriptions and analysis of artistic and literary works).
- Identify and describe the basic processes used for the creation of artistic works.
- Identify and analyse similarities, differences and interrelationships among the arts.
- Make and explain informed evaluations of artistic events and literary works.

Note these objectives focus more on the process rather than knowledge as content. A model of aesthetic development was established (Erwin and Halpern 1997) called Stages of Aesthetic Development. The five stages briefly stated are:

Stage One: Closed-resistance.
Stage Two: Descriptive-literal, superficial, socially desirable.
Stage Three: Elements – attempt to analyse, some sensory qualities, judgement criteria based on depth of feelings.

Stage Four: Traces significance – judgement criteria based on art community standards, articulates historic and cultural points of view.

State Five: Evaluates worth-judgement criteria, evaluation of worth based on social and human terms, mastery of vocabulary in interpretation, technique and style.

Moving through the stages represents greater cognitive complexity.

In each area of technology/information seeking and aesthetic development, new assessment methods were constructed. Before an assessment method is constructed, a table of specifications or test blueprint should be outlined weighting the programme objectives for planned coverage on the method.

Assessment stimuli need not always be words. In the example of the aesthetic development assessment method, students are presented with three representations of artistic experiences: a musical selection called, 'Prélude à l'après-midi d'un faune' – Claude Debussy, images of orchestra; a visual selection, Rembrandt – 'Aristotle Contemplating the Bust of Homer'; and a video selection: 'Antigone' by Sophocles – portrayed by actress Juliet Stevenson. After each artistic experience, open-ended questions were posed to students and rated independently using the five stages of aesthetic development. These questions were:

1. What was the most clearly recognizable subject matter of the piece? Name at least three elements that led you to this conclusion.
2. Visual artists use a variety of elements with which to evoke a response. Which element(s) in the visual arts were you most aware of in the piece?
3. The performing arts (theatre and dance) utilize a variety of artists and forms to create and structure audience response. What element(s) of the performing arts were you aware of in the piece?
4. What sound and musical qualities were you the most aware of in the piece?
5. Choose one of the four areas you just commented on (1–4) and discuss its effectiveness.
6. All arts generally seek an empathic or sensory response from their audience. Did you experience a sensory response? Please describe the response and explain which elements led you to this response.
7. Are you able to classify the piece shown as being representative of any style or having roots in a particular historic period? Which one? Explain which elements led you to this conclusion.
8. Is this a 'good' work of art? Why or why not?

Assessment methods may generally be described as selective response formats or constructed response formats. Selective response formats, which may be more common in the USA, present alternative answers such as multiple choice for the students to choose a single best answer. Contrary to popular belief, higher-order thinking can be tested with selective response formats (Roid and Haladyna 1982), but much preparation and skill is required (see also Millman and Greene 1989). Constructed response formats elicit the student to perform, produce, process or exhibit. Unfortunately, some teaching staff stop at the construction phase such as the collection of portfolios. Constructed response formats require the use of a checklist or rating scale to evaluate these performances, products, processes or display of personal traits. Briefly described, checklists display all aspects of quality about these constructions, but the raters merely indicate the presence or absence of these behaviours. Rating scales are more evaluative allowing the raters to indicate the degree of performance displayed, not just its presence or absence as in a checklist. There are various types of rating scales, but the optimum type are behaviourally-anchored rating scales. Behaviourally-anchored rating scales list typical student behaviours ranging from poor to superior for each aspect of the performance or product. Listing specific behaviours reduces the subjective element facing raters, instead of guessing what 'good' or a '3' means. More about selective and constructed response formats may be found in Erwin (1991).

Interrater reliability is typically calculated with constructed response formats. See generalizability measurement theory (Brennan 1983) for further information. In the fine arts example above, low teaching staff agreement to the students' constructed responses to the open-ended questions led to further definition of the stages and discussions about the nature of the curriculum. Other issues about the quality of assessment methods are too lengthy to be covered adequately here, and the reader is referred to Erwin (1991) and Linn (1989).

When to collect the information remains another key step in the assessment process. UK and European practices of programme final examinations are ideal occasions. Readers may also consider assessing at matriculation and the mid-point of the undergraduate curriculum. Marks collected with modules or programme units may also be helpful. In my institution's assessment programme, students are assessed at the beginning, middle and end of the four-year baccalaureate programme.

A fourth step in the assessment process is the analysis of the data. Again, the issues become more complex to give full coverage, so some broad considerations will be presented. Generally, four analytical strategies are used in analysing assessment information.

First, do students change over time? Typically, at least two comparison groups of students are used: one participating in the educational programme (e.g. entire degree programme or individual course module) and the other control group who has not participated in the educational programme. Do students who participated in the designated programme or experience, change to a greater extent than students who did not participate?

Second, if a pretest measure is not available, do students who participate in the educational experience score or rate higher on the average than students who did not participate? Without a pretest measure, however, one cannot attribute how much learning existed prior to the beginning of the programme or service.

Third, what is the relationship or correlation of the outcome measure compared to other measures of student performance or success? For example, are module marks related to end of programme outcomes? Are end of degree programme outcome measures related to measures of later job performance or citizenship?

Fourth, are students performing at expected levels of competency? This strategy may seem confusing to some UK or European readers; however, in the USA completion of a degree is usually determined by successful accumulation of courses (modules) rather than end of programme exit examinations.

End of degree programme outcomes in the USA often carry little weight for individual students. If students do not reach competency, as can happen, on end of the degree programme measures, then why? Incidentally, determining passing levels or setting competency levels can be a very technical procedure; see Erwin (1991) or Zieky and Livingston (1977) for ways to set competency levels. For example, often the difficulty level of the assessment method is ignored.

Using and reporting the assessment information and results requires planning and forethought. One criterion for evaluating an institutional assessment programme is how or if the assessment information is used. Merely collecting information without improving the educational programme is insufficient. Ideally, course modules will be changed by varying content of material or style of delivery. For instance, students may or may not be performing well in some area of the curriculum, and this area might need renewed emphasis with subsequent students. Style of delivery such as multimedia technology receives much attention now. For particular subject matter, do students learn best under lectures, the web, CD-ROM or interactive-video?

Deans, departmental heads, and teaching staff may use the assessment information for guidance in appointment decisions, for planning instructional strategies such as technology use, and for allocating or reallocating resources. Presidents/vice chancellors/principals may use assessment information in programme reviews and strategic decisions about institutional direction. Are institutional goals being met? Is the institution accomplishing what is stated? University heads can use assessment information to petition boards and government officials for additional resources. These institutional heads should be able to characterize the uniqueness and effectiveness of institutions with brief assessment summaries about student learning. Basing resource requests on assessment information has been a more powerful argument then merely basing the requisition on logic or persuasive ability of the requester.

New roles for assessment centres

The section above outlined steps in the assessment or programme evaluation process for higher education. Organizationally, how will these functions be accomplished in a credible way? The term 'credible' is used because our information and progress must be credible to audiences external to the academy. In the past, our criteria focused on satisfying persons primarily within higher education. As was mentioned, external audiences may play the major role in our future. Testing centres already exist in the USA and UK, but they must be refocused to handle the new political, technical and collaborating demands for assessment.

In the USA, testing centres spend considerable resources on scoring classroom tests and tallying student perceptions of teaching surveys. In the past ten years, new assessment centres have been set up to consult with teaching staff for improvement of assessment methods to evaluate degree programmes, general education/graduateness and basic skills.

In the UK, external examiners focus on both the individual performance to ensure fair play and on cohort reference to ensure standards. The external examiner system is to be further strengthened in the UK following the Dearing Report. Marking schemes are mainly concerned with approval of student competencies for graduation. These functions will probably continue, but external demands for programme evaluation, or examining group data, are emerging. Organizations for staff development such as UK Staff and Educational Development Association (SEDA) also offer helpful advice through publications and conferences to teaching staff about assessment and evaluation and are playing a great role.

Whatever organizational structure or unit is used, accountability and assessment functions will become more critical for single institutions. First, individual teaching staff and discipline departments will be under pressure to produce clearer programme objectives and credible assessment methods. In the USA, the credibility of course grades, similar to module marks, or transcripts holds questionable value for employers (Morrison 1997). More voices in the USA are calling for agencies external to the universities for certifying learning and the granting of degrees (e.g. Romer 1996; Morrison 1997). For example, the virtual university discussed earlier may likely have Sylvan Learning Centres, a for-profit organization, serve as testing centres for certifying competency and be independent of any college or university.

Second, it is of benefit to individual institutions to have available and report assessment data about its programmes and services. Institutional funding and accreditation or external programme reviews are, and will be, affected to a greater extent. Some educators refer to these type of uses as 'high stakes' testing. Yes, the stakes, or consequences of decisions, are being raised, and institutions responding in systematic ways with assessment information will benefit.

The furnishing of any data will not satisfy our critics. The information must be reliable and valid. The technical definitions of reliability and validity cannot be adequately addressed in this short chapter, but systematic research about the quality or worth of our assessment methods should be conducted on an ongoing basis. Staff in these assessment centres need to possess knowledge about measurement or testing methods. The expertise in one's own discipline or the long-time experience of a master teacher is not sufficient.

The new technology in testing is directed towards computer-based testing. Computer-based testing integrates measurement, artificial intelligence and cognitive psychology through the multimedia capabilities of the microcomputer. Computer-based testing will naturally follow the use of technology as an aid or replacement to traditional instruction.

If institutions refuse to develop their own sound measurement procedures for programme assessment, governments will be likely to fill that vacuum. In the USA, states such as Tennessee and Missouri have mandated particular tests for programme assessment and score results affect institutional funding. In some states such as Virginia, statewide tests, which can dictate the nature of the curriculum, have been avoided through these institutions' design of credible assessment methods and use of noticeable assessment information for programme improvement. This has not as yet happened in the UK, but it may only be a matter of time before very much further direction of assessment processes is implemented.

Conclusion

The calls for accountability and change in the academy necessitate a collective, systematic approach to address the questions and concerns about higher education. Institutions in the Western world still have time to respond in ways that reflect and emphasize their values. However, naysayers even within the academy point a different lifestyle ahead. Peter Drucker, a well-known management professor who correctly predicted earlier US college enrolment trends and the replacement of manual labours with knowledge working as the core work force, portends:

> Thirty years from now the big university campuses will be relics. Universities won't survive. It's as large a change as when we first got the printed book. Do you realize that the cost of higher education has risen as fast as the cost of health care? And for the middle-class family, college education for their children is a much of a necessity as is medical care – without it the kids have no future. Such totally uncontrollable expenditures, without any visible improvement in either the content or the quality of education, means that the system is rapidly becoming untenable. Higher education is in deep crisis.
>
> (Lenzner and Johnson 1997: 127)

Recognition of this looming crisis would certainly help move higher education to action. Our action or lack of action will help shape our destiny. Progressive institutions that will keep or garnish new resources will develop systematic approaches to collecting and using assessment information. Can you answer these questions about your institution to external audiences?:

- What are the major purposes of your institution?
- How would you describe what all students learn at your institution?
- What changes have you made at your institution based on this information?

These are questions that will not fade away but will be voiced louder. Our responses will help shape our future.

References

Anderson, M. (1992) *Imposters in the Temple.* New York: Simon and Schuster.

Baumol, W. and Blackman, S. (1995) 'How to think about rising colleges costs'. *Planning for Higher Education,* 23(4), 1–7.

Blumenstyk, G. (1995) 'Campuses in cyberspace: Western governors will explore the establishment of a virtual university'. *Chronicle of Higher Education,* 42, (December), A18–21.

Brennan, R. (1983) *Elements of Generalizability Theory.* Iowa City, IA: The American College Testing Program.

Brown, S. (1997) (ed.) *Facing Up to Radical Changes in Universities and Colleges.* London: Kogan Page.

Brown, S. and Knight, P. (1994) *Assessing Learners in Higher Education,* London: Kogan Page.

Candy, P.C. (1997) 'Some issues impacting on university teaching and learning: implications for academic developers' in S. Brown (ed.) *Facing Up to Radical Changes in Universities and Colleges.* London: Kogan Page.

Davis, S. and Botkin, J. (1994) *How Business is Mastering the Opportunity of Knowledge for Profit: The Monster Under the Bed.* New York: Simon and Schuster.

Desruisseaux, P. (1994) 'Assessing quality'. *Chronicle of Higher Education,* 7 (December), A41–42.

Ehrenfeld, T. (1996) 'What to chop?' *Newsweek,* 29 April: 59–68.

Erwin, T.D. (1991) *Assessing Student Learning and Development: A Guide to the Principles, Goals, and Methods of Determining College Outcomes,* San Francisco: Jossey-Bass.

Erwin, T.D. and Rieppi, R. (in press) 'A comparison of multimedia and traditional classrooms teaching undergraduate psychology courses'. Paper presented at the Annual Conference on Teaching of Psychology, March, Ellenville, NY.

Erwin, T.D. and Halpern, L.C. (1997) 'Perceptual abilities in the arts: a model for undergraduate education'. Submitted for publication.

Ewell, P.T. (1984) *The Self-regarding Institution: Information for Excellence.* Boulder, CO: National Center for Higher Education Management Systems.

Huber, R.M. (1992) *How Professors Play the Cat Guarding the Cream: Why We're Paying More and Getting Less in Higher Education.* Fairfax, VA: George Mason University Press.

Institute for Research on Higher Education (1997a) 'Turning point'. *Policy Perspectives,* 7(2), 1–12.

Institute for Research on Higher Education (1997b) 'The landscape: adding it up. The price-income squeeze in higher education'. *Change,* May–June.

Knight, P. (ed.) (1995) *Assessment for Learning in Higher Education.* London: Kogan Page.

Lenning, O.T. (1977) *The Outcomes Structure: An Overview and Procedures for Applying it in Postsecondary Education.* Boulder, CO: National Center for Higher Education Management Systems.

Lenzner, R. and Johnson, S.S. (1997) Seeing things as they really are, *Forbes,* pp. 122–8.

Linn, R.L. (ed.) (1989) *Educational Measurement.* New York: American Council on Education and Macmillan.

Mahoney, D. (1990) 'The demise of the university in a nation of universities: effects in current changes in higher education in Australia'. *Higher Education,* 19, 455–72.

McAleese, R. (1997) 'Technology in education to technology of education: concepts, conflicts and compromises' in S. Brown (ed.) *Facing Up to Radical Changes in Universities and Colleges.* London: Kogan Page.

Millman, J. and Greene, J. (1989) 'The specification and development of tests of achievement and ability' in R.L. Linn (ed.) *Educational Measurement.* New York: Macmillan.

Morrison, J.L. (1997) 'Looking back from 2005'. *On The Horizon,* 5(3): 2–3.

Pearce, A. (1997) 'Splitting the atom of education' in S. Brown (ed.) *Facing Up to Radical Changes in Universities and Colleges.* London: Kogan Page.

Perelman, L.J. (1992) *School's Out: A Radical New Formula for the Revitalization of America's Educational System.* New York: Avon Books.

Princeton Survey Research Associates (1997) *Newsweek,* 129 (Spring/Summer Special Edition): 8–9.

Roid, G.H. and Haladyna, T.M. (1982) *A Technology for Test-Item Writing.* Orlando, FL: Academic Press.

Romer, R. (1996) 'Making quality count – a governors' perspective on higher education' in *Educational Commission of the States, Making Quality Count in Undergraduate Education: A report of the ECS Chairman 'Quality Counts' Agenda in Higher Education,* pp. 1–4. Denver, CO: Education Commission of the States.

Sanchez, R. (1997) 'Colleges turning virtual classrooms into a reality: Growth of online degree programs offer new opportunities, presents new challenges'. *The Washington Post,* 27 March: 1, 18.

Smith, P. (1990) *Killing the Spirit: Higher Education in America.* New York: Penguin.

Strosnider, K. (1997) 'For-profit university challenges traditional colleges'. *Chronicle of Higher Education,* 6 June: A32.

Sykes, C.J. (1988) *Prof Scam: Professors and the Demise of Higher Education.* Washington, DC: Regency Gateway.

Terenzini, P.T. (1997). *Student Outcomes Information for Policy-making: Final Report of the National Postsecondary Education Cooperative Working Group on Student Outcomes from a Policy Perspective.* Washington: National Center for Education Statistics and US Department of Education.

Westerheijden, D.F. and van Vught, F.A. (1995) 'Assessment of quality in Western Europe'. *Assessment Update,* 7(2), 1–11.

Zieky, M.J. and Livingston, S.A. (1977) *Manual for Setting Standards on the Basic Skills Assessment Tests.* Princeton, NJ: Educational Testing Service.

4

Using Assessment Strategically to Change the Way Students Learn

Graham Gibbs

Introduction

Assessment is the most powerful lever teachers have to influence the way students respond to courses and behave as learners. This chapter will use a case study of a radical change in assessment within an otherwise conventional course to analyse the functions of assessment and the dramatic ways in which students can be reoriented and their performance improved. The framework derived from this analysis is used to explain how a range of assessment innovations can change the way students learn, with examples of each. Details of how to implement some of these assessment methods are elaborated in other chapters. Here I will provide a rationale for choosing between these methods.

Strategy and tactics

Much of what is presented as good practice in assessment is described in terms of tactics: specific techniques such as using criteria on feedback sheets to students. This chapter is about using assessment strategically, regardless of specific tactics, to achieve particular strategic goals. In order to see how to operate strategically, it is important to understand something of the changed context in which assessment in higher education is operating.

By the late 1990s, modules at Oxford Brookes University were designed in such a way that students were supposed to spend, on average, three-quarters of their total learning time outside of class. In some final-year modules, especially project-based modules, they were supposed to spend nine-tenths of their time out of class. When the ratio of in-class to out-of-class learning time is about 1 : 1 what happens in class exerts considerable leverage over what students do out of class. Preparation before tutorials or labs and reading or writing up after lectures or practical classes dominates what students do in their studying. A lecture may inspire a student to read more. A seminar may induce preparation to avoid social embarrassment. Once you get to a ratio of class time to independent study time of about 1 : 3 the class contact becomes less dominant. Students become more strategic in allocating their out-of-class time to what counts: to what is assessed. In-class hours may influence some of the hours out of class but much of this time is probably more influenced by the nature of assignments, by assessment criteria, by perceptions of what the important topics are and which might be examined, and so on.

Qualitative studies of the way students respond to assessment, or at least to their perceptions of assessment, provide a vivid insight into its central importance in their lives. At MIT, Snyder (1971) painted a vivid picture of how students learnt to see behind the formal curriculum and orient themselves to what he termed the 'hidden curriculum'. In particular, he showed the extent to which students constructed their own understanding of the curriculum from messages, explicit and implicit, about what counts in assessment.

> 'Just don't bother doing the homework now. I approach the courses so I can get an "A" in the easiest manner, and it's amazing how little work you have to do if you really don't like the course.'
>
> (Snyder 1971: 50)

In a study of students' orientation to the assessment system at Edinburgh University (Miller and Parlett 1974) researchers distinguished between students who sought out information about what counted in assessment ('cue seekers'), those who were aware of these cues and responded to them ('cue conscious'), and those who missed the cues no matter how often they were told and sometimes misoriented their efforts ('cue deaf'). The extent to which students were cued in to assessment demands was found to be a strong predictor of their overall performance. In both the Snyder and Miller studies the assessment system was found to be the dominant influence on the way students learnt: on how much effort they put in and what they allocated this effort to.

Interviews undertaken at Oxford Brookes University in the mid-1990s during studies of students' responses to class size reinforced this picture. In transcripts of the interviews, almost every paragraph contained references to the assessment system and the way it affected students' study patterns. These findings suggested that teachers' preoccupation with what went on inside large classrooms was misplaced. It was found that differences between the assessment regimes used in small and large classes were strongly related to differences in student performance (Gibbs and Lucas 1997). At Leeds Metropolitan University the extent of students' orientation to assessment has been quantified through extensive diary studies, logging exactly how students spend their time (Innis 1996). It was found that not only did assessment take up the majority of students' time out of class but this trend increased markedly over time. By Year 4 about three-quarters of student learning time was spent out of class and almost all of this time was spent on assessed tasks with only about 5 per cent of student time spent on out-of-class activity unrelated to assessment.

The increase in the extent to which students behave strategically is in part a cultural and economic phenomenon (MacFarlane 1992). Students who work in the evenings to pay off debts, and who worry about the competition for employment after graduating, tend to make very careful use of their time and effort. Faced with contexts as powerful as this, teachers have little choice but to go with the tide and use assessment strategically. If it is going to have a profound influence on what, how and how long students study then it might as well be designed to have educationally sound and positive influences rather than leaving the consequences to chance.

The focus in this chapter is on strategically manipulating the global response of students to the total assessment system. A variety of tactics might achieve similar strategic goals and it is the rationales behind these tactics rather than the details of their operation which will be explored. The strategic goals which are worthwhile pursuing will emerge as we analyse case studies.

A case study in cheap and effective change

This first case study illustrates how a modest change in an assessment regime achieved dramatic improvements in student performance. Its analysis draws out the principles which underlie this success, principles which can be used to guide strategic change in assessment in any context. This case study, like the others used here, is based on a real course but has been idealized to present a clearer picture of what went on.

The course was a compulsory second-year module of an engineering degree. Traditionally, it had been taught by twice-weekly lectures and weekly problem classes at which students worked on problem sheets handed out at the lectures. The problem sheets were marked by lecturers and handed back each week and the problem classes were relatively small with about ten students. Assessment was by exam and contained problems similar to those on the problem sheets. Average marks were about 55 per cent, much the same as on other modules, and the failure rate was acceptably low. As student numbers increased and eventually doubled, several problems emerged. In problem classes of over twenty, students could hide simply by avoiding eye contact and not asking questions, and as a result they could get away with having prepared poorly. The marking load became crippling and marking of weekly problem sheets had to be abandoned. The lectures, problems and exam remained the same as before but the average mark dropped to 45 per cent with a substantial failure rate.

The department could not afford to reinstate weekly marking of problem sheets and could not afford small problem classes. They looked around for possible alternative solutions and found one from Australia (Boud 1986) which involved peer assessment. Their implementation of peer assessment had the following features:

1. Students met in a lecture theatre on six occasions during the course, bringing with them all the problem sheets they had tackled up to that point and since the last peer-assessment session. They handed in their problems and these were randomly redistributed along with the kind of marking sheets which a postgraduate student would need to mark the problems. Students then marked whatever problems they found in front of them, using the marking sheets for guidance. They did not mark in careful and rigorous ways, there was no quality control over their marking and they were personal and forthright in their comments. They could see whose problem they were marking, but when students got their own problem sheets back it was not possible to tell who the marker had been.
2. The problem sheets were then handed back immediately but marks were not recorded and did not count towards course marks. Teachers were not involved at all in this process.
3. Students were required to complete a specified number of problem sheets, about three-quarters of the total. The problems which they had tackled were logged at the peer-assessment sessions. If they did not get sufficient sheets logged then they could not sit the exam and so failed the course.
4. Lectures, problem sheets, problem classes and the exam remained unchanged. The only change to the course was these six peer-assessment sessions which did not contribute to course marks.
5. For the purposes of distinguishing between students, the final examination was marked and all the problems undertaken and marked during the course were ignored. For the purpose of providing an external examiner with samples of student work to assure standards, again the exam was used and the coursework ignored.

The average marks in the exam increased from about 45 per cent to about 75 per cent with almost no failures and a good many outstanding performances. Marks were considerably better than during the previous years when teachers had marked problem sheets regularly and had held problem classes with much smaller groups.

When a transformation in performance on this scale occurs, it is likely that some important principles are involved. What are the most likely explanations, and what are the accompanying underlying principles? First, students actually did the problems. Previously when they had not been marked and there was no social pressure in problem classes to turn up prepared, they had simply stopped doing enough problems to learn. There are two underlying principles here. The first is 'time on task'. This is one of the 'Seven Principles for Good Practice in Undergraduate Education' (Chickering and Gamson 1987) shown in Table 4.1. This principle is based on research about the time students spend studying and the effect this has on their performance. Basically the principle is, 'If you don't spend time on it, you won't learn it'.

Table 4.1   The 'Seven Principles for Good Practice in Undergraduate Education' (Chickering and Gamson 1987)

1. Good practice encourages student-faculty contact.
2. Good practice encourages cooperation among students.
3. Good practice encourages active learning.
4. Good practice gives prompt feedback.
5. Good practice emphasizes time on task.
6. Good practice communicates high expectations.
7. Good practice respects diverse talents and ways of learning.

Assessment is an excellent way of getting students to spend time on task. However some assessment, such as final exams, distributes this time ineffectively, concentrating it immediately before the assessment rather than evenly across the course. Coursework assessment usually succeeds in capturing student time during the course but may focus it on a narrow subset of the course material at a particular point in time, for example on one essay question in week seven rather than evenly across all topics in all weeks. Making the tackling of problem sheets a weekly task and requiring sufficient problem sheets, to be completed by six intermediate deadlines, as in this case, both captured student time and distributed it reasonably evenly.

The second principle here is that not only did the assessment generate enough learning activity, it generated appropriate learning activity. The best way to learn how to tackle problems is to tackle lots of problems. Time spent in other ways (e.g. reading lecture notes) is unlikely to be as effective. Many assessment tasks generate uniquely appropriate learning activity which disappears if the assessment task disappears. For example, the reduction in the use of coursework essays forced on many courses by increased student numbers and resource constraints has in all probability led to a change in the nature of the reading students do. To write an essay you need to 'read around' a topic to develop an argument. Reading for a seminar or to prepare for an exam is qualitatively different. If you take the essay away, this kind of 'reading around' probably declines or even disappears. Assessment substitutes such as multiple-choice questions are extremely unlikely to generate this kind of reading. Appropriate assessment engages students in exactly the kind of learning activity you want to take place. Not all widely used conventional assessment tasks succeed in doing this. For example, writing up lab reports after lab sessions designed by the lecturer is unlikely to develop experimental design skills.

In this case study, the assessment in addition generated new forms of appropriate learning activity. Not only did students tackle the problems, they also marked other students' attempts at the problems. In doing this, they will have noticed other ways to succeed with problems than those they worked out for themselves, solutions to problems they could not solve, errors just like the silly ones they made themselves and other errors which they will have been alerted to avoid. The care and trouble other students take and the sloppiness of some other students is made visible and helps to calibrate the level of effort which is required and the standard which is expected. The model answers used will have provided clear reference points to reflect on their own solutions. The act of marking brings with it a heightened focus of attention to detail and a new perspective on one's own work which simply tackling the problems may not achieve. Note that this use of peer assessment did not involve marks which counted towards students' grades for the course: only the exam contributed marks. The value in the peer assessment came substantially from the act of marking: it created appropriate learning activity.

The third principle illustrated by this case study concerns the role of feedback. It is a truism that learners require feedback in order to learn. To get better at playing darts you have to be able to see where the darts land. When students stopped having their problem sheets marked, they stopped getting feedback and their performance declined. But there is more to feedback than it simply happening or not happening. It has to happen reasonably soon after the learning activity: 'Good practice gives prompt feedback' is another of the 'Seven Principles for Good Practice in Undergraduate Education' and the keyword here is 'prompt'. In the face of increasing student numbers, it is common for feedback to be slow: the sheer volume and logistics of commenting on and returning student work within a week defeats all but the most committed and organized teacher. And three weeks after submitting an assignment, students have moved on to another topic and are tackling another assignment for another course. They may not care about anything except the mark and may not even read feedback which has been carefully and expensively provided. It is common on courses lasting a single term or even a semester for coursework submitted two-thirds of the way through the course not to be returned until after exams. This is next to useless for the purpose of guiding and improving learning. Providing feedback on students' work is one of the most expensive components in their education but it is often not an effective investment simply because it happens too slowly. In the case above, students received feedback on their problems at six points during the course, and only one hour after submitting the problems for marking. The quality of feedback may in circumstances like this be less important than its frequency and timing. But even timely feedback may not have much impact if students do not pay serious attention to it.

The next principle involved here is that students pay attention to feedback which has a social dimension. By this I mean that students care what others think about them. A piece of work submitted confidentially and given a dreadful mark by a tutor they hardly know, may have little impact. A face-to-face meeting with a tutor who they know socially, about the same piece of work, is likely to have quite a different effect. And their peers and friends, seeing and judging the same hopeless work, in public, in front of others, is likely to have quite a dramatic impact. When students present work on posters which are displayed on the walls of classrooms or laboratories, and other students notice sloppy mistakes, slapdash presentation and shallow background studying, the social pressure makes students pay attention in ways which impersonal and confidential marking does not. In the case study, the assessment changed from a context where poor work was hardly noticed, even by the tutor, to one where a peer wrote comments all over your work, knowing it was you.

The final principle here concerns the internalization of criteria for quality and depends on who does the assessment. When academics submit an article for publication in a journal they spend a considerable amount of time making sure that, as far as they can ascertain, it is good enough for publication. Rejection is embarrassing and wastes time so drafts are read and improved several times before submission. Academics have a pretty shrewd understanding of the standards required from having read many journal articles and also from having acted as a referee for journals themselves. They have internalized what the threshold standard consists of and are reasonably good at judging when they have exceeded it. Students, in contrast, often hand in work which they have not even glanced through. They have no idea if it is good enough, no idea of the standard required and even if they did, it would not have occurred to them to apply this standard to their own work. After all, marking is what lecturers are paid for, right? When students object to self-assessment or peer assessment it is often because they do not understand the importance of internalizing standards in order to be able to supervise one's own work. The significance of peer assessment in this case study is likely to have been partly in the impact it will have had on the quality of self-supervision. Because students learnt how to assess others' problems, they learnt how to assess, and improve, their own, before they submitted them.

The functions of assessment

From analysing this case it can be argued that assessment has six main functions:

1. Capturing student time and attention.
2. Generating appropriate student learning activity.
3. Providing timely feedback which students pay attention to.
4. Helping students to internalize the discipline's standards and notions of quality.
5. Marking: generating marks or grades which distinguish between students or which enable pass/fail decisions to be made.
6. Quality assurance: providing evidence for others outside the course (such as external examiners) to enable them to judge the appropriateness of standards on the course.

Functions (5) and (6) are expensive to perform but this is not too much of a problem because they need to happen only rarely. In many undergraduate degree programmes it would be possible to predict final-degree classifications on the basis of about half a dozen carefully selected components of assessment, such as the final-year project or other large, complex open-ended tasks. In practice, undergraduate students may be marked over a hundred times in three years, but most of this marking contributes little either to distinguishing between students or to quality assurance. An analysis of marks in a science faculty programme at Portsmouth University suggested that as little as 5 per cent of the separate assessments undertaken may be sufficient to produce exactly the same degree classifications for students. The sheer volume may instead trivialize the nature of assessment tasks and result in a poor quality of attention by students, markers and examiners alike – and at great cost.

In contrast, if learning is to be supported, functions (1–4) have to happen frequently: as frequently as possible. Alverno College in the USA use assessment as a primary learning activity (Alverno College Faculty 1994): assessment happens constantly, especially in class, but not for the purpose of grading. In the case study, functions (5) and (6) were performed once only – in the exam. Functions (1) and (2) were performed every week as students tackled problem sheets. Functions (3) and (4) were performed six times during the course. Functions (1–4) were performed at a total cost of six administrator-hours in a lecture theatre. Because functions (5) and (6) need to be performed fairly, reliably and validly, they can be expensive. It matters little whether functions (1–4) are performed reliably. In the case study, student feedback could have been unfair or even plain wrong but it still worked because it generated the learning activity and quality of attention required for learning, Performing functions (1–4) can therefore be cheap or, as in cases discussed below, even free.

Using tactics to implement assessment strategies

Two broad tactics for changing student learning behaviour are illustrated here with examples in the form of cases. The first tactic is to change the assessment method, for example by changing from assessing every lab report to only sampling them for assessment, as in the 'Case of the mechanical engineer'. The nature of the assignment remains largely unchanged, but the way students go about tackling it changes in quality as a result of some change in the assessment method. The second broad tactic involves changing the assignment or learning task. Here the assessment method, such as using an exam, is retained, but the nature of the questions used in the exam is changed in order to change how students prepare for it, as in the 'Case of the philosopher of education'.

Tactic 1: Change the assessment method

The case of the pharmacist
In a pharmacy course, students handed in lab reports every week. They made similar errors every week, despite careful marking and commenting,

and the average marks for these lab reports increased only slightly, from about 5/10 to about 6/10 over the course of a semester. The time spent marking was substantial, about 20 hours a week, but seemed to have little impact on the quality of student work. The lecturer responsible for this course decided to introduce peer assessment – not for marks but for feedback. In the first week, he handed students several lab reports of mixed quality and asked them to mark and comment on them, without giving them any advice on how to do this. He then showed and explained his own marks, talked students through the marking scheme he used and asked them, in pairs, to re-mark the reports using his scheme. He then explained that from then on, every week, the first thing that would happen in each lab session is that each student would mark another student's lab report and hand it back immediately. Fifteen minutes were allowed for this. He sampled students' work and marked it himself to see if they were being rigorous. Their marks proved very accurate but, if anything, a little tough. The average marks went up to over 8/10 – an increase of 20 per cent as a result of the teacher not marking any more. These marks did not count towards course marks but the quality of reports, and presumably the quality of attention students paid to them, went up markedly. About 18 hours a week of marking time was saved. The purpose of the tactic of peer assessment here is to operationalize the strategy of getting students to internalize quality criteria and apply these criteria to their own and to others' work, in order to improve quality, in a way which tutor marking had failed to do.

The case of the mechanical engineer

On a practical engineering course, students undertook regular workshop-based practical work and wrote up this work in 25 reports. The marking load was very heavy and the quality of student work patchy, with crucial objectives concerned with communication skills, data handling and safety very poorly addressed. Regular marking was abandoned. Students were told that they had to hand in a complete portfolio of reports at the end of the year and that unless all 25 reports were present, they could not sit the exam. This solved the 'time on task' problem and made sure students did all the work. To ensure quality of effort as well as quantity, four of the reports were extracted from the portfolio at random and marked, and these marks counted towards the overall course marks. This ensured that students could not afford to drop their standards for any of their reports. Previously, so few marks were associated with each report that students did not care if they submitted the occasional weak report, but in the new regime they could lose 25 per cent of their coursework marks for a weak report. Sampling reduced total marking time to about 25 per cent of what it was previously.

What would have been lost by sampling like this was regular feedback – so the course used a variety of economical feedback methods to give students various types of feedback on each report as it was written: model reports, oral feedback in a lecture on the basis of reading a sample of reports, peer feedback at the start of practical sessions, and so on.

The case of the accountant

An accountancy course was taught by lectures and assessed entirely by an end-of-course exam which contained questions on the material and procedures covered in the lectures. Despite the close matching of the exam to the lectures, student performance was extremely poor with a substantial minority failing both the exam and the re-sit exam and very few gaining high marks. The diagnosis was that students were not working regularly on the problems and methods explained in the lectures and were not getting feedback on their misunderstandings or mistakes. Regular tutor marking and feedback could not be afforded. The course adopted a method borrowed from a preclinical medical course at a nearby university. Students were formed into learning teams of four, allocated randomly. They were told that, although they would sit the exam on their own, they would be allocated the average mark of their team of four. Students were told of the positive impact of this method elsewhere and they approved of the change. Not trusting each other not to let others down, they all taught each other furiously, making sure that each of the other three in their group was completely on top of the content every week. Exam marks increased dramatically with few individual fail marks. Individually failing students had to re-sit an exam, but the re-sit mark still counted towards the group mark, so the other students tutored the failed student through the re-sit, and almost all passed at the second attempt. There were also many high marks – in fact, the changed grade distribution benefited the best students more than the poor students. The act of tutoring others greatly increased their learning and their marks. There were no changes in the lectures or in the exam and the innovation was at zero cost.

The tactic here was the use of learning teams and shared exam marks. The strategy was to capture enough learning time, distributed evenly across the course, to make the learning activity productive, and to provide regular feedback.

Tactic 2: Change the assessment task

The case of the philosopher of education

A philosophy of education module which was part of a Certificate in Teaching in Further Education course used a final exam in which students were asked questions in the form: 'Compare and contrast the philosophies of X and Y in relation to classroom practice Z.' Students who had diligently attempted to memorize features of each philosopher they had covered in the course duly listed several features of each, the bright ones spotted a difference and the really bright ones understood a practical implication. All students attempted to 'fake good' – to make out that they knew more philosophy than they really did. The main problem with this assessment is that it did not generate appropriate learning activity. As it was possible to pass the course by memorizing some factual details, this is all most students did. In lectures and in their reading they tried to spot the facts they should note down about each philosopher for later use. Attempting to show understanding was dangerous in that they could be wrong – so they played safe with facts. A new course leader transformed the course, not by changing the content or the teaching, but by changing the exam questions. Students were told that there would be two compulsory exam questions. In the exam, they would be shown a 10-minute video of a teacher in a further education classroom and asked to 'Comment on what is going on in this class from a philosophical point of view' and to 'Advise this teacher on her future practice, from a philosophical point of view'. The same question was used every year. All that changed was what was on the video. One year it might illustrate issues of power and control, the next year issues of ethics, equality of opportunity, or whatever. There was no way a student could prepare for such an exam by memorizing facts about philosophers. The only sensible way to prepare was to look at what went on in classrooms from a philosophical point of view and to discuss and tune up this point of view by using ideas gleaned from the lectures and the reading. Students took themselves off to observe classrooms, borrowed videos of classrooms, and sat and discussed what they had seen with other philosophy students. The learning activity was then appropriate. The syllabus, lectures and reading list were all largely unchanged, but the learning outcomes were completely transformed. The tactic here was to change the exam question. The strategy was to use assessment to change the nature of student-learning activities to make them more appropriate.

The case of the Norwegian engineer

Engineering undergraduate courses are normally assessed in large part by a series of exams on specialist subtopics such as mechanics, materials, mathematics or management. Exam questions often relate closely to the type of problems students have tackled as they have progressed through the course. Students prepare for such exams by practising the problems on their problem sheets and in their lecture notes. Students tend not to practise tackling real-world complex problems of the kind engineers face, which involve mechanics, materials and management, all at the same time because – as students – they are rarely, if ever, tested in exams which span these topics. The result is that students memorize algorithms for predictable small-scale problems but tend not to learn how to tackle unpredictable large-scale problems such as those they will encounter in work, except perhaps in a final-year project. In a Norwegian engineering programme, the final exam consisted of one very large, complex real-world problem. Instead of each problem being able to be tackled in about 10 or 20 minutes, they had all day and were not expected to finish – they were assessed on how much progress they had made. In addition, they could take into the exam any kind of aid they liked. Professional engineers use computer programs which solve equations, manuals, books, notes – in fact, every kind of support they find helpful. They do not try and remember everything. So students were allowed the same kind of aids, including their lecture notes, books, laptop computers with any kind of software they liked, and so on. The result of such an exam is that students focus their revision and their preceding study, not on how to tackle predictable problems from memory, but on how to prepare for unpredictable real-world problems, just like a practising engineer. The tactic was to change the exam and exam question. The strategy was to generate appropriate learning activity.

Planning strategic change

Throughout this chapter, the emphasis has been not so much on assessment methods and tasks *per se* as on their consequences for student learning. Students are tuned in to an extraordinary extent to the demands of the assessment system and even subtle changes to methods and tasks can produce changes in the quantity and nature of student effort and in the nature of learning outcomes out of all proportion to the scale of the change in assessment. In planning such strategic change, the following questions can help generate ideas and an appropriate focus of attention.

- How well are students currently performing, and what are they poor at?
- What do students currently do with their time out of class and do they spend enough time, distributed evenly enough?
- How is their learning behaviour influenced by the current assessment methods and tasks?
- In particular, are some aspects of learning behaviour dysfunctional as a by-product of the assessment?
- Do students gain the feedback they need on their progress and on their main learning activities, when they need it?
- How else might they gain useful feedback quickly enough and cheaply enough?
- How might students' learning time be captured in sufficient quantity and with an appropriate distribution across the course, without increasing tutor effort, for example by introducing course requirements?
- What learning benefits might accrue from students doing some of the assessment for themselves and/or each other that teachers currently do for them?
- How could students be supported in internalizing what quality means in your context so that they actively review their own work rather than leaving such judgements to the tutor.
- How could social pressures be brought to bear to increase students' sense of responsibility to others and their cooperation in learning?

Using these questions, assessment can be used strategically to change the way students learn.

References

Alverno College Faculty (1994) *Student Assessment-as-Learning at Alverno College*, 3rd edn. Milwaukee, WI: Alverno College Institute.

Boud, D. (1986) *Implementing Student Self-Assessment.* Green Guide No. 5. Kensington: Higher Education Research and Development Society of Australasia.

Chickering, A.W. and Gamson, Z.F. (1987) *Seven Principles for Good Practice in Undergraduate Education. Wingspread Journal,* 9(2), special insert.

Gibbs, G. and Lucas, L. (1997) 'Coursework assessment, class size and student performance 1984–94'. *Journal of Further and Higher Education,* 21(2), 183.

Innis, K. (1996) *Diary Survey: How Undergraduate Full-time Students Spend their Time.* Leeds: Leeds Metropolitan University.

MacFarlane, B. (1992) 'The "Thatcherite" generation of university degree results'. *Journal of Further and Higher Education,* 16, 60–70.

Miller, C.M.L. and Parlett, M. (1974) *Up to the Mark: A Study of the Examination Game.* Guildford: Society for Research into Higher Education.

Snyder, B.R. (1971) *The Hidden Curriculum.* Cambridge, MA: MIT Press.

Part 2

Exploring the Effectiveness of Innovative Assessment

Earlier chapters have argued for changes to assessment. In this part, the chapters address explicitly the question of innovation, and provide practical advice about how to begin to approach it.

Phil Race in Chapter 5 urges us to ask for whom assessment takes place, what its purpose is and what the various stakeholders in higher education want and need. Answering these questions takes him to a position where he advocates innovation despite the risks associated with it. He concludes that because traditional methods are not fulfilling their purposes – they fail to measure the knowledge, skills and attributes which we mean them to – we have no choice but to look to new ways of assessing. Our choices will involve us in making decisions about the timing and content of assessment, and about the balance between collaborative and individual work and that between assessing content and performance. In each of these decisions, Phil Race helps by providing us with prompting questions.

Liz McDowell and Kay Sambell (Chapter 6) in drawing our attention to the student perspective suggest that we do not yet know enough about the use of innovative methods in practice. We do not know whether they fulfill successfully the aspirations that, in them, teaching, learning and assessment are integrated into a meaningful unity. Their chapter makes it clear that innovative assessment is not necessarily beneficial to students and may not be entirely welcomed by them, although their research indicates that there may be considerable advantages over what students see as combative approaches in traditional assessment. To realize the potential of innovative assessment, we need to involve students and to share with them the intentions and implementation of new methods and approaches. They suggest that there are seven steps which can guide the teacher in implementing new assessment approaches more effectively, and that it is worth the effort – not least for students!

Finally, in Neil Fleming's chapter (Chapter 7), we are cautioned against an uncritical adoption of innovation. Like any other form of assessment, innovative assessment carries risks with it, and indeed may be more open to bias than more traditional methods. Bias does not necessarily operate against the student: it can inflate assessment outcomes as well as unconsciously disadvantaging students. We are taken on a tour through the major sources of bias before Neil Fleming identifies some of the steps which can be taken to reduce such effects through moderation, sample marking, the development of explicit and public criteria, and through training.

5

Why Assess Innovatively?

Phil Race

Introduction

If traditional assessment practices and instruments were working perfectly, there would be no need for innovative assessment. With something as crucial as assessment, it is essential that innovation is not approached lightly, or engaged in for its own sake. The future careers and lives of students are at stake, and the scope for experimentation must be carefully delineated and planned. Before justifying the need to assess innovatively, it is important to be convinced that traditional methods are not serving the purposes for which they were designed. In this chapter, we take a fresh look at the role of assessment in higher education, including discussion of the various client groups that assessment should be serving, and the needs of these groups. We then explore how some traditional approaches to assessment are failing, in that they are not measuring the intended learning outcomes that we claim are important for students to develop, and are often promoting surface approaches to learning. The ways that students perceive their learning, and the ways that academics perceive their teaching, are all significantly dependent on the nature and formats of assessment. Therefore, changing assessment can best be justified if the quality of both teaching and learning are improved as a result, and if the assessment itself can be shown to be demonstrably fairer, and better related to the intended learning outcomes. It is argued that assessment must play a better part in the ways that teachers teach and learners learn.

I will conclude with checklist questions about some of the principal factors that can be adjusted either separately or in combination, to form the basis of innovations in assessment. The questions aim to be an aid to fuel productive innovation, to counter the dangers of overassessment, and help to ensure that assessment may be used to promote deeper approaches to learning.

Assessment for whom?

Higher education is often talked about using industrial and commercial metaphors. The sector has been described as being driven by market forces. Management systems which may work well in commerce and industry are increasingly transposed into higher education, however inappropriately. Students themselves are much better informed about their rights as consumers in this market, and their awareness and sensitivity to the performance criteria of educational institutions has never been more acute. Whether we like it or not, the most significant product of higher education is now the qualifications that students gain, rather than the quality of their learning experience. Part of the aim of this chapter is to point to ways of balancing assessment so that it enhances and enriches students' learning experience, as well as leading to qualifications that are valid and appropriate for their future lives and careers. The client groups served by assessment are diverse, and it is relevant to look at the respective expectations of students themselves, the employers who will take them on when qualified, and other significant stakeholders in higher education such as the teachers who work in the system, subject reviewers who review the system, parents who increasingly pay for the system, and society in general for whom the system should be geared.

What should assessment do for students?

Ultimately, assessment should be for students. It should not only serve to ensure that their qualifications are valid and relevant to their career development, but also should be a formative part of their learning experience. Other chapters in this book explore in detail how assessment can deliver much more significant learning payoff to students than is often the case with familiar, traditional approaches. Various contributions to Knight's (1995) book show the extent to which assessment practices can let students down. At present, students often feel that they are excluded from the assessment culture, and that they have to use trial and error to make successive approximations towards the performances that are being sought in assessed work. Students developing their technique the best tend to succeed in assessment, and it is not always the students who could have most to offer to the future development of the fields in which they are studying.

What do employers want from assessment?

Employers have a vested interest in assessment. Students' achievements are the principal basis of selection for employment. Employers wish to be able to make well-informed decisions when short-listing candidates for interview. They also wish to be able to tell, from assessment data, whether students are going to turn out to be good employees, and not just subject experts.

Employees need to be able to work together, to communicate effectively, and to think creatively, and it is not enough for them just to be knowledgeable about the subjects that they have studied. Employers, therefore, have a strong interest in what is assessed, as well as in how fairly the assessment practices and instruments function. Employers also want it to be easy for them to use students' assessment data in short-listing and recruitment. This often means that they find it more acceptable to use degree results as a quick indicator of candidates' suitability for posts, even when such results may be poor indicators of actual employability potential. Employers also tend to remember assessment as it was when they themselves studied, and this can make them more reluctant to think about the benefits that may be linked to innovations in assessment. It is therefore necessary to be able both to spell out these benefits to them, as well as to explain why the innovations are necessary in terms of what was wrong with some of the assessment formats they themselves encountered.

What do parents expect of assessment?

Parents remain a very significant factor in students' learning. This is not least because the monetary aspect of their vested interest has increased significantly, as their financial contribution to students' education has become more important. Parents increasingly subsidize the time their offspring spend in higher education, and are naturally concerned about all factors contributing to quality in teaching, learning and assessment, even though they are often distanced from the day-to-day experience of students. They need to be assured that assessment processes and practices are fair, equitable and valid, and that students are well informed about the rules of the assessment game. Parents too, however, may distrust innovations in assessment, especially if they believe that such innovations are made merely to save money.

What do teaching staff need of assessment?

For most teaching staff, designing and implementing assessment instruments and processes, and marking students' work, are crucial parts of their day-to-day work. However, lecturers and tutors now have less face-to-face time with individual students, and often carry out most of their dealings with students in large-group situations. Their ability to base assessment results on really knowing students is reduced, and therefore they need to take steps to ensure that assessment practices and instruments are well designed and valid. In an educational system where the prominence of institutional and departmental performance indicators has increased dramatically, they need to ensure that assessment (which is one of the most public performance indicators) is measuring what it is intended to be measuring. With syllabus content expressed in terms of intended learning outcomes, and with standards associated with graduateness becoming increasingly public, the onus is on lecturers to be able to demonstrate that assessment is measuring well what it is intended to measure. The increased need to make assessment robust and valid comes at a time when most lecturers are under increasing pressure to make their research output more significant, as well as to cope with unprecedented administration and bureaucracy in higher education. There is a significant risk that assessment becomes an intolerable burden on them, and it is not surprising that the assessment innovations which are most attractive to lecturers are those which can make their work more efficient.

What do subject reviewers expect of assessment?

In the UK, and in many other parts of the world, the funding of higher education depends on assessments of the quality of teaching, learning and assessment. Various models of quality audit, and quality review are in operation. In England, for example, the Quality Assurance Agency for Higher Education and the Higher Education Funding Council for England organize 'subject reviews' in universities and colleges, and among other aspects of provision, assessment processes come under the spotlight for inspection. The English system of teaching quality assessment continues to evolve, and universities are now required to furnish substantial evidence of the student's own work, alongside assessment data. Some of the guidance, in the form of checklist questions, given to subject reviewers to help them to interrogate the quality of assessment, is presented below (adapted from UCoSDA 1996):

1. Do the assessment tasks or questions link closely with the learning objectives of the course? What is the evidence for such linkage?
2. Is there a sufficient diversity of assessment methods used?
3. Are the assignments and tasks sufficiently challenging?
4. Do the assignments encourage deep, active, reflective learning?
5. Do the assignments provide opportunities for students to apply their knowledge and understanding to different problems and contexts?
6. Is the oral/written feedback provided to students meaningful and helpful?
7. Is the marking accurate and consistent?
8. Is there a system for checking the consistency of the marking of assignments and examination papers?
9. Are the students aware of the criteria or marking schemes used for marking assignments and examinations? Are the criteria sufficiently explicit?
10. Is there a system for identifying assessment workloads for students and staff?
11. Is it working?

Although these questions do not directly refer to innovations in assessment, they provide a useful frame of reference to ensure that innovations can be seen to address the principal requirements being made regarding the quality of assessment.

What does society require from assessment?

Taxpayers and electors are naturally concerned that funding spent on all aspects of education is well managed. With a much higher proportion of the population aspiring to degree qualifications, the level of interest in assessment has increased. The extent to which people regard themselves as stakeholders in education has increased accordingly. This leads to a greater demand that the outcomes of higher education are relevant to society in general, and that successful students are well qualified to contribute to society.

Why innovate? – there's no need if it's working!

One of the most significant dangers facing higher education is that of trying to replace things which aren't broken. Any risks associated with innovations in assessment are far more serious than any dangers linked to innovations in teaching practices, learning environments or syllabus content. Assessment directly affects students' immediate futures and their whole future careers. Even decades after students complete their last examinations, their assessment results continue to be scrutinized when they apply for promotion, or change jobs or career directions.

Before investing the time and energy necessary to introduce innovations in assessment, it is important to be convinced about the areas where traditional methods are not fulfilling their purposes. Those opposing innovations in assessment often refer to traditional methods as being tried and tested. This can be a strong argument against innovation. Anything new brings with it its own risks. However, it is equally valid to propose that when something is indeed tried and tested, there is a tendency to become blind to the shortfalls and weaknesses that are involved. McDowell and Sambell in Chapter 6 present interesting evidence of students' reactions to innovations in assessment, showing that students themselves are all too aware of some of the shortcomings of traditional assessment methods.

There is widely shared concern that assessment does not measure the knowledge, skills and attributes that are intended to be assessed. In other words, assessment is often simply not valid. For example, traditional unseen examinations tend to measure students' skills to perform in this particular environment, which is in most respects one far removed from both the working environment, and the lifestyle, for which higher education should be aiming to equip them. Similarly, assessment tends to be dominated by measurements of things which are relatively straightforward to assess, such as written answers, essays, reports and dissertations. The students who fare best in such assessments are those who develop those skills which relate directly to succeeding to extract marks from assessors marking such work. Again, what is actually measured may only be a pale reflection of students' real learning.

I therefore continue this chapter with a short analysis of some of the principal weaknesses of two of the most familiar kinds of assessment, traditional unseen written exams and continuous assessment. In each case, I present first some of the tensions that can occur between these kinds of assessment and the quality of students' learning, then move on to some of the operational weaknesses that can easily jeopardize the validity and reliability of these assessment formats, however safe, familiar and comfortable they may seem to be to assessors.

Some failings of traditional unseen written exams

Much has been written about the weaknesses of unseen traditional examinations. I do not wish to suggest that such examinations should be abandoned altogether, and elsewhere in this book are suggestions about ways of using many other forms of examination. Alternatives include open-book exams, time-unconstrained exams, take-away exams, multiple-choice exams, computer-delivered assessments, oral exams and assessed presentations. However, the unseen written exam continues to dominate many educational programmes. In particular, this assessment format seems to be at odds with the most important factors underpinning successful learning. For example, Brown *et al.* (1998) in an edited collection of articles on student motivation, demonstrate fundamentally how assessment can affect (and often damage) students' enthusiasm to learn. Of particular significance are the chapters by Mortimer (Brown *et al.* 1998: 173–88), advocating the benefits of portfolios over traditional assessment methods, Newstead (ibid.: 189–200), presenting startling evidence about the frequency of cheating, and Leach, Neutze and Zepke (ibid.: 201–11) giving insight into the links between assessment and motivation from studies in New Zealand. Moreover, there is abundant evidence that assessors are not particularly good at making exams valid, reliable, or transparent to students. Some of the principal concerns that can be expressed are summarized below.

Firstly, there are tensions between examinations and the quality and depth of students' learning experience. Exams do not do much to increase students' motivation in terms of their want to learn. They may, however, cause students to need to learn, which is a significant driving force for learning, if not the happiest one. Students often make choices in modular schemes so that they avoid this kind of assessment if they can. This can lead them to choose subjects in which they are less interested than those which they fear to select because they will be subjected to such exams. Most exams are not ideal learning experiences in their own right. Though students may do a lot of learning before formal unseen written examinations, their actual experiences of learning in such situations is very limited.

Secondly, traditional exams are cause for concern in the context of a further important aspect of deep learning: feedback. The amount of feedback that students receive after most kinds of exam is not optimal. Feedback plays a vital role in learning, yet most systems require exam scripts to be regarded as secret documents, not to be shown to students on any account! Traditional unseen written exams can, in this situation, be said to be lost learning experiences. Exams do not do much to help students make sense of what they have learned. While during the time leading up to exams, there may be a significant amount of making sense of what has been learned, the assessment experience itself does little to help students to gain any further deepening of their knowledge or skills.

Thirdly, exams usually force students into surface learning, and into rapidly clearing their minds of previous knowledge when preparing for the next exam. Students are encouraged by the assessment regime, to clear their brains of the knowledge they have stored for each exam in turn. One of the defences of those supporting the continuation of unseen written exams, is that these concerns about the tensions between assessment and learning quality are not important as the intention of the assessment is summative rather than formative. They argue that feedback to students should be handled elsewhere in an educational programme, rather than in the context of examinations. However, I argue that the extent of the tensions exceeds that associated with the contribution of feedback to learning quality.

Fourthly, there are concerns about validity and reliability of traditional unseen written exams. Examinations scripts are usually marked far too quickly. Most staff who mark exams agree that the task usually has to be completed in haste, in preparation for timetabled exam boards. It can then be said that one of the most important things that we do for students is performed as a bolt-on addition, rather than a well-planned central part of the design of their education. Lecturers and examiners are often tired and bored when marking students' scripts. Because of the speed with which exam scripts need to be marked, and the pressure to do the task well, staff are not functioning at their best while undertaking the task. This leads to increased danger that the assessment is not reliable. Even under good conditions, there is abundant data on the problems both of inter-assessor reliability and intra-assessor reliability. This suggests that even the best groups of assessors find it a difficult and complex process.

Finally, there is cause for concern that traditional unseen written exams do not really measure the learning outcomes which are the intended purposes of higher education. Brown (Chapter 8) expands on this concern in the context of assessing practice. Exams tend to favour candidates who happen to be skilled at doing exams, rather than at anything more important. If we look at exactly what skills are measured by unseen written exams, the most important of these from the students' point of view turns out unsurprisingly to be the techniques needed to do unseen written exams! This can be interpreted as a serious threat to the validity of such exams; in other words, what is being measured may be much less important than what should have been measured. There are many important qualities which are not tested by traditional exams. For example, unseen written exams are limited or useless for measuring teamwork, leadership, and are rarely a suitable vehicle for measuring creativity and lateral thinking.

Some failings of continuous assessment systems

The umbrella term 'continuous assessment' tends to be applied to ongoing measurement of the work that students do throughout a course rather than at fixed end-points. The term 'formative assessment' is often mentioned in such contexts, particularly when continuous assessment is coupled with the provision of feedback to students on their work. However, there is still the need for much of continuous assessment to play a summative role, in that it is counted towards overall assessment, including sometimes final-degree classifications.

Firstly, there are tensions between continuous assessment and the learning payoff which is associated with the time students spend doing assessed work. When students are under too much coursework pressure, their 'want to learn' is damaged. When almost everything that students do is measured, they naturally adopt strategic approaches to their learning, and only concentrate on those things that are going to be assessed. Students' learning becomes driven by assessment, and students may only do those things that are assessed. Such strategic approaches can be made beneficial if the nature and range of the assessed tasks are adjusted to make all the learning that students do in their assessed work as relevant as possible to the intended learning outcomes. Furthermore, the range of learning experiences associated with continuous assessment can be too narrow. For example, essays and reports make up the majority of students' continuous assessment formats in many disciplines, and the skills tested are primarily those associated with preparing essays and reports, rather than the deeper knowledge or understanding that may be intended. The value of feedback to students may be eclipsed by marks or grades. Students pay most attention to their scores or grades when they get back marked work, and often are quite blind to valuable feedback which may accompany their returned work. Furthermore, students may not have the opportunity to make sense of the feedback they receive. Particularly when there is a long delay in getting feedback to students, they may already have moved on to learning other topics, and they do not then find learning from the feedback a priority. Students are often quite unaware of the criteria used to assess their work. When students are practised in interpreting and making use of assessment criteria, the standard of their assessed work rises dramatically. Alerting students to the detail of the assessment agenda is regarded by some staff as a move towards 'spoonfeeding'. However, enabling students to demonstrate their full potential is a desirable goal.

Secondly, there are concerns about validity and reliability of continuous assessment. For example, it can be difficult to detect unwanted collaboration. Particularly with assignments submitted in word-processed formats, it is hard, if not impossible, to detect every instance of plagiarism or copying. For teaching staff, continuous assessment often results in too much time spent in marking. In many courses, lecturers continue to try to use the same continuous assessment processes that worked quite well when student numbers were much smaller. This leads to reduced reliability of assessment. Students have their own problems with continuous assessment, and may get the balance wrong between ongoing assessment and exams. For example, students feeling under pressure to submit coursework by stated deadlines, may still be attempting such work at a late stage in their studies on a particular module, when they would be better advised to cut their losses regarding coursework and prepare for important exams.

The failings both of traditional unseen written exams in particular, and continuous assessment regimes in general, should not be taken as sufficient causes to abandon all traditional approaches to assessment. Despite these failings, traditional assessment systems have worked for a long time, and much of the experience that has been developed in making them work continues to represent valuable foundations for further development of assessment processes and practices. I suggest that innovations in assessment need to build on this experience, and that innovations need to be made incrementally, and tested and refined on an ongoing basis. It should not surprise anyone if an assessment innovation proves not to work well at first. As long as each innovation is carefully regulated to ensure that any teething troubles do not translate into casualties in students' learning experiences or their subsequent qualifications, there remains every reason to experiment with and research into the validity and reliability of innovative approaches to assessment.

Dimensions of innovation

There are many variables which can be the basis for experimentation, research and analysis in redesigning student assessment. Any of these variables can be adjusted independently, or two or more can be the basis for innovations. I suggest that the most productive way of deciding upon directions for innovation is, however, to interrogate each of the variables separately at first, and to have good reasons for wishing to adjust them before planning the implementation of any innovation. The dimensions I will consider are timing, content, choice of assessment methods, the balance between individual and collaborative work, and the balance between assessing performance and assessing evidence. The anticipated effects of each and every adjustment should, I suggest, be interrogated against the following five questions:

- How can the innovation increase the learning payoff associated with the assessment experience?
- How can the innovation claim to make the assessment more valid? (In other words, how does the new assessment instrument or process get closer to measuring students' genuine and direct achievement of the intended learning outcomes?)
- How can the innovation be defended in terms of the assessment being more reliable than that which it is replacing?

- How can the innovation be seen to make the assessment workload of the staff involved more realistic, productive and relevant to students' qualifications?
- How can the innovation reduce the extent to which students are forced to jump repeatedly through the same hoops?

In the foregoing, I suggest that each of the questions above should be used together with the separate questions I will propose about each of the dimensions of innovation addressed in turn.

Timing of assessment

In traditional educational programmes, there has always been a tendency to have most of the important assessment episodes towards the end of a course or module. While this can be justified in terms of this being the time when students should have learned enough to be ready for assessment, a consequence is that too much weight is placed on students' performance during a period of a few hours spread over a week or two. Moreover, the assessment of all the different subjects being studied tends to converge at these times. This is bad news for the significant numbers of students who do not happen to be at their best during this narrow bandwidth of time. Some questions about timing which may fuel innovations are presented below.

- Is that which is measured in three hours much more reliable than that which could have been measured in 30 minutes? A short exam, for example, can measure some things just as well as a much longer one (and take much less time to assess, with more chance of the assessment being done in a reliable way).
- Is speed so important? What is the desired balance between students doing something well and doing the same thing quickly? How significant is the danger that we force all students to do things quickly, then end up measuring how well they do them under such conditions, missing out measuring how well they could have done them? When speed is deemed to be important, are we in danger of measuring speed too often?
- Why can a three-hour exam be justified? What is it that can be measured in three hours that could not be measured in much shorter assessment episodes? There are indeed good answers to these questions, but then we might ask two further questions: How often do we need to measure these things? Are we in danger of using a lot of time to measure these same things repeatedly?
- Do all summative assessments have to occur during the same weeks? An alternative would be to have modules spanning different lengths of time, and starting and finishing at different times of the year. This would at least allow students to concentrate their energies on assessments (coursework or exams) in one subject at a time. It can be argued that this will be

fairer in terms of students demonstrating their optimum performance in each subject.

- With coursework, what is the learning payoff per unit time involved? For example, how much greater is the learning payoff of writing a full essay, than of producing a clear essay plan? How many times do we need to get students to produce full essays (or reports) to show that they can do so? How often could we use short-form assessments to generate significant learning payoff over much shorter timescales?

Content being assessed

The validity of assessment needs to be the prime directive in deciding how the content agenda is addressed. What are we actually measuring? Some content-related questions which may fuel innovation in assessment are listed below.

- What are we trying to assess? Is it merely how much students can remember about what they have read? Is it merely how well they can write about what they remember about what they have learned? Is it how well students can handle a given body of information? Is it how well students can find their own way through all the available information, and pick out what is the most important information?
- Is assessment measuring what has been learned, and not just what was taught? The Quality Assurance Agency in England emphasizes the importance of this in the briefing of subject reviewers.
- Are we measuring learning, or are we paying too much attention to the ways that students communicate their learning in writing? If the latter, are we giving appropriately weighted credit to students' communication skills, and making sure that we are not measuring the same skills more frequently than we need to?
- What content agenda are we trying to measure? How much of it is what has been covered in lectures? How much of it should be what students have found out for themselves? How do we communicate to students the content agenda that we intend to set for them? How can we show them what we will be looking for in their assessed work, without stunting their own initiative and creativity?
- Where the content has already been delineated in terms of learning outcomes, how appropriate is the assessment method to the measurement of students' actual achievement of the outcomes?

Selection of assessment methods

Throughout this book are mentioned different assessment methods. A wide range of assessment methods are discussed by Brown and Knight (1994).

These range from traditional unseen written exams, through many kinds of alternative exam formats, to a wide variety of other 'measurables' that can be products of students' individual work or of their collaborative work. Each assessment method advantages some students. Each assessment method disadvantages other students. The following general questions about assessment methods can be the starting point for productive innovations in assessment.

- Is there a sufficient diversity in the mixture of assessment methods being used on each course? Does this allow students who happen not to show themselves at their best in particular assessment situations adequate opportunities to demonstrate their full potential through other assessment situations?
- Does the amount of time devoted by students to their work related to each assessment method reflect the relative importance of what is being measured in each instance?
- Are we using diverse assessment methods to ensure that we are not measuring the same things again and again?

The balance between collaborative and individual work

As mentioned earlier in this chapter, and in many other places in this book, employers value collaborative skills. Indeed, most avenues of working life or professional development involve collaboration at least as much as individual effort or personal achievement. Traditionally, assessment has tended to measure individual achievement, not least because this is easier to measure 'fairly' or 'objectively', but I have placed these words in quotes because it is often the individuality that is measured thus, rather than that which it should have been intended to measure fairly and objectively. When trying to measure collaborative work objectively, there is the danger that 'if we can assess it, it probably isn't it!' A couple of questions about the balance between assessment of individual work and collaborative work, which may provide food for thought for assessment innovations, are given below.

- Is the difficulty in attributing individual achievement standing in the way of using assessed collaborative tasks to measure valuable skills and attributes? It is likely that in the overall assessment profile of the course, individual achievement will already be addressed substantially. Therefore, it may be worth striking a balance between the value of the collaborative work and the objectivity of some aspects of its assessment.
- Are there ways in which triangulation of individual achievement within collaborative work can be made? For example, when it is only possible to measure the overall product of collaborative work, can a viva or presentation be used to make a realistic estimate of the individual contribution to the work?

The balance between assessing performance or assessing evidence

To achieve a realistic, rounded assessment, any assessment programme needs to balance the measurement of students' performance alongside that of the evidence which they produce. With some kinds of evidence, there may be concerns about the authenticity of the ownership of the work being assessed. Yet some aspects of performance are too difficult or overly time-consuming to attempt to measure directly, and assessment may need to concentrate on evidence arising from the performance. The balance between evidence and performance needs to be a consideration in all forms of assessment. Even with as familiar an assessment format as traditional unseen written exams, the evidence which is assessed relates both to students' learning achievements and to their performance under the conditions of the assessment. The following questions are intended to provide some starting points for assessment innovations addressing the need to optimize the balance between assessing evidence and performance.

- Are the conditions under which the assessment takes place appropriate? For example, if the real intention is to assess performance of some kind, does the assessment method lend itself to measuring this objectively, and are the assessment criteria relating to the performance clearly understood by the students themselves?
- Are the same elements of performance being measured too often? Some aspects of performance are easier to measure than others, and there is the danger of measuring the same ones again and again, while failing to try to measure other (perhaps more important) elements. For example, the assessment of essays in written exams at least partially reflects the performance of writing an essay in handwriting (rather than using a word-processor) under exam conditions, and good performance at this task may be repeatedly rewarded, and cumulatively may play too significant a part in distinguishing a first-class degree from a lower one.
- Where it has been decided that a particular performance aspect is important, is the measurement being done in a way that promotes learning and provides feedback to students? Using self-assessment of performance as a contributory factor can cause deepening of the associated learning experience. Using peer assessment of the performance can lead to greater reliability of the assessment, and can provide increased richness of feedback to students about their performances.

Conclusions

The dimensions of innovation I chose to discuss in this chapter are by no means exhaustive. They are intended to be indicative, and to illustrate just some of the possibilities regarding assessment innovations. They should enable readers to find their own rationale in looking for ways in which innovative assessment can be introduced, not least because we are increasingly aware that the familiar, tried-and-tested methods are not matching up to the requirements of a widening range of stakeholders in higher education. Most importantly, however, assessment innovations are the best way forward in researching and evaluating the effects of assessment on the two most vital factors involved: the quality of students' learning and the validity of their qualifications.

References

Brown, S. and Knight, P. (1994) *Assessing Learners in Higher Education*. London: Kogan Page.

Brown, S., Armstrong, S. and Thompson, G. (1998) *Motivating Students*. London: Kogan Page, SEDA.

Knight, P. (ed.) (1995) *Assessment for Learning in Higher Education*. London: Kogan Page, SEDA.

UCoSDA/Loughborough University (1996) *Making the Grade*. Sheffield: UCoSDA.

6

The Experience of Innovative Assessment: Student Perspectives

Liz McDowell and Kay Sambell

There has been considerable diversification in the methods of assessing student learning in higher education in recent years. Few courses in the UK now rely solely on the conventional finals examinations supplemented by essays or, in scientific subjects, laboratory reports. The diversity of assessment practice is well illustrated by the survey carried out in Scotland by the ASSHE project (Hounsell *et al.* 1996). There are a growing number of texts from various parts of the world reviewing alternative assessment practices (for example Cross and Angelo 1988; Birenbaum and Dochy 1996; Brown *et al.* 1997). Other authors focus on specific aspects or forms of assessment, such as self-assessment and peer assessment (Boud 1995), profiles (Assiter *et al.* 1992) or group-based tasks (Thorley and Gregory 1994).

Examples of alternative or innovative assessment which are now recognized are described elsewhere in this volume in Chapters 1 and 8. In many cases, new forms of assessment have been introduced because of some sense of dissatisfaction with conventional assessment methods among academics and other stakeholders such as employers and professional bodies. There is a view that a broader range of assessment methods may provide a more accurate representation of students' knowledge and understanding, that alternative approaches may be more appropriate to the kinds of abilities now demanded of graduates and that this may also enhance learning and teaching (Brown and Knight 1994).

We may be moving from a testing culture into a new assessment culture as suggested by Birenbaum (1996). One of the main changes which she identifies as part of the new assessment culture, is the integration of assessment, teaching and learning, replacing the view of testing as a separate function which takes place after teaching and learning have occurred. She also perceives a shift in the role of students; they are seen as active participants in both learning and assessment rather than being the 'victims' of the assessor. A further major change is in the nature of assessment tasks which are authentic, meaningful and engaging and are more akin to realistic contexts than the artificial time-constrained exam or multiple-choice test. This summary of the kinds of change taking place will seem familiar to many readers but, despite a considerable amount of development activity, we do not yet know enough about the use of innovative assessment methods in practice. Are they indeed fulfilling some of the hopes placed in them by assisting in the integration of assessment, teaching and learning, facilitating the active participation of students and providing authentic, meaningful and engaging tasks?

The Impact of Assessment project at the University of Northumbria at Newcastle

The Impact of Assessment project has investigated students' perceptions and behaviour when experiencing new forms of assessment, thus providing some revealing insights into the effects of such assessment. Thirteen case studies of innovative assessment in practice have been undertaken, covering a range of subjects and a variety of assessment methods such as: individual research projects; self-assessment and peer assessment; assessment by oral presentation; group case study, research and development projects; open-book exams; poster presentation; simulated professional tasks; portfolios and profiles. In each case, extensive data have been collected from interviews with staff and students, documentary evidence and observation of students and staff. The emphasis has been on semistructured interviews with students, adopting a qualitative approach to illuminate and understand the perceptions and experiences of students.

The outcomes of the project may be used to illuminate what happens, from the student perspective, when innovative forms of assessment are implemented. The student quotations used are drawn from across the case studies and illustrate the themes which have emerged from the analysis of case study data. The issues raised may help those implementing new forms of assessment to avoid some of the pitfalls and make better informed decisions and also highlight questions and issues which those evaluating the efficiency and effectiveness of assessment may wish to consider.

Introducing innovative assessment

The way in which any form of assessment is introduced to students will have a significant effect on their perceptions of it and their subsequent behaviour. This is true for all kinds of assessment, even the most 'conventional'. For example, it is a mistake to assume that all higher education students know what constitutes a good essay and it is frequently the case that students' views of what is required by an exam differ markedly from the views of their lecturers. However, it is particularly important to introduce students carefully to a new form of assessment since the new approach may well be demonstrably less effective if this vital stage is ignored.

Students do not necessarily welcome innovative approaches to assessment. Although students are often critical of conventional assessment methods, there is safety and security in the routine and the familiar which any changes may threaten:

> [With normal assignments] you get them out of the way, you know what mark you've got, you know how you're doing.

Students may be concerned about possible impacts on their marks or grades and on their workload. For example, a common concern about the possibility of lower grades is expressed here in relation to a group project:

> If you've got people in the group that aren't prepared to do the work then your grade [for this project] might pull you down.

Students may also question the motives behind the introduction of a new form of assessment and wonder whether it is really intended to benefit them or has been introduced for some other reason such as cost reduction. A possible, and not infrequent, reaction to the introduction of self-assessment and peer assessment is:

> What I think they are trying to do is relieve some of the work for them . . . release lecturers to do other things.

However, there are some convincing and compelling reasons for innovative assessment which students do readily understand and accept. Students generally welcome a form of assessment which to them seems fairer, that is, one which asks them to carry out a reasonable task, perhaps one which relates to the 'real world' and measures what they see as genuine learning:

> It's [assessing] the sort of level of knowledge you're more likely to hang onto long term and actually apply as well . . . It's the sort of thing that's more likely to crop up in a conversation in industry.

These views form a stark contrast to student views of 'normal assessment' such as exams and essays which often appear to them as irrelevant and pointless tasks, unlike anything they would ever be required to do outside academia and often not measuring real learning:

> Everything else we do here, like essays and so on, are just not relevant to real life. Exams here are so pointless, the questions are so precise. You're never going to need to know that kind of useless information.

Others have noted similar student perceptions. Hampson (1994) reported that students contrasted the meaningful exercise of undertaking a dissertation very strongly with normal assessment. A dissertation was:

> Definitely much better than set pieces of coursework that have been answered over a thousand times before.

Tang (1994) discovered that students believed that performance in exams was due, to a large measure, to luck and therefore they felt that such exams could not be considered fair tests of their abilities.

Some students welcome the broadening of assessment methods because they feel that it will give them, as individuals, a better chance to demonstrate their learning:

> If you have come from a working background, exams are not a lot of use to you . . . They suit people who have come straight from school, who've been taught to do exams and nothing else. I'm out of that routine.

For other students a change in the standard routines of assessment can add interest and rekindle motivation:

> It's just a break, a change from normal.

A first step in introducing innovative assessment may well be to discuss with students how they might benefit from it. A further issue is to help students to understand the requirements of the assessment and in particular how their performance will be judged. Assessment is a complex matter for students, even though it may seem straightforward and unproblematic to an experienced lecturer. Students encountering a variety of forms of assessment, including here a statistical task with self-marking and a group case study project, said:

> I didn't like the exercise that much to start off with because we had no idea . . . what the marks were going to be given for.
> It wasn't clearly explained . . . we weren't sure what was expected or how much we could ask [the lecturer].

Briefings and handbooks of information are useful but students often need a more substantial induction particularly to help them to understand assessment criteria (Orsmond *et al.* 1996). Without an understanding of assessment criteria students may well misdirect their efforts and fail to learn in the ways intended. However in-depth understanding of assessment criteria really means that the ways of judging what is good, bad or acceptable within the subject discipline or professional area, have been internalized and understood by students and this is not easily or quickly achieved. For example, in one of our case studies (also reported in Mowl and Pain 1995), two lecturers in geography ran a workshop in which two substantial group exercises were used to introduce students to self-assessment and peer assessment and which had some success in helping students to understand assessment criteria. The first exercise involved a marking task based on two short essays (Brown *et al.* 1994) followed by class discussion which led to the development of assessment criteria. The second exercise required students to sort a set of feedback statements about a piece of work and discuss the grades which the statements would indicate.

Experiencing innovative assessment

Student motivation and effort

A major advantage of many innovative forms of assessment is that they encourage students to work hard by promoting intrinsic motivation and interest in the tasks involved. We noted that such interest tends to be generated by assessment tasks which appear meaningful and relevant to students, and which are clearly vehicles for learning and developing useful knowledge and skills which will be of long-term benefit to students. Personal involvement can also be enhanced when students have some choice over the nature of tasks and the ways in which they are carried out. Students carrying out a range of projects as forms of assessment made comments such as:

It became a real personal project for me.

You're doing something you need to do for yourself and it's interesting.

I think [this assessment] gives a much better indication of what you know. It gives you more chance to express your ideas. You can actually put more into your work and promote yourself into your work.

However, in implementing innovative assessment, such motivation needs to be built upon and maintained when students find themselves dealing with challenging tasks and competing demands upon their time from other assignments. One student undertaking a group case study assignment said:

[It was] very stressful, demanding, a real headache. The assignment seemed to hang over us constantly and took up too much time, emotionally and physically.

Interim deadlines can be vital on assignments which extend over a period of time and feedback and guidance from the lecturer or fellow students can also be helpful in sustaining motivation and interest and providing reassurance:

We know we've got to reach our target for that date and then we'll go and see [the lecturer].

You've got the others [fellow students] there to help you if you're stuck. You know, they can show you where you've been going wrong.

It would be misleading to suggest that in every case of innovative assessment every student maintains high levels of motivation. The potential is certainly there, but student behaviour is affected by other contextual factors and their underlying aims in studying. For example, one student commented on the amount of time and effort needed to complete a design-and-build project saying:

At first I thought this was brilliant. But you need a lot of motivation . . . the thing is that half of us lot just want to get out . . . it's just a case of finishing the course and passing.

Authenticity and genuine learning

One of the things which can make innovative assessment successful is that it offers students authentic tasks such as working on a case study which places their learning in a realistic context, or undertaking individual investigations and presenting the outcomes. (See also Chapter 8.) Students tend to see these kinds of activities as more relevant to things that they might have to do in 'real life'.

> This is more like an actual work situation. You're given a task to do and it's up to you to just get on and do it . . . I think you need to work in a group . . . when you're out in the real world you work in teams, you all put your brains together to get the thing done.

They may also view innovative assessment tasks as ways of developing knowledge and capabilities which then will remain with them and thus be of long-term benefit:

> . . . your abilities are actually far more important – your abilities to research, analyse, dissect an argument, your abilities to bring forward information out of a set of data. Those kind of analytical abilities I think are important in day-to-day life and they are going to come across far more in progressive assessment than they ever are in exams.

However, it is sometimes difficult to sustain authenticity, especially when it is based on the task closely mirroring situations outside the university. Students may therefore complain, like this student referring to a professional practice simulation:

> In industry you would ring them up and say, 'Look, I've got a bit of a query on this. Is there any way you could come over and discuss this item?' – but there was none of that.

There may also be more substantial conflicts between the goals of a task within an academic context and an employment context. In the academic context, the overriding aim of an assessed task is to enable students to learn and demonstrate their learning, while in a working context the major focus may be the successful completion of the task.

Nevertheless, an assignment which is perceived as authentic and meaningful by students has the potential to promote genuine learning or deep approaches to learning, as opposed to one which is viewed by them as jumping through assessment hoops. One technology student contrasted an open-book exam with the conventional kind of closed-book exam:

> I think the open-book exam helps you learn better, personally, because you sit there and actually read the stuff, rather than just sit there and commit it to memory . . . I found myself questioning key concepts and ideas rather than hard facts about things. I was trying to understand the subject rather than memorise things.

Members of another student group in a humanities subject made the following comments about a 'normal' essay, and then the experience of undertaking an individual research project:

> Often with essays all you have to do is go to the library, look up the relevant books and just copy down the relevant chapters in a different language.

The personal research project, however, develops abilities which can be applied elsewhere:

> This is something you can apply to anything. I mean we're looking at it from the point of view of [specific topic] but it's something you can apply to anything you were researching at all.

Control and dependency

Innovative assessment often involves students in individual and, to varying extents, unpredictable tasks. This is different from the standard essay or the exam questions which are the same for everyone. For example, portfolios required students themselves to decide upon the actual evidence to include in order to demonstrate their achievements. Some of the projects and investigations which we examined were on topics self-selected by students; others were not, but still developed in different directions depending upon the ways in which the individual or group of students approached them. In all of these cases, the level of close control exercised by lecturers over student activities was reduced.

Students were not necessarily willing or able to accept higher levels of independence and responsibility. So, one student taking part in a year long group project, showing a high level of dependency on the lecturer, said:

> He [the lecturer] will say whether it's right and we'll get on with the next bit.

Another student experiencing the same assignment appeared to demonstrate more willingness to take responsibility, although he still wanted the lecturer to be there as back-up:

> We all try and figure it out for ourselves which I think is good. We don't feel that he's hanging around all the time looking over our shoulders. But you know where he is.

There is always a balance to be made in higher education between student independence and tutor control. Usually, it is the tutor who judges and marks assessed work in the end. One of the key ways in which students can be assisted to act independently and take responsibility for themselves is if they are given a clear framework and guidelines within which to work. This enables them to exercise responsible choice without worrying that they are completely 'off track'. It can be particularly important to understand the assessment criteria and the ways in which marks will be allocated. Students are then in a position to take more control of their own performance. One student explained how she began to take control of her own essay writing by making sure that she addressed all the criteria (the 'questions') after involvement in a self- and peer assessment exercise:

> I thought about it a lot more. If I do an essay normally, I just tend to do it. Having the criteria was good because I looked at them a lot, thinking 'Now have I answered all the questions?'

Grading and marking

It appears, from reviewing the student experience, that it is generally much easier to develop assessment tasks which are valuable learning tools and which motivate students than to mark or grade such tasks fairly and accurately. We find complaints from students such as this one in relation to a task which was a simulation of professional practice:

> I think you do get more out of the exercise but that isn't reflected by the marks.

Gibbs (1995) suggests that when a new form of assessment is introduced to replace, say, an essay or exam but the assessment criteria do not change, students may seem to perform differently because they have learnt slightly or even significantly different things. The assessment criteria and marking need to fit the nature of the tasks and the actual learning achievements which can be expected from a particular method of assessment. A mismatch here may be one explanation for the problems which students sometimes perceived. It also seems to be the case that when students have more sense of ownership and personal investment in assessment tasks, they may also be more likely to complain if marks do not reflect the genuine efforts and achievement they think they have made. In contrast, a common attitude found suggests that students are less likely to be concerned about the fairness of marks awarded in an exam where:

> You think 'Just let me remember this for the next hour-and-a half' and then you don't care.

All methods of assessment, including innovative approaches, may be seen to be biased in favour of certain students or those with certain kinds of abilities. Many students believe that exams favour those with good memories. Other forms of assessment may be seen to favour those with other qualities such as, in an oral presentation:

> The confident ones . . . It's something you can't really change. It's just your natural behaviour.

Many forms of innovative assessment also raise issues about the assessment of the process of undertaking a task and the end-product produced. Group assignments which are meant, in part, to assess abilities in teamwork are often marked on the basis of a final product such as a report. A student commenting on the assessment by oral presentation of a research task said:

> No matter how well you've researched, if you present it badly you've had it and then even if you've done minimal research but you present it really well, you can make it sound very good.

Assessment criteria and marking schemes which emphasize the products of assessment tasks can lead to students missing out on vital learning opportunities. In a group assignment intended to help students to develop IT skills in the analysis and presentation of data, one student reported that:

> the less good tended to let the good ones go ahead on the computer while they sat watching.

In many cases of innovative assessment, students are involved in allocating marks though self-assessment and peer assessment. This is almost always done in conjunction with tutor marking and may therefore be more appropriately called co-assessment. However, self, peer-assessment and co-assessment are invariably not included. Often innovative assessment tasks such as group projects, assessment via oral presentation or by portfolio are used but marking remains in the hands of the lecturer, as was the situation in a number of our case studies.

Where self-assessment, peer assessment and co-assessment were used in the cases which we studied, it had a number of benefits. Firstly, involving students in self-assessment and/or peer assessment capitalizes on the personal investment and interest which many students display in relation to innovative assessment. Students may want to have a say and they will almost certainly want to know how marks are allocated. Involving them and opening up the process will reduce the likelihood of serious dissatisfaction and challenge. Self-assessment and peer assessment are also congruent with the aims of giving students more freedom, responsibility and autonomy which many lecturers implementing innovative assessment espouse. Active participation in marking is a way in which students can develop a better understanding of assessment criteria:

> [peer assessment] improved my understanding of how judgements are made about work because before . . . I thought I knew what constituted a good essay and a bad essay, and then I went into more detail.

Knowing how such judgements are made in their subject is a very important aspect of students' academic development. Peer assessment can also be beneficial because it requires students to look at the work of other students, which can expand their repertoire of ideas and ways of approaching academic tasks:

> You were able to jot down things which you thought would be good in your essay.

It should be noted that some of these benefits can be gained through informal assessment, involving students in feedback and review rather than marking. This might be considered more appropriate if there are concerns about students actually awarding marks, although a number of studies have shown that students can be reliable markers, in close agreement with lecturers in some circumstances (Boud and Falchikov 1989; Stefani 1994).

Lessons for innovative assessment

Evidence from students shows that the benefits of innovative assessment are potentially very significant. However, the full potential is not always attained. Sometimes this is due to wider contextual factors but in many cases there are things which lecturers can do to promote success. Some useful guidelines are as follows:

- *Consider student workload carefully.* Students will work hard in many cases of innovative assessment and may spend more time on it than you think. Many of us have limited experience of the size of research task a student can reasonably be expected to undertake in a given period of time or how long it takes students, on average, to prepare for an oral presentation. This is something on which we need to learn from experience drawing on student feedback.
- *Take steps to maintain motivation.* Interim deadlines, guidance and feedback are important on any but the shortest of assessment tasks. Although students may find what they are doing interesting, we all tend to need the additional push of a deadline to meet to help us focus and find our way through competing pressures on our time!
- *Introduce a new form of assessment carefully.* There are good reasons for students to accept and benefit from innovative assessment but their initial reactions may be negative, even hostile. A discussion on students' normal experiences of assessment may provide a good context for promoting a newer form of assessment which may overcome some of the disadvantages which students will readily identify for themselves.
- *Establish a clear framework and guidelines.* When students are working on tasks which are not conventional, routine or the same for everyone, clear guidelines are needed as a safety net to ensure that students do not completely misunderstand what is expected. Students are also better able to act independently and make their own decisions when they feel reasonably secure about the overall parameters for their work.
- *Help students to understand assessment criteria.* Many forms of innovative assessment involve students in the assessment process, perhaps as self-markers or peer markers. In other cases, more openness about assessment criteria and marking will almost certainly be required. This is something to be welcomed as a significant potential benefit to student learning since it is a way of them developing their understanding of how judgements are

made in the subject they are studying and also developing the assessment abilities which they may need as lifelong learners.

- *Pay careful attention to organizational details and procedures.* Procedures tend to be very well established for conventional assessment. We know what to do if a student misses an exam for some reason. We may be less sure about what to do if a student fails to contribute to the group work needed to complete an assignment. It is far more likely that innovative assessment will run into trouble because some of the practical details are inadequate than because it is flawed in principle. Student interest and motivation may soon turn to cynical disengagement if the assessment turns out to be unfair or unreasonable in its requirements.

- *Pay particular attention to how you award marks and for what.* Marking new forms of assessment products such as group design projects, oral presentations or portfolios can present problems. Again, we have less experience of marking them than we have of marking exam questions or essays. One particular danger is a mismatch between the aims of the assessment, for example, to develop and assess teamwork abilities, and the ways in which they are judged. It is much easier to allocate marks to the completion of a group task than to the process by which it was completed. Once again, we need to learn from experience about what can reasonably be judged and how, using feedback from students about their experiences and approaches.

The guidelines above may appear to be daunting. Is it then worthwhile to innovate in assessment? The experience of current students suggests that it is. Many of them find newer forms of assessment tasks, for example, assignments based on problem-solving, or design and development work, intrinsically motivating. One reason for this is that students are more able to find intrinsic worth in tasks which they perceive as having some meaning outside the purely academic context. To some students, conventional forms of assessment appear to have no relevance to anything outside the university and are all about judging them, sometimes on a somewhat arbitrary basis, rather than involving them in genuine learning. Students appreciate assessment tasks which help them to develop knowledge, skills and abilities which they can take with them and use in other contexts such as in their subsequent careers. Assessment which incorporates elements of choice, perhaps about the topic for research or the method of approaching a development task, is also beneficial. It can give students a greater sense of ownership and personal involvement in the work and avoid the demotivating perception that they are simply going through routine tasks which have been done by many students before them. Collaboration with fellow students rather than working in isolation can also help to maintain student motivation and improve the quality of their learning as it opens up the possibilities for discussion, new ideas and varying approaches. Innovative assessment therefore has the potential to encourage students to take an interest in their studies, work hard, engage in genuine or deep learning and produce good outcomes which will have long-lasting benefits.

References

Assiter, A., Fenwick, A. and Nixon, N. (1992) *Profiling in Higher Education: Guidelines for the Development and Use of Profiling Schemes*. London: HMSO/CNAA.

Birenbaum, M. (1996) 'Assessment 2000: Towards a pluralistic approach to assessment' in M. Birenbaum and F.J.R.C. Dochy (eds) *Alternatives in Assessment of Achievements, Learning Processes and Prior Knowledge*. Kluwer: Dordrecht.

Boud, D. (1995) *Enhancing Learning Through Self Assessment*. London: Routledge.

Boud, D. and Falchikov, N. (1989) 'Quantitative studies of self-assessment in higher education: a critical analysis of findings'. *Higher Education*, 18(5), 529–49.

Brown, S. and Knight, P. (1994) *Assessing Learners in Higher Education*. London: Kogan Page.

Brown, S., Rust, C. and Gibbs, G. (1994) *Strategies for Diversifying Assessment in Higher Education*. Oxford: Oxford Centre for Staff Development.

Brown, G., Bull, J. and Pendlebury, M. (1997) *Assessing Student Learning in Higher Education*. London: Routledge.

Cross, P.K. and Angelo, T.A. (1988) *Classroom Assessment Techniques: A Handbook for Faculty*. Ann Arbor, MI: National Center for Research to Improve Post-secondary Teaching and Learning.

Gibbs, G. (1995) *Assessing Student-centred Courses*. Oxford: Oxford Centre for Staff Development.

Hampson, L. (1994) *How's Your Dissertation Going?* Lancaster: Unit for Innovation in Higher Education, Lancaster University.

Hounsell, D., McCulloch, M. and Scott, M. (eds) (1996) *The ASSHE Inventory: Changing Assessment Practices in Scottish Higher Education*. Edinburgh: University of Edinburgh, Napier University and the Universities and Colleges Staff Development Agency.

Mowl, G. and Pain, R. (1995) 'Using self and peer assessment to improve students' essay writing: a case study from Geography'. *Innovations in Education and Training International*, 32(4), 324–35.

Orsmond, P., Merry, S. and Reiling, K. (1996) 'The importance of marking criteria in the use of peer assessment'. *Assessment and Evaluation in Higher Education*, 21(3), 239–50.

Stefani, L.A.J. (1994) 'Peer, self and tutor assessment: relative reliabilities'. *Studies in Higher Education*, 19(1), 69–75.

Tang, C. (1994) 'Effects of modes of assessment on students' preparation strategies' in G. Gibbs (ed.) *Improving Students' Learning: Theory and Practice*, pp. 151–70. Oxford: Oxford Centre for Staff and Learning Development.

Thorley, L. and Gregory, R. (1994) *Using Group-based Learning in Higher Education*. London: Kogan Page.

7

Biases in Marking Students' Written Work: Quality?

Neil D. Fleming

Introduction

We build a huge edifice based on the grades and marks given by teachers in higher education, yet there is serious doubt about the validity and the reliability of those marks. Recently, higher education has had a great deal of rhetoric, discussion and energy about the measurement of quality. While there have been a number of initiatives in the 1990s that have focused on the meaning of 'quality' and how it might be enhanced, audited or assessed, the business of marking student scripts still remains as the most significant quality event in the lives of the students and the academics. It is at this early stage that the system has to have integrity. If not, then everything that is built on that fragile base of a set of marks will collapse. If we as academics cannot hold our heads up and say that in the process of marking student scripts we have been thoroughly professional, then the statements made by deans, provosts, and vice chancellors about quality are in error.

Clark (1993), in a study about blind marking, states that,

> Given that students are subject to the assessment process, it is a funda-
> mental requirement that the assessment process be reliable and valid,
> and perhaps above all else, equitable. Notwithstanding these laudable
> ideals, educators should be aware that the assessment process is not as
> scientific as it may sound. In fact, the assessment process is subject to
> error and bias.

This chapter identifies the sources of bias in the marking of students' scripts. It examines some of the research literature and it suggests ways of lessening the effects of the bias where those exist. Where this is not possible, biases are better acknowledged than hidden and academic staff should have opportunities to discuss the biases that will not 'go away'. The word 'marking' is used throughout this paper synonymously with the word 'grading'.

Quality teaching has few measurable outcomes and so too does quality learning. The universal measure for the latter is the test, the assignment, the project, the event, the artefact or the examination. In a search for indicators of quality learning, there has been a spate of courses and seminars to tease out the dimensions and the components of quality but these are built on top of an assumption that the assessment of students is valid and reliable and that may not be the case. Many senior tertiary administrators would prefer not to open the Pandora's box and ask the question 'Are our students being assessed without bias?' or 'Can we rely on the quality of our marking systems?' If these questions are never asked, nor answered positively, then no amount of massaging means, medians, quartiles, margins of error and levels of significance will do anything to redress the basic errors in the raw data. One solution that is not well received by administrators would be to be more tentative in making decisions, as suggested by MacGinitie (1993). It would be difficult to get acceptance of a student's results as being 'somewhere between 55 per cent and 65 per cent'.

Innovative assessment, like any other innovation, carries with it some risks. Although it has the potential to level the playing fields for those students for whom traditional assessment is disadvantageous, it may be more open to bias and unfairness than traditional assessment. The movement towards impression (or holistic as termed in the USA) marking is an example where there is conflicting evidence about its validity. The 1990s pendulum swung towards objective testing. That was caused by too much marking for the increases in class size. Innovative assessment retreated on many campuses. Is it possible to have innovative assessment and larger classes? Is it possible to have innovative assessment and still speak about the quality of an institution's marking and grading?

Lest the reader believes that multiple choice and other 'objective' tests are excused from these statements about unreliability, there are doubts about the objectivity of any test. Even when it is marked objectively (true or false, multi-choice) there is the strong likelihood of bias in the design of the questions – especially in the choice of distractors, choice of content to test or the choice among 'correct' answers. This chapter is not about the bias in setting questions, although it is important to recognize that such bias is evident. It is about the biases that exist when academics mark students' written scripts for essays, projects, short answers, fill-in-the blank questions, and so on.

Research into sources of bias appears regularly in the literature with contributors conducting studies into the various sources of bias and recommending procedures to lessen the risks. What follows is not an exhaustive literature review. Some of the significant contributions have been cited merely to underpin the point that there are a range of biases 'out there' and that we still have much to do to reduce the impact of biases in higher education. If we do not reduce the impact of biases, should we rely on our marks and grades as being deserving of a quality stamp of approval or an ISO 9002 rating?

Sources of bias

The signs that bias might be present are often remarkably easy for students to detect. Two students at my own university worked collaboratively on an essay and there was no difference in the content and style of the two essays that were then given to two tutors assigned to mark their essays. The difference between the marks given by Tutor A and Tutor B astounded the students. When this happens with the same tutor or teacher, the astonishment turns to total disbelief in fairness. Academics at Lincoln University in New Zealand have also been known to accidentally mark the same script twice during a marking 'run' only to find a wide discrepancy in the two marks given when the double marks were later 'discovered'.

Gabb (1980), writing in an in-house academic newsletter, quoted the results from research indicating that consistency in marking was a major problem with one study showing correlations between re-marked scripts as low as 0.28 and 0.4 and differences as high as 20 per cent between the two scores. There are numerous references to problems with interrater reliability. Russikoff's (1994) study of 392 faculty in the California State College system is one where the holistic scoring of essay examinations written by limited-English-speakers was examined and found wanting.

Gender bias

Gender bias is frequently cited although its effects are not consistent. Handwriting alone can identify the sex of the writer at a level significantly greater than chance but that does not prove gender bias. Eames and Lowenthal (1990), in a study of the effects of handwriting on assessment of essays, found that university teachers were not influenced. Archer and McCarthy (1988) concluded that there is evidence of likely biases from gender, physical attractiveness and prior knowledge. Goldberg (1968) is frequently cited for his study identifying that the work is more highly rated when attributed to a man. Some earlier studies about 'domain bias' are more worrying. They note that students perceived as 'masculine' were judged higher in understanding in a 'masculine' subject – physics. In a 1984 study, Spear got preliminary results that revealed that both male and female teachers tended to differentiate between the work of boys and girls in similar ways. In a primary school study (Sprouse and Webb 1992) teachers exhibited gender biases concerning handwriting, with illegible handwriting being wrongly attributed to males more than females.

Ethnic bias

Howell *et al.* (1993) found that biases in the assessment of writings by ethnic minority students were evident. Oliver (1995) used the services of

20 preservice teachers to grade two sets of essays both before and after some instruction on such things as assessment, pedagogy and issues of diversity. She found: that the preservice teachers' scores on these essays were lower than experts; that the first scores either remained constant or were raised substantially by the end of the semester; and that the essays that received large jumps in scores were written by students whose ethnicity was very apparent in their work. At Lincoln University, with more than 20 per cent of students being international students, some academics claim to be able to identify Asian students' scripts because of sentence structure, grammar and handwriting. Whether bias then results is not mentioned.

Halo effects

Clark (1993) stated:

> academic staff can be influenced if the identity of the student is known when marking a script. Headlines such as EXAMS MARKED BY NUMBERS TO AVOID DISCRIMINATION CLAIMS and RISK OF EXAMINER BIAS PERSISTS in the *Times Higher Educational Supplement* (circa 1992) serve only to emphasize this perception.

Knowledge of the student appears to lift their marks, with Bradley (1984) indicating that blind markers marked significantly lower than the actual teacher (supervisor) of the class. Scott (1995) argues that teachers knowingly or unknowingly use grades to reward and punish students for their behaviour, attitude, appearance, family backgrounds and lifestyles as well as writing ability. This was from a self-study and an experiment in anonymous grading to determine the extent of these biases.

Although there are few studies of the possible effects of physical attractiveness on assessment at university level, there are some that indicate that bias exists. A number of authors talk about the informal assessment that happens. Archer and McCarthy (1988) note that 'decades of halo-effects . . . provide substantial evidence for a pervasive effect of prior knowledge of a target on judgements of the targets' subsequent performance'. These 'halo-effects' may spread through academic staff discussing students, their physical descriptions and their performances even in different subjects. Archer and McCarthy state that our schemas influence our interpretations of ambiguous stimuli (examination answers) and that a pre-existing schema is perceived more readily.

Contrast effects

Daly and Dickson-Markman, in a 1982 study, set out to examine the potential for bias introduced by the quality of preceding essays on the evaluation of subsequent essays. Referred to as the 'contrast effect', this concerns visual perception, attraction ratings of females, social judgements, and many others.

In marking scripts, what is happening is that the order of marking is having some effect on the results. They cite research by Hales and Tokar (1975) and Hughes *et al.* (1980) who found significant effects attributable to the quality of preceding papers. Daly and Dickson-Markman's research replicated these two studies. Although a low-quality essay was not downgraded when read after high-quality ones, an average essay read after a series of high-quality ones was rated lower than when it was preceded by a group of low-quality ones. This is an expression of Helson's theory (Helson 1964) that when we meet with a stimulus 'significantly different from the established norm we adjust or contrast the new stimulus with a more extreme position than is warranted by the object's true value'. Their study also indicated a tendency for judges to move towards an average evaluation as they read more essays. In other words, the best students should ask that their essays are marked first!

Presentation bias

Massey (1983) concluded that for a GCE (UK) English Literature exam, the examiners were successful in avoiding the danger of crediting candidates for presentation rather than content and says that this was contrary to some previous research. A study by Peterson and Lou (1991) of 103 US ninth graders who wrote essays on the same topic found that short papers were seldom rated higher than long ones but there was no evidence of bias between papers that were handwritten and the same papers that were wordprocessed. Arnold *et al.* (1990), however, found that papers converted to wordprocessed format received lower scores than the original handwritten ones.

Sprouse and Webb (1994) found that illegible samples received lower grades and a higher number of spelling errors than did legible ones. Well-scribed (legible) essays received mean scores 18 per cent higher than the same essays in illegible condition.

Sweedler-Brown (1991) found that, although typed essays were of higher quality than handwritten essays, well-written essays received significantly lower scores when they were typed than when they were written. Markers are influenced by the appearance of an essay such that student work receives its highest mean score when it is nicely handwritten. Sweedler-Brown makes the strong point that 'whether students are allowed . . . [to progress] . . . should not be determined by their good or poor handwriting'. There are other dimensions to presentation bias. Often the way in which a project or case study or essay is bound, has the potential to signal the social or financial status of the student. That may bias the marker positively or negatively.

Causes and explanations

Some general psychology texts suggest that as human beings we move into an area of doubtful validity when we start to sort into more than 15 different

Table 7.1 Grades (*n*) awarded by different tutors to their tutorial groups. Same subject. Same assessed task

Tutor	A+	A	A-	B+	B	B-	C+	C	D	E
Jim	0	2	0	1	2	2	1	4	5	3
Mary	5	3	4	12	6	4	0	1	0	0
John	15	2	3	1	1	0	0	0	0	0
Susan	9	11	2	2	2	2	0	0	1	0
Binti	2	2	4	7	4	4	4	7	3	1
Din	5	14	2	7	4	2	0	1	0	0
Rashi	4	4	5	4	5	5	3	3	4	1
Tamara	1	5	1	2	3	3	4	6	7	1

categories. This poses some problems with marking schemes that use a range of 0 to 100 for a single piece of work. Even subdividing that scale into subscales for content and presentation and argument and other criteria may not improve the limits of our human ability to discriminate finely. When teachers argue that this student has clearly earned a mark of 59 per cent and not 60 per cent and these marks are the summation of a number of assessed events, one doubts the validity of the judgements being made and what might result if there was a challenge by the student.

The greatest bias in marking comes from the 'like me' effect. This is the subjective desire that some markers have when they expect students to model the way that they themselves write, think, spell, organize, use headings, set out bibliographies or arrange paragraphs. Our own self-image gets in the way of deciding in an objective way whether the student has, or has not answered the question at a particular level of competence. This is made worse when we are marking the content knowledge that is so important to our discipline. There may be an argument for the use of markers who have not been involved in the teaching, but there are disadvantages to that as well. Consider the interrater reliability of the real results in Table 7.1 (they are fictitious names from an actual example from an unnamed New Zealand university!). Which tutor group would you want to be in? Clearly there are advantages being in John's class where two-thirds of the group got A+ results compared with zero in Jim's group.

Solutions

Training markers may be essential to improve the quality of grading but 'in everyday classrooms, teachers and readers seldom receive training prior to evaluating essays' (Daly and Dickson-Markman 1982). Before we invest in training, however, we should note that Sweedler-Brown (1992) found that training had no effect on grader bias in assessing handwritten (poor and good) and wordprocessed scripts. She had assumed that markers were unaware of the effect of their bias on their marking behaviour and that it would be eliminated or diminished when they were made aware of it. Even the experienced graders showed no reduction and she hypothesized that the short training sessions were not enough to offset years of habit. Less-experienced markers may be more susceptible to training! She goes on to suggest that, having the appearance of an essay explicitly marked, may help to remove the bias because the markers would then focus only on the content. She concludes with: 'Holistic grading as a sole means of assessment may not provide the most accurate judgement of students' writing ability.' In the same study, she states that: 'Contrast effects persisted despite the use of model essays and explicit instructions.' In citing from Nisbett and Ross (1980), Archer and McCarthy (1988) state that trying hard to be accurate does not, as a rule, immunize one's judgements from the effects of bias.

As well as using blind marking, 'the operation of the halo-effect might be further minimised by marking each question independently, to avoid building up expectations based on the marks for a previous question or questions' (Archer and McCarthy 1988). Although some academics claim to carry in their heads implicit standards from one year to the next without any diminution in quality or changes in rigour, that is unlikely.

In most countries, higher education staff could learn much from their colleagues in schools in which they are more often trained to mark. They also have the opportunity to check marks and be part of large national marking panels where the principles and the practices of marking are taught and learned under skilled guidance. This is not such a familiar scene for lone academics in higher education although, in increasing numbers of universities worldwide, the issue of training for assessment is being taken seriously.

There are other ways to reduce the effect of bias and it is not the purpose of this chapter to write in detail about each one. For example, there are double marking and moderating devices that are frequently used for senior work in universities. Having explicit criteria against which to judge the quality of a script is a good start, not always observed in universities. Randomizing the order of materials before marking so that a script has an opportunity to be first or last or to follow or lead good or bad scripts is another strategy.

Conclusions

Table 7.2 sets out some of the main biases discussed in this chapter. In many of the examples, note that there can be both positive and negative effects. For example, noting the poor grammatical skills of an international student may lead to compensatory marks: 'Well it's the best she could do.' Or reduced marks: 'Until he learns to spell our English words he is not going to get top marks from me regardless of his competence in the subject!'

There are a number of practical and readily-actionable methods that can be used to reduce bias and enable greater reliability and validity in marking. To do so, it is possible to do the following:

Table 7.2 Biases

Type	Description	As recognized by . . .
The halo-effect	Previous performance is personally known through: having marked a previous question or recalled their other work, or	'This is not like Jenny.' 'He has not done well on his first two questions so . . .'
	recognition of some aspect of their style, handwriting . . .	'This is too good to be Sam's!'
The contrast effect	The script(s) preceding this one have an effect on this one, which is an advantage or a disadvantage	'How nice to get a good one occasionally.' 'After the Lord Mayor's carriage comes . . .'
Group membership, clan or sect	Membership is detected from cues like handwriting, name, language, e.g. ESOL clues, format (wordprocessed), presentation (glossy folder), examples given, question choice so that the following biases could come into play.	
	Gender (some research indicates that women are marked harder by women than men)	'Not a bad answer on feminist theory for a lad.'
	Ethnicity	'They always have trouble with pronouns and tense.'
	Social class	'With a folder like that and laser printing she has to be from the northern suburbs'
	Ability level – 'like me'	'First student I've ever had to use the word *paradigm* correctly.'
Marker factors	Marking when tired, irritable, stressed, or fresh, vibrant and alert!	
Script order	Marking paper X first	'That's not what I expected.'
	Marking paper X last	'Hurrah! I've nearly finished.'
	Marking without knowing what was taught	'I wonder if that's her example or not?'
Interrater unreliability	Uneven standards between markers marking the same assessed task	(See Table 7.1)

- Evaluate all answers to one question before going on to the next one.
- Shuffle the order of the papers after each question.
- Blind mark. Don't use names on papers – use numbers.
- Obscure the marks previously given for other questions.
- Make a *conscious* effort to eliminate bias from our judgement by thinking about our biases before marking. Be honest!
- Use a marking schedule with clear criteria.
- Have one marker for each question or assessed event.
- Tighten up the questions. The greater the freedom allowed to candidates in assembling their answers, the more likely the marking is susceptible to bias.
- Obscure any signs of group membership – 'after randomly and artificially labelling pairs of identical essays as from "regulars" or "honours" students, scores given by experienced teachers to the honours essays were significantly higher than those given to the identical regular essays' (Gronlund and Lynn 1990).
- Mark only those aspects that match with the assessment objectives.
- Resist midstream changes in criteria – sometimes an excellent student will add another valid and important criterion to those already expected by the marker. Depending on when this student's work is marked (early–middle–late) there will be an effect on other papers. Be prepared for creative responses.
- Use points or mark values that are easy to assign. Competent markers can seldom categorize across more than 15 points. Most find a range of 8–10 more comfortable.
- Use all of a scale, not just marks between 35 and 70.

It is unlikely that bias in assessment will be entirely eliminated, but it is up to all academics to strive to do so as far as possible, if we are to do justice to our students and promote confidence in our abilities as assessors.

References

Archer, J. and McCarthy, B. (1988) 'Personal biases in student assessment'. *Educational Research*, 30(2), 142–5.

Arnold, V. *et al.* (1990) *Do Students Get Higher Scores on their Word-Processed Papers? A Study of Bias in Scoring Hand-Written vs. Word-Processed Papers*, Rio Hondo College, Whittier, California.

Bradley, C. (1984) 'Sex bias in the evaluation of students'. *British Journal of Social Psychology*, 23, 147–53.

Clark, M.B. (1993) Towards the Reduction of Bias when Grading Examination Scripts. (Unpublished paper, available from the author: Accountancy Department, Lincoln University, Canterbury, New Zealand)

Daly, J.A. and Dickson-Markman, F. (1982) 'Contrast effects in evaluating essays'. *Journal of Educational Measurement*, 19(4), 309–16.

Eames, K. and Lowenthal, K. (1990) 'Effects of handwriting and examiner's expertise on assessment of essays'. *Journal of Social Psychology*, 130(6), 831–3.

Gabb, R. (1980) 'How consistent is examination marking?' *Educational Services Unit, Newsletter*, 2, Lincoln University, New Zealand.

Goldberg, P.A. (1968) 'Are women prejudiced against women?' *Transaction*, 5, 28–30.

Gronlund, N.E. and Lynn, R.L. (1990) *Measurement and Evaluation in Teaching*, 6th edn. New York: Macmillan.

Hales, L.W. and Tokar, E. (1975) 'The effect of the quality of preceding responses on the grades assigned to subsequent responses to an essay question'. *Journal of Educational Measurement*, 12, 115–17.

Helson, H. (1964) *Adaption-Level Theory*. New York: Harper and Row.

Howell, K.W. *et al.* (1993) 'Bias in authentic assessment'. *Diagnostique*, 19(1), 387–400.

Hughes, D.C., Keeling, B. and Tuck, B.F. (1980) 'The influence of context position and scoring method on essay scoring'. *Journal of Educational Measurement*, 17, 131–5.

Lowenthal, B. (1989) 'Sources of assessment errors'. *Academic Therapy*, 24(3), 285–8.

MacGinitie, W.H. (1993) 'Some limits of assessment'. *Journal of Reading*, 36(7), 556–60.

Massey, A. (1983) 'The effects of handwriting and other incidental variables on GCE "A" level marks in English literature'. *Educational Review*, 35(1), 45–50.

Nisbett, R. and Ross, L. (1980) *Human Inference: Strategies and Shortcomings of Social Judgement*. Englewood Cliffs, NJ: Prentice Hall.

Oliver, E-I. (1995) 'Pre-service teachers assess the writing quality of language minority and non mainstream students: an experiment'. Paper presented at the Annual Meeting of the American Educational Research Association, San Francisco, CA, 18–22 April.

Peterson, E. and Lou, W.W. (1991) 'The impact of length on hand-written and word processed papers'. Paper presented at the Annual Meeting of the Oregon Educational Research Association, Portland, OR, October.

Russikoff, K.A. (1994) 'Hidden expectations: faculty perceptions of SLA and ESL writing competence'. Paper presented at the Annual Meeting of the Teachers of English to Speakers of Other Languages, Baltimore, MD, 8–12 March.

Scott, E-L. (1995) '*Mokita*' The truth that everyone knows but nobody talks about: bias in grading. *Teaching English in the Two Year College*, 22(3), 211–16.

Spear, M-G. (1984) 'The biasing influence of pupil sex in a science marking exercise'. *Research in Science and Technological Education*, 2(1), 55–60.

Sprouse, J.L. and Webb, J.E. (1994) 'The Pygmalion Effect and its Influence on the Grading and Gender Assignment on Spelling and Essay Assessments'. Masters Thesis, University of Virginia, 63pp.

Sweedler-Brown, C.O. (1992) 'The effect of training on the appearance bias of holistic essay graders'. *Journal of Research and Development in Education*, 26(1), 24–9.

Sweedler-Brown, C.O. (1991) 'Computers and assessment: the effect of typing versus handwriting on the holistic score of essays'. *Research and Teaching in Developmental Education*, 8, 5–14 .

Part 3

Assessing Practice

Assessment of practice throws up a number of problems that do not arise when assessing the more theoretical elements of curriculum delivery. This is particularly important when key skills such as numeracy, the use of information technology, communicating orally and in writing, working as a member of a team and managing one's own learning are increasingly regarded as important and integral elements of effective study. There are many tried and tested ways of assessing practice used to test skills and abilities as well as knowledge and understanding. Many of them are concerned with how to capture what is often ephemeral experience, in ways that are reliable and verifiable. Crucially assessment of practice relies on evidence rather than assertion, which is, where possible, triangulated, using a number of sources to support a claim of competence against explicit, available and relevant criteria.

In this part, Chapter 8 by Sally Brown explores the practicalities of assessing practice, looking especially at the methods that are best suited, the contexts in which such assessment takes place and appropriate timing to ensure that the essential learning is captured effectively and meaningfully.

In Chapter 9, Garth Rhodes and Freda Tallantyre explore how best the key skills most of us aim to integrate into our learning programmes can be assessed. There is considerable agreement nationally and internationally on what are the key skills we wish to see our students demonstrate, but less on issues such as the extent to which it is important to map, develop and assess key skills and very little indeed on issues associated with level of achievement and demonstration of progression. This chapter, based on work undertaken at the University of Northumbria, describes one model and addresses the crucial associated questions.

Three examples then follow which describe the assessment of practice in different contexts: Gill Young in Chapter 10 first considers the use of portfolios as a means of assessing students on a postgraduate Certificate in Teaching and Learning in Further and Higher Education, exploring both the advantages and the disadvantages of the method. Group-based assessment is the topic of Chapter 11 by Mike Heathfield, particularly focusing on the way that it can shape and improve the nature of learning. Gordon Joughin in Chapter 12 then describes eight dimensions of oral assessment in the context of legal education, considering them in relation to student approaches to learning.

As the volume of assessment of practice we use in higher education increases, we need to explore different ways to help us access and accredit the experience of students' learning in ways that are meaningful and reputable. The chapters that follow shed some light on the approaches that can satisfy us that students have achieved work of the appropriate standard and enable students to find the process of assessment a means of integrating their learning into practice.

8

Assessing Practice

Sally Brown

The pragmatics of assessing practice

In order to establish whether or not a student is a competent practitioner in a professional context, it is essential to use experiential approaches for the testing of skills, otherwise we risk missing the very heart of what it is that we are aiming to assess. It is not sensible to assess practice in ways that traditionally have been used to assess learning in universities, as we are likely to miss important elements. If, for example, we want to assess the skill of hedgelaying, we should not just ask the student to write a history of hedgerows, provide a set of instructions for tackling a neglected and overgrown hedgerow or write an account of the kinds of species we might find in a typical 200-year-old hedge (although the ability to converse knowledgeably about these areas would be expected of an expert hedgelayer). In the final analysis, we would need to judge the hedgelayer's skill at actually laying hedges. This rustic analogy can be applied to any of the professional disciplines we encounter in institutions of higher education.

This chapter explores some of the issues that arise when practice is to be assessed, and provides descriptions of some of the principal evidence-based means which are used. It is based on experience of working with staff in universities and colleges who assess students aiming to become nurses, lawyers, vets, hotel and catering staff, occupational therapists, accountants, doctors, social workers, artists, quantity surveyors, librarians, chemists, fashion designers, engineers of all kinds, playworkers, medical laboratory scientists, actors and teachers (but in fact, to date, no hedgelayers!). It also draws on the work of others, notably the Assessment Strategies in the Scottish Higher Education project (Hounsell *et al.* 1996), which presents an inventory of 120 accounts of innovative assessment, many of which relate to the assessment of practice. In addition, my work as a member of The Impact of Innovative Assessment project at the University of Northumbria (McDowell 1995) and Chapter 6 in this volume has informed my thinking.

Table 8.1   Competence Checklist

Date observed	Date returned	List of competences to be achieved	Date ready to be assessed	Date of assessment	Further comments/tutor recommendations
		• _____ • _____ • _____ • _____ • _____ • _____ • _____ • _____ • _____			

Instruments for assessing practice

To assess practice, as I have suggested in Chapter 1, we need to broaden the range of assessment methods we use beyond the written account that is the customary basis of most essays and unseen time-constrained written exams, to encompass instruments which can provide us with confidence in the capabilities of our students as practitioners. Some of the methods we might wish to use to assess practice include these discussed below.

Competence checklists

These are used by a number of professions to assure that a range of activities have been undertaken and assessed, often more than once. Table 8.1 provides an example of one such competence checklist in landscape format, with columns in which students can indicate when they observed an activity, rehearsed it, estimated themselves to be ready to be assessed, the date at which the assessment took place, the outcome, the tutor's name and any further comments. For some competences, all these activities might take place in a single day, others might be completed over a period of time, often paced to fit students' own estimation of preparedness to be assessed. Such a checklist would normally be completed by the student and tutor together, and would provide a written record of negotiations and discussions concerning practical activities beyond the scope of the checklist alone.

Projects

Projects are widely used as a means for students to report on learning undertaken away from or independently within institutions. Their value for assessing practice is enhanced when students are encouraged to move away from a merely descriptive approach and to adopt a critical/analytical stance to their experiences of learning.

Case studies

Case studies can also be used to enable students to apply learning evinced in professional contexts to materials and examples provided in document-ary form or on-line, requiring them to provide recommendations, offer solutions or analyse data in realistic scenarios which encourage application of knowledge and problem-solving abilities. Students can also be asked to write their own case studies based on their experiences in practice, adopt-ing a similarly interrogative and critical approach.

Logs, diaries, reflective journals, critical incident accounts

These are all variously used as instruments by which students could be assessed on practice and reflection. At their simplest, logs can comprise simple checklists to record prescribed activities, with or without reflective commentary. A diary tends to be a personal narrative account of activity, which usually itemizes actions undertaken and includes a level of personal response. Reflective journals are sometimes more selective in the narrative detail they introduce, focusing instead on a much greater level of reflection, referring back to theoretical perspectives provided by the course and analys-ing process as well as outcome.

Critical incident accounts have been developed in a number of discip-lines such as social work and nursing, where it was felt that logs were rather instrumental, or that diaries tend to be used by students as rather rambling and pedestrian blow-by-blow accounts of what happened without much learning taking place and that reflective journals were sometimes found to be problematic such as in cases where the content turned out to be extremely emotionally-laden and personal. For example, a nursing tutor found herself very concerned to be reading an account of a student who was working on a geriatric ward nursing patients dying of cancer, when at home she was caring for her own mother who was dying of cancer. Assessing that particu-lar reflective journal was a harrowing experience, and the tutor concerned found herself questioning the acceptability of what she found to be a rather prurient experience.

Typically, students being assessed by a critical incident account would keep a personal journal or diary as an entirely private document, but would be asked to extract from it two or three particularly critical incidents on which to focus. In each case, they would typically be asked to provide the following:

- A brief description of the context.
- Perhaps a brief photocopied extract of a non-sensitive passage from the journal relating to the incident.
- A description of what the student as practitioner actually did.
- Some demonstration of the ways in which theory learned on the course influenced the student's actions.
- An account of the outcomes of the student's actions.
- What alternatives were considered and rejected and why.
- How the student would tackle the incident differently on another occasion and why.
- What learning the student took away from the incident and how this would affect future practice.

This method, therefore, enables students to draw strongly upon personal experience and to adopt a positively self-critical and analytical approach to professional practice.

Portfolios

Portfolios are widely used nowadays in higher education as a means to enable students to provide evidence of competence from their practice. A good way to approach the use of a portfolio is to provide students with a ring binder, with sections labelled with the learning outcomes that are to be assessed by the portfolio and then ask them to fill each section with selected representative data in a variety of media (letters, reports, diagrams, treatment plans, work schedules, peer comments, computer programs, checklists, teaching materials, audio and video tapes, and so on) which they feel demonstrates their professional capability in the specified area. Portfolios are an excellent means of helping students to assess their own level of competence by asking them to select the evidence that best demonstrates their ability, but students need considerable guidance if they are not to use a 'supermarket trolley' approach to portfolio assembly ('just shove it all in') and if they are to become proficient at selectivity, structuring and demonstration of excellence.

Observation of the demonstration of skills in practice

This is widely used in a range of professional contexts, particularly perhaps medicine and teaching, frequently with a tutor or workplace supervisor watching how professional tasks are undertaken and providing feedback and evaluation on performance. Checklists are commonly used, but subjective responses are also relied on, using the experience and judgement of the evaluator to provide a standard towards which the student must strive. This can, on occasions, be problematic when evaluators are new to the task, have little experience of assessment, see very few students against which they can compare performance or have unrealistic expectations of what can be achieved.

Effective and valid assessment by observation and demonstration relies on clear, explicit and available criteria against which the student is to be judged and which are available to all stakeholders in the process, together with clear justification from the tutor that does not rely simply on gut reaction.

Artefacts

These are frequently the outcome of students' professional practice, including for example sculptures, meals, computer packages, scientific rigs, vehicles, dental bridges and fashion garments. As outlined above, the importance of clear criteria against which artefacts can be assessed is of paramount importance. A helpful way of enabling students to understand how these criteria are applied is to provide opportunities for them to discuss with tutors and each other how samples of artefacts from previous students have been judged, so they can see what is recognized as good practice. It is also valuable to have interim critiques of work in progress, so that a major investment of time and resources is not made by students who do not really understand what is expected.

Expert witness testimonials

These are sometimes used as components of portfolios but may also be used as free-standing means to demonstrate competence. They often comprise a statement written by a professional who has been acting in the capacity of mentor, line manager or supervisor of the student and who is able to provide testimony to the student's ability. In some professions, such people sometimes find it difficult to find the time to assemble and write up such testimony, in which case students can be encouraged to provide an account of professional competence that the expert can therefore carefully check and verify as accurate.

In-tray exercises

Such exercises have been widely used for a number of years in accountancy and nursing among other subjects. In this kind of assessment, students are likely to be presented at the start of an exam with a dossier of documents to read, but at this stage no exam question. For example on a nursing course, using the papers which represent the in-tray of a ward manager, the nurses will need to work out for themselves which documents are likely to be relevant, which are just routine and which are red herrings. After a period of time for perusal, perhaps half an hour, the students will be given tasks, for example, drawing up a treatment plan for a particular patient and prioritizing the workloads of junior staff. After a further interval, new information will be given: perhaps the patient has been transferred to another ward or a major road accident means that as many beds as possible have to be cleared. The examinees will need to react fast to the changed circumstances, move onto different tasks and demonstrate many of the skills that a professional ward manager would need to use in real life. In some cases, in-tray exercises can last a full day, with new tasks or information being given at intervals. Students are told that during their lunch period they can talk to whoever they like (each other, their tutor, their partner, whoever), consult any reference sources they like (their notes, the Internet, textbooks), but nothing should leave the exam room and nothing new be brought back into the room. Colleagues report that in-tray exercises are an excellent means of getting students to demonstrate that they can put into practice what they have learned.

Objective Structured Clinical Examinations (OSCEs)

Widely used in medicine and professions allied to medicine, OSCEs typically involve students undertaking a set of prescribed tasks (perhaps eight in 90 minutes), at a series of assessment stations. (This is rather like circuit-training exercises in the gym.) These provide opportunities for students to demonstrate their skills at, for example, interpreting clinical data, obtaining information from real or simulated patients (both actors and computers are used to save excessive stress on actual patients) and analysis of slides or X-rays. The methodology enables assessors to judge students' competence at a range of practical skills they are likely to need in their professional lives. The content of data contained within tasks can be changed at intervals to prevent students passing on information to other students. Other disciplines are beginning to modify the process to suit their own professional assessment needs.

Posters and presentations

As I have described in more detail elsewhere (Brown and Knight 1994), these can be used by individual students or groups to demonstrate the outcomes of the work undertaken on placements, thus providing insights to students' approaches and values and allowing the students to interpret their experiences of professional work in ways that are meaningful to them. An advantage of these methods is that they are amenable to peer assessment. The advantages in terms of sharing of learning and development of students' understanding of their own competence is described in Part 4.

Oral assessments

Oral assessments of all kinds can be used to interrogate the understanding that underlies practice, as Gordon Joughin describes in Chapter 12. Any kind of oral assessment introduces the element of performance into practice assessment, and appropriate decisions need to be made about the weighting that this element should be allocated. We would expect, for example, that lawyers and actors should be able to demonstrate high levels of oral competence, but this is likely to be less important for some other professions (although all professions need to be able to communicate orally and in writing at well above a basic level).

Learning contracts

These are often used to enable students to be involved in setting their own goals and to respond to changing learning situations. They are usually described (Brown and Baume 1992a, b) as having four stages: entry profiling, needs analysis, action planning and evaluation. Students individually, or in small groups, typically map out their levels of relevant competence and skills at the beginning of a programme, via a discussion with tutors, a self-assessment proforma or both, then set about deciding how these can be built upon in order to satisfy the learning outcomes required. This is developed into an action plan, which is then reviewed. Frequently, these four stages are cycled through on a number of occasions over a period of time, with the students having chances to renegotiate targets when they have exceeded their own expectations, or where they have been overambitious or when progress has been hampered by adverse circumstances.

Learning contracts are an extremely valuable means of involving students in recognizing their own expertise and helping them to set realistic self-managed targets for professional practice.

The choice of instruments for assessing practice involves a number of complex decisions. These will include not only the nature of the task to be assessed but also the context in which it is being undertaken. We now explore where assessment takes place and how this impacts on students and on assessors.

Contexts for assessing practice

The contexts in which practice can be assessed are diverse. Inevitably, students on placement and students undertaking work-based learning will be assessed in their workplaces, either by line managers, practice tutors or supervisors. This is valuable in that these are likely to be the people who are best placed to evaluate a student's performance at work, but there can be some problems concerning role boundaries and potentially even greater problems in trying to ensure equivalence of experience and interassessor reliability, when the workplace assessors may be hundreds of miles away from the institution and each other. Where work-based assessment of practice takes place, there is a need for effective briefing of assessors (who ideally will receive training by the institution about level and sufficiency of achievement), support during the process, moderation of outcomes and opportunities for two-way feedback to ensure the validity of the process.

Many disciplines nowadays use *simulated workplace environments* of various kinds where students can develop their abilities in safe environments prior to working in actual professional contexts. Training restaurants, for example, often give opportunities for students on Hotel and Catering courses to practise on their peers before the public are invited in as clients. Trainee doctors in some London hospitals can practise taking histories from patients using actors as rehearsal for working with actual patients. Simulated workplaces are expensive to set up and run, but give students invaluable experience and rehearsal, which builds confidence and develops skills. They are increasingly widely used in the further education sector.

Many universities go further and provide *learning environments* in which students interact directly with the public as part of a learning experience (as indeed do Hotel and Catering students and trainee doctors after the rehearsal phase). For example, at the University of Northumbria, staff have established a Student Law Centre and a Building Advice Centre to enable students working under supervision to give advice on actual cases. The students in the Law Centre work under the supervision of qualified solicitors to offer advice on cases brought in by fellow students, staff and the general public and, where necessary, to pursue the cases through the courts. Students from the Building Advice Centre visit clients' buildings and offer professional advice on matters such as cracked ceilings, rising damp and other structural issues.

As communication and information technologies start to play a greater part in students' learning and assessment experiences, it becomes more likely that the assessment environment will be students' own homes, from which they will be able to interact via the Internet or intranets. However, other than in a few specific disciplines, it is less likely that the assessment of practice will take place virtually using electronic means than by other means of assessment. This is a factor that needs to be taken into account by those universities that are moving towards information technology-based assessment as the norm.

Whenever off-site assessment takes place we need to be very clear about how we are to ensure that assessment is consistent and reliable. It is more difficult to monitor and moderate assessment when students and their assessors are distributed and when the standards attained are difficult to compare due to variations in context. It is therefore even more necessary to ensure that assessor briefings are provided, with an emphasis on equivalence of experience when it cannot be identical.

Timing of assessment

The point in a programme at which assessment takes place is a crucial decision, influenced by a number of factors (Brown *et al.* 1996: 10). With the assessment of practice, there are particularly high stakes, since in many professions, the assessment decisions we make will ultimately affect the lives and fortunes of their clients. Many traditional assessments provide only a snapshot of a student's ability at a single point in time but this may not be enough to assure us of a student's fitness to practice or professional competence. Fletcher (1992: 78) argues for a flexible approach to the timing of assessment and I would argue for approaches that enable us to assess students when they feel ready to demonstrate competence rather than when it suits our systems. For example, returning to the midwifery course at Northumbria, it is proposed that assessment can be offered to any midwife who feels ready to be assessed after week 7 of a 15-week course, enabling them them to spend time on extension tasks and enabling staff to concentrate their energies on supporting the remainder, so all have completed by week 15. The approach indicated in Table 8.1 also demonstrates a means by which students can indicate readiness following observation and rehearsal.

'Mastery' learning approaches at Otago University (New Zealand) and Sunderland University similarly focus on a number of key competences to be mastered by students over a period of time. Teams concerned, in this case, with medical laboratory officers, identify a limited range of competences that students need to 'master' (in the unfortunately gender-specific term) in order to succeed on the course. These techniques, such as making up of slides and correct setting up of microscopes, are taught intensively and then assessed after an hour in, say, a three-hour session. Those who demonstrate mastery are able then to leave to undertake a library or information technology-based extension task, and the staff then work with the remaining students, testing at intervals and providing, if necessary, one-to-one support until all students are competent in the required skills. Staff suggest that this intensive focus on basic competences saves hours of remedial teaching in labs late in the course and has great benefits in terms of developing student confidence.

Professional disciplines require practitioners to regularly develop and update their competences. It is not enough for a professional to have once been able to do something; practice must be current and ongoing. For this reason, *Continuing Professional Development* (CPD) and in-service training are requirements of many professions, with individuals perhaps required to provide evidence under a points scheme (law) or through a professional portfolio (nursing) in order to maintain membership of their professional bodies. Assessment of CPD needs to be as rigorous and demanding as any other kind of professional evaluation, particularly as the agenda for life-long learning becomes more apparent.

Problems and issues with the assessment of practice

The most commonly discussed issue concerning the assessment of practice tends to be how to cope with large numbers of pieces of student work in ways that are realistic and manageable for staff. Practice assessment tends to be more labour intensive than traditional forms of assessment like essays and exams, since it often involves high levels of interpersonal interaction, with discussion, negotiation and feedback. Anyone who has ever marked large numbers of portfolios or been involved in setting up OSCEs will recognize why some colleagues sometimes hark back to the 'good old days' of the domination of written examinations.

As indicated in Chapter 1 in this book, the problem of volume assessment can be ameliorated to some extent by using a range of assessors including practice supervisors, mentors, line managers, university tutors, peers, proctors and the students themselves. Both inter- and intragroup peer assessment can be extremely useful. Peers can be invaluable at providing down-to-earth feedback on, for example, other groups' performances or artefacts (intergroup), but need extensive preparation and briefing before they can be accepted to assess reliably to the same standards as tutors (Brown 1998).

If we want to assess process as well as outcome in group work, the best agents to do this are fellow students in their own group (intragroup). They are well placed to indicate whether their peers have contributed effectively, worked hard and collaborated purposefully (Brown 1996).

Assessment of professional skills often involves assessing the values that underpin students' performance and this can be highly problematic. It is difficult to be certain whether what is being observed is the student's espoused values or values translated into actions that the student believes the tutor or assessor wants to see but does not necessarily own. Midwives, for example, assert the centrality of mother-centred approaches but students' practice will often be influenced by deference to medical practitioners, concerns about hierarchies and personal religious and ethical beliefs. There is often debate about whose values predominate.

The assessment of practice is often uncomfortable, approximate and problematic, but it is not an issue academics can evade, as increasingly the nature of what we assess in universities is changing from a focus on knowledge and understanding towards students' abilities to do useful things with what they have learned. As we become more and more committed to lifelong approaches to learning, the greater the relevance of assessment and accreditation of learning which does not necessarily fit into familiar patterns. There is a need to monitor and review continuously the approaches we use for practice assessment and to commit ourselves to ongoing enhancement to assure the reliability and validity of the process.

References

Brown, S. (1996) 'The art of small group teaching' in *New Academic*, 5(3), Autumn 1996.
Brown, S. (1998) *Peer Assessment in Practice*. SEDA Paper No. 102. Birmingham: SEDA.

Brown, S. and Baume, D. (1992a) *Learning Contracts. 1: A Theoretical Perspective.* SEDA Paper No. 71. Birmingham: SEDA.

Brown, S. and Baume, D. (1992b) *Learning Contracts. 2: Some Practical Examples.* SEDA Paper No. 72. Birmingham: SEDA.

Brown, S. and Knight, P. (1994) *Assessing Learners in Higher Education.* London: Kogan Page.

Brown, S., Race, P. and Smith, B. (1996) *500 Tips on Assessment.* London: Kogan Page.

Fletcher, S. (1992) *Competence Based Assessment Techniques.* London: Kogan Page.

Hounsell, D., McCulloch, C. and Scott, M. (eds) (1996) *The Assessment Strategies in Scottish Higher Education (ASSHE) Directory.* The Centre for Teaching Learning and Assessment, Edinburgh University and Napier University, Edinburgh, in association with the Universities and Colleges Staff Development Agency (UCoSDA), Edinburgh.

McDowell, L. (1995) 'The impact of innovative assessment on student learning'. *Innovations in Education and Training International*, 32(4), 302–13.

9

Assessment of Key Skills

Garth Rhodes and Freda Tallantyre

The University of Northumbria at Newcastle (UNN), has held a view for long before the Dearing Report that key skills are important to graduates, and indeed its mission, framed in 1987, pledged:

> dedication to the development of the full human potential of its students and to their better preparation for employment, through the development not only of intellectual abilities but also enterprise, competencies and personal skills.

In 1988, UNN became one of the first eleven universities to implement the UK's Enterprise in Higher Education (EHE) initiative. Throughout that five-year programme, we worked with a checklist of thirteen skills which were collated from those which employers most frequently claimed to be desirable. They were, however, neither further differentiated as to importance, nor further defined in meaning. The emphasis of EHE was upon development and assessment of skills, but course teams applied their own interpretations and priorities. The whole picture was very patchy and unsystematic, even within single programmes, let alone within or across institutions.

While EHE was operating, however, other developments were taking place which were considerably to refine models for key skills. There had previously been Business and Technical Education Council (BTEC) Common Skills, though these were somewhat underrated by higher education. In the 1990s, though, National Vocational Qualifications (NVQs) were beginning to register a strong presence, and although higher education found much that was unpalatable in the discourse of 'standards' and 'competence', they did find value in the notion of articulating more clearly what graduates should know and be able to do as a result of their courses. The language of learning outcomes became widespread and the foundation for many modular curricula. The progress of the Management Charter Initiative helped make this more respectable at the higher levels.

Model design

By 1994, then, we had become more conscious that if we wished to assess key skills in higher education, then we needed a much clearer model that would:

- identify priorities and distinguish the essential from the desirable
- address issues of level, in the interests of student progression into and within higher education
- allow for overlap and interrelationship between the skills
- clarify potential performance criteria
- offer examples of the skills in practice
- achieve compatibility with the leading models that exist in the field and which various programmes would need to incorporate.

Our first recourse was to scrutinize the models already available to us which included at the outset:

- NVQ and General National Vocational Qualification (GNVQ) key skills
- BTEC Common Skills
- Management Charter Initiative (MCI) competencies
- the Department for Education and Employment (DfEE) Personal Effect-iveness model
- Enterprise models
- Alverno College's key abilities
- Confederation of British Industry (CBI) priorities
- individual university templates, such as those for De Montfort University.

In this period, there emerged more sophisticated and detailed models in terms of level descriptors associated with generic skills for graduates, including:

- the South East England Consortium (SEEC)/Wales skills and levels descriptors
- the New Zealand Qualifications Authority competencies
- the University of Portsmouth Partnership Programme skills and attain-ment matrices
- the Further Education Unit (FEU) key skills common approach.

Ownership

Rather than adopt any of these individual models in their totality, it was determined that we would learn and extract from them as appropriate, but would go through a protracted, but worthwhile, process to design our own (Appendix 1). The advantage of this, we felt included the following:

- Our model could be tailored and structured to fit the range of our programmes.

- The requirements of relevant awarding/accrediting bodies could be taken into account.
- The knowledge and experience of our own staff could inform the model, and build confidence in their competence to deliver it.
- The process would build assurance that much relevant work was already going on across the curriculum.
- The input of our own key skills 'experts' would give the model credibility among fellow academics.
- Those who assisted in design could become faculty champions to assist implementation.

Consequently, a working party, with six subgroups convened around each of the key skills, refined their elements and produced sets of performance criteria, based upon their experience in developing skills and upon evidence of external demand. Some of the dialogue which resulted naturally from this process was among the most stimulating in educational terms that many of us had experienced in years of staff development. The discussion went right to the heart of the purpose of higher education and of individual programmes, and challenged us to consider what we believed learners needed to know and be able to do, and how they might best learn. It established much common ground and hammered out unusual understandings between practitioners from quite distinct subject areas.

What is 'key'?

The emergence of our model was by no means free from dilemma. One of the first issues was to separate out what was 'key', and what subsidiary, in workable groupings. There is a practical necessity to do this to aid curriculum and assessment design, even though it may belie the complex process by which key skills interplay with one another, and with more specialist skills, in their acquisition and development. The models we drew upon used many and varied ways of making relationships, though in many communication, IT and numeracy commanded a prominent presence. In fact, our earliest model rolled these three together as all parts of communication, but we eventually bowed to the weight of external developments and separated them.

The heart of a higher education model we considered to be 'Managing and applying intellect', as an incontrovertible objective, and although the articulation of the model appears linear, in fact we have also a diagrammatic model which puts it in the centre of more functional skills (Appendix 2). 'Self-management' and 'Working with others' were added to the other four. The first of these was considered vital to successful performance in both study and work. Also, both are very prominent in employer wish lists and graduates are generally expected to exercise, at least in time and often more immediately (as self-employment becomes more common), supervisory and management responsibility in which organizational and people skills are fundamental. It was gratifying when Dearing's recommendation 21 proposed a very similar list to that which we had arrived at independently.

The concept of 'key' suggests that these skills should all be obtained by all students. However, this presented some problems that were both practical and attitudinal. For example, foreign language skills are part of our communication skill, yet institutional resources would not yet allow us to make these mandatory for all students. Moreover, a UNN 1997 survey of 50 employers to rank 29 different skill areas still, disappointingly, placed languages last (UNN 1998). It is becoming more possible to ensure a threshold in IT for all students, but some subject areas remain resistant to the notion of numeracy as essential, and it would certainly raise issues of staff competence. Originally, therefore, we proposed to recommend some elements as essential and others as desirable, but we were advised to leave that distinction to programme areas.

Progression and level

The greatest challenge has been the notion of attaching level to key skills. It is not difficult to get agreement to the fact that students should progress in key skills from pre-higher education, through higher education and beyond graduation. Moreover, it is easily discernible that improvement is both potential and actual in individuals. However, despite the major contributions to this argument made by the SEEC/Wales and other level descriptors, in practice, puzzling problems present themselves.

In the beginning, we set out to build level into performance criteria for each skill area, and succeeded surprisingly well with written and oral communication which were so widely accepted that staged progression seemed capable of articulation in a way relevant to most programmes. However, with the less extensively integrated and recognized key skills, exit levels in some programmes would be deemed barely more than entry level in others, and although it was possible to specify threshold exit levels for all students, it was not possible to reflect by means of level where and when these should be achieved within programmes. In the cases of IT and numeracy, the subgroup eventually arrived at the conclusion that the threshold exit level for all graduates was remarkably close to the Key Stage 4 curriculum, normally associated with 16-year-olds, and now mandatory though not so when most present participants in higher education were 16 years old.

There are difficult questions too around what to do in terms of the assessment of prior experiential learning (APEL) to avoid repetition for individuals who already possess the threshold skills, by comparison with those who have considerable progress to make. We did, however, wonder whether development was always linear, or whether transferability was achieved through practice in breadth of context. Eventually, we had to conclude that the most acceptable way to make progress in a standard fashion across the university was to specify threshold exit levels for graduates in key skills, and leave programmes to determine where and how they were integrated and developed.

Mapping

Our preferred approach to implementation is by integration, as opposed to bolt-on, because of the evidence that accumulates that only thus do students take key skills seriously, perceive their relevance, link them to context and get sufficient opportunities to develop, practise and be assessed. However, this is no easy option, as the Open University project, Changing the Higher Education Curriculum (Open University 1996), demonstrated. It is very demanding in terms of curriculum, systems and assessment design, and underpinning resource and staff development. Nevertheless, it seems to us at this stage that the advantages of integration are that:

- it allows for more systematic horizontal distribution and vertical progression
- it avoids overload on staff and repetition by students by limiting learning outcomes per unit
- it allows one to build upon different expertise in staff and clarify each person's area of responsibility
- it needs no additional curriculum space, and can be designed into existing units and assignments
- it achieves greater visibility and value with both staff and students.

The starting point, therefore, is a curriculum-mapping exercise to ensure comprehensive and systematic coverage. This is no mean feat in modular curricula, where one cannot easily control student choices to enable them to cover everything. However, our curriculum exists mainly in the form of named routes, with optional pathways and electives, so that it is possible to build teaching and assessment into core areas, with opportunities to develop and practise in optional and elective components. The mapping process involves an audit of the entire curriculum, module by module if necessary, to identify the actual and potential opportunities for students to develop, practise and be assessed in each element of each key skill, at appropriate levels. A balance in terms of attention may then be designed in, which can be reflected in the learning outcomes associated with each module, thereby assisting learners in exercising choice to achieve the most systematic coverage.

Development

Development of skills is intimately related to, but should not be confused with, their assessment. Students need opportunities to learn what each key skill comprises and means and to practise them, just as in assessment they need to be able to demonstrate the necessary underpinning knowledge and understanding as well as to perform competently.

EHE and other programmes have shown that there are a wide variety of approaches to teaching and learning key skills, and the politics and structures of institutions will determine how far these can be standardized. In UNN, we have preferred to leave considerable discretion to programmes and routes, with support and guidance from the centre, because approaches are then fully owned by their creators and tend to fit better the culture of the disciplines in which they are embedded.

Experience to date suggests that many programmes choose a model whereby some strong foundation work is laid down in introductory modules, where generic and subject-specific skills can be introduced and interwoven by staff with stronger competence in these aspects. These can be subsequently rehearsed in other components. Experiential activities prove important for development and assessment opportunities for many key skills in practice, so project work, placements, presentations, role plays, groupwork and so on are more likely to be assessed and accredited than in the past. Independent study packages and materials can be used to help students who are operating at very different levels to balance their abilities, and to deal with the problem of highly differentiated staff competence to teach key skills.

The assessment process

Key skill assessment should be capable of identifying the student's ability to:

- demonstrate the skill within a range of contexts and complexities
- apply the relevant underpinning knowledge and understanding
- assess the degree of autonomy involved in performing each key skill

Therefore it is unlikely that any one assessment tool will be able to do this. Indeed, the opportunity to assess any one skill via a number of methods is more likely to achieve a more accurate result.

The assessment process should be based upon sound principles and procedures (Figure 9.1) which include the following:

- Transparency for the student in what is required of them.
- A learning programme described in terms of outcomes of performance which specifically identify the key skills.
- A range of opportunities for an individual to demonstrate such outcomes/ skills.
- Negotiation between tutor and student in order to establish an action plan, describing opportunities for learning, and for formative and summative assessment.
- A system of monitoring and review.
- Formative assessment.
- Judgement of evidence.

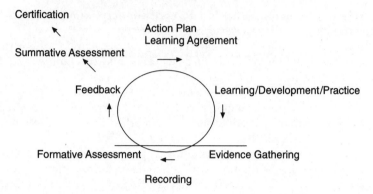

Figure 9.1   The cycle of assessment

- Feedback to the learner.
- Summative assessment.
- Certification.

The nature of evidence

Evidence of achievement comes in a variety of forms and includes the following:

- *Performance evidence*, whereby the individual is assessed by observation, preferably in a real situation, for example while on a work placement. Where this is not possible, use could be made of simulation, or possibly skills tests or even examination. Usually such forms of evidence should be supported by questioning (oral or written) to determine evidence of transferability, underpinning knowledge and understanding.
- *Product evidence*, whereby an individual submits a product such as an artefact, project, video, etc. which he/she has produced, and by which the assessor can judge by inference, the individual's ability to meet the specified learning outcome.
- *Prior learning.* A most important aspect in key skills is the assessment of students' entry competence and/or prior learning, because many will enter university already possessing the required level in particular key skill areas. We need to be able to introduce quick and reliable methods of confirming such skills. This could be in the form of accepting specific certificated learning, e.g. GCSE mathematics to confirm mathematical skill or via entry tests which are simple to implement and assess and which could conceivably be computer based. Alternatively, students could be asked to produce a Claim for Prior Learning, identifying evidence which can corroborate the claim.
- *Evidence from current learning outside the university*, e.g. from part-time work, voluntary work, travel, etc.

Assessing evidence

Assessment tools can be quite diverse. As indicated above, the closer one can get to the actual performance or authentic product of the skill, the more valid and reliable assessment will be.

Diagnostic tests may capture prior learning and dispense with the need to collect unnecessary evidence in specific areas, and *self-assessment materials and packages* can contribute efficiently to both formative and summative assessment.

In some areas, assessment is loaded into experiential components like placements, projects, presentations and using observation, but also mechanisms like *logs, diaries* and *learning contracts.* Tutors, students, peers, work supervisors can all be engaged in these assessments.

Where direct experience is not possible to arrange, *simulations* or *case studies* can be used instead, and *oral questioning* test underpinning knowledge and transferability.

For many aspects of key skills, staff may integrate performance criteria into existing assignments, so that student grades for overall performance (and implicitly degree classification) include a reflection of key skills. However, this method cannot clearly indicate that students are equally competent in all key skills.

Recording evidence

There are significant benefits to individuals in playing a major part in recording their own key skills achievements, including:

- the opportunity to recognize and own their abilities
- identify areas for development
- the ability to plan learning and career development
- the opportunity to bring together and synthesize the whole learning experience
- exercise self-responsibility.

In a curriculum where key skills will be demonstrated over a range of academic units, and where students can opt for a variety of optional units, it is important that a system for recording draws together all aspects of an individual's progress and achievement from across such a programme. Particularly useful is a *profile*, which is not a method of assessment but rather a multidimensional way of presenting information about a student's achievements and performance over a wide range of knowledge, skills and personal qualities. A *portfolio* of evidence may be collated and owned by the student, to support and contextualize the demonstration of performance in specific skills, and in so doing be a complete and permanent record of progress during the period of study. *Profiling* is a versatile system which, instead of isolating individual subject areas into artificial segments, draws upon learning from across the curriculum and builds up an overall picture of the individual's abilities (synthesis). Its strengths include:

- establishing the principle of student participation
- increasing motivation through the recognition of personal achievement
- providing a focus and system for diagnosis of achievements and learning needs; for definition of the action plan and assessment opportunities; and for recording their subsequent achievements
- placing assessment at the centre of the learning process
- freeing up the curriculum, and allowing for individual negotiation of the learning programme
- offering a meaningful summative leaving document.

The main weakness may be that, while performance can be reflected in a systematic, qualitative way, it does not thus contribute to degree classification.

Quality assurance

There are various issues that need to be addressed to ensure that skills assessment practices are robust. The more closely integrated with the normal institutional systems, the more readily they are likely to be accepted.

Validity requires that assessors get as close as possible to the actual skills performance, and that evidence is direct. The evidence must show clearly the authenticity of the student's evidence and that the performance belongs to them. Decisions may need to be taken about how recent the performance needs to be to assure *currency* of competence. *Reliability* and *sufficiency* require that the student provides enough evidence, in an appropriate range of contexts, to assure that performance is reproducible and transferable.

In addition, a system of *moderation* is desirable to ensure that standards are common, not only within, but across programmes. Staff development and support are important to ensure that assessors are sufficiently competent to assess within those areas which may lie outside their subject expertise.

Certification

There are a number of issues concerning recognition of key skills. First comes the question of whether their achievement is to be *mandatory*, with subsidiary questions about whether learners must meet *all* skills and criteria all, at what point they are deemed competent, and whether they will fail to achieve an award purely on grounds of failure to satisfy in key skills. Many staff remain resistant to the idea that a student might fail a degree if demonstrably not competent in all key skill areas, while good in subject knowledge.

Second comes the issue of *how* to recognize key skills within the final award, whether it be by *integration with the degree classification,* or by a complementary *qualitative profile.* The former would require marks or grades for skills to be awarded, though they do not lend themselves well to such systems. The criterion referencing of a profile is more appropriate, but tends to leave the certification as additional to, rather than integrated with, the award.

Practical questions surround the ability of institutional management information systems to track the performance of students in key skills to appreciate when certification becomes appropriate.

Finally, all efforts to encourage and recognize key skills may fall on stony ground unless we can persuade employers and other recipients of students on graduation to take seriously and use the modes of recognition provided.

Expectations of, and support for, students

Research has shown that many graduates are poor at identifying and articulating their key/employability skills, especially to sell their attributes to others, including employers. As indicated, the very acquisition of key skills is best underpinned by the student taking responsibility for his/her own learning, for identifying the opportunities to develop and demonstrate these skills and for gathering and recording the evidence of their learning. This does not mean that they should be unsupported however. In order for them to manage their key skills programme they will need to be able to:

- be familiar with and understand the model and the key skills criteria
- understand their own roles and responsibilities
- evaluate their own strengths and weaknesses
- identify and present appropriate current and prior learning/abilities
- negotiate their action plan
- manage and evaluate their own learning
- record their achievements
- understand types of evidence, e.g. product, process
- identify and gather evidence from various sources and synthesize it
- present their evidence to best advantage
- synthesize and cross-reference evidence
- identify learning and assessment opportunities
- receive feedback and act upon it.

To be successful in this, they will need information, explanation and guidance, especially at the outset. To maintain momentum, they will need a transparent and reliable system for action planning, reviewing progress and arranging assessment, if it does not come automatically. They may need help in arriving at balanced coverage across and beyond a modular curriculum, and in arranging remedial opportunities in areas of weakness.

Expectations and support for staff

Introducing an abilities-based cross-curricular model like key skills will have a major impact for many academics where they will be expected to play an active part throughout the assessment cycle. Not only will they be faced with new challenges of how to assess key skills, possibly using a variety of unfamiliar and non-traditional assessment tools, but also within areas where they may not see themselves as specialists. This will require them to cooperate and collaborate with other academic staff outside of their subject areas. They will need to be able to guide and support their students in the identification, development and assessment of their core skills and be able to record such skills within a sophisticated recording system.

In this cultural shift, institutional support in the form of direction and policy from senior management, quality assurance procedures, training and staff development and the development and dissemination of key documentation and exemplar material will be critical to achieving in staff an understanding of, value for, commitment to and competence to deliver and assess key skills.

In order to promote quality procedures in the assessment and verification of key skills, a cross-institutional team of lead internal assessors and verifiers can perhaps support others through networks. Our university has over a number of years offered a staff development programme for the training of assessors and verifiers, commonly known as the 'D' units, which are taken from the National Standards for Training and Development (Training and Development Lead Body, TDLB). Through these programmes staff develop a 'toolbox' of skills in order to assess students' performance, other than by the traditional assignment and examination. Assessor skills such as observing natural performance, examination of product evidence, oral questioning techniques, witness testimony and assessment of prior experiential learning (APEL) are explored. Such skills must be demonstrated and assessed by the 'candidate assessor' in order for them to gain their awards.

Real resource and real time has to be dedicated within the curriculum to establish and support key skills. It is essential that the institution recognizes the burden of work under which many academics work and use effective mechanisms to soften the blow of the introduction of key skills. We have found it helpful to work with pilot teams initially, and to allow for sufficient flexibility in the model for it to be taken on in different ways, and therefore owned, within different disciplines. Audits and mapping should serve to emphasize that much relevant work is already taking place. The availability of flexible support materials can also reduce the burden. It is desirable for staff to have ready access to key skill experts who can provide ongoing support and guidance. Within our university we have a small team of such staff who work from our Quality Enhancement Unit.

Increasingly, excellent management information systems for tracking student progression can take the sting out of such developments for staff. Much of the input of student progress into such systems could be done by the students themselves. Institutions could vastly reduce time spent on the recording and tracking of students by making the resources available in order to identify, develop and implement such systems. Experience and feedback from staff has shown that assessment recording documentation has to be simple to understand, easy to operate, and not reliant on vast amounts of additional bureaucracy.

Case study – Students into Schools Module

Students who undertake this academic unit, work alongside teachers in local primary and secondary schools, helping pupils with their work and giving them an idea of what it is like to be a student. This is a joint module between the universities of Newcastle and Northumbria.

Students have, as a requirement of their work experience placement, to demonstrate key skills in the areas of 'Managing and applying intellect', 'Self-management', 'Working with others' and 'Effective communication'.

Some considerable developmental work was undertaken by the module team prior to the introduction of the key skills to produce support and review mechanisms, along with the associated recording and assessment documentation, but the benefits of this seem to have paid off.

Before going out on placement, students are given a thorough introduction to the skills, their purpose and examples of how they can be demonstrated and recorded. Each student maintains a log book of their experience, records and self assesses their performance. They are supported through this process by student managers (students who themselves have previously undertaken the module). The course leader, who is a trained TDLB assessor, formally assesses the student's evidence at the end of the module.

The students also meet in groups to share their experiences and to discuss problems and issues of good practice, and in this way the students learn from each other. The evidence which students have presented has, through a critical examination of their own practice, been of an exceedingly high quality and clearly shown that by the end of the process, they have not only internalized the concept of key skills but also demonstrated competence over a wide range of skills.

Feedback from students at the end of the process indicates that, while they at first found difficulty understanding the key skills and were concerned about how much work and responsibility was being given to them to record and demonstrate their skills, once they had grasped the concept, they found the experience invaluable. In particular, they expressed support for being given specific skills targets to aim for, which gave structure to the experience and also helped them to recognize the skills which they had attained:

> 'Improvement in many skills such as communication and an insight into the way children learn.'
>
> (Sophie Ingleby, student in Business Management,
> Newcastle Business School, UNN)

'I improved my organizational skills and ability to adapt in unexpected situations. I felt useful and believed that I had made a difference.'
(Zoe Sylvester, student of Mathematics, University of Newcastle)

References

Open University (1996) *Changing the Higher Education Curriculum: Towards a Systematic Approach to Skills Development.* Milton Keynes: Open University.
University of Northumbria at Newcastle (1998) *Report for the Department for Education and Employment: Project to improve the relevance and responsiveness to employment of teaching and learning through partnerships with graduates.* Newcastle: UNN.

Appendix 1   Key skills at the university of Northumbria at Newcastle

Key skill	*Element*
1. Managing and applying intellect	1.1 Identify problematic issues and situations 1.2 Exercise an enquiring and critical capacity 1.3 Search for, retrieve, extract and synthesize information 1.4 Reason conceptually and develop argument 1.5 Arrive at judgements and decisions 1.6 Evaluate reflectively 1.7 Demonstrate initiative, inventiveness, new ideas
2. Self-management	2.1 Organize tasks to meet priorities and deadlines 2.2 Accept responsibility for and manage personal learning and development 2.3 Evaluate own performance and capabilities 2.4 Maintain and improve upon standards 2.5 Exercise self-control over emotion and under pressure 2.6 Identify and work within values, including equal opportunities and global perspectives
3. Working with others	3.1 Build, maintain and improve positive relationships 3.2 Make a positive contribution to groups and teams 3.3 Lead the process of determining collective goals and working towards them 3.4 Work well under supervision
4. Effective communication	4.1 Use clear, appropriate and accurate written styles 4.2 Use clear and appropriate oral and aural styles, including presentation, listening and discussion 4.3 Use visual and media styles to enhance communication 4.4 Communicate in one or more languages other than the mother tongue
5. Information technology	5.1 Demonstrate an understanding of standard information technology concepts and applications 5.2 Demonstrate constructive values and attitudes in relation to information technology 5.3 Use generic information technology skills
6. Use and application of mathematics	6.1 Communicate mathematically 6.2 Use mathematical reasoning to arrive at decisions and solutions 6.3 Demonstrate mathematical skills and knowledge

Appendix 2   'Managing and applying intellect'

Although the key skills in this model are described in a linear way, we feel that the relationships between them within higher education may be better expressed by the following diagram.

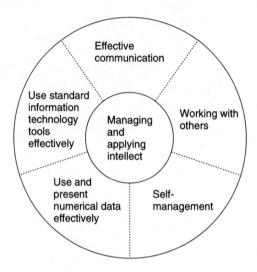

The field of 'Managing and applying intellect' is perhaps the highest-order skill and is best represented as a cyclical process, owing much to Kolb's model of how learning takes place.

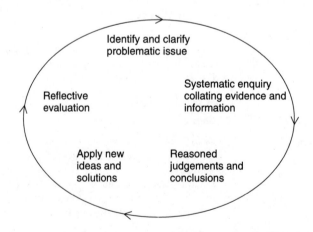

Self-management is a prerequisite for approaching the problem in a disciplined and systematic fashion. Effective communication allows one to read, write, discuss and listen, often in conjunction with others, drawing upon quantitative and qualitative evidence, and increasingly using IT to access rapidly remote sources of information.

Eventually new approaches and solutions can be applied, tested and evaluated, and then the process begins again to take us further forward in understanding. This interlocking set of abilities is even more critical for today and tomorrow than in the past, given the pace of change we all need to address in our living, working and studying environments over our own lifetimes.

10

Using Portfolios for Assessment in Teacher Preparation and Health Sciences

Gill Young

Introduction

This chapter will initially consider the use of a portfolio as the assessment method for Thames Valley University's (TVU) postgraduate Certificate in Teaching and Learning in Further and Higher Education. The reasons for this choice of method, how it has been evaluated as an assessment method, and what changes have been made are described. The chapter will also look at the use of portfolios generally, including their advantages and disadvantages. It will then go on to describe how this method of assessment has been developed further for use in nursing and midwifery programmes in the Wolfson Institute of Health Sciences at TVU.

Portfolios for teacher preparation

The development team creating this postgraduate Certificate in Teaching and Learning in Further and Higher Education in 1994 were interested in the philosophy of innovative assessment. Many of the team members were involved in the university's Enterprise in Higher Education scheme. The team, drawn from all ten schools of the university (as the university was structured at the time) and the Learning Resources Centres, were united in a common goal to improve the quality of students' learning. The team subscribed to the idea of learning through assessment. During the development of the programme, assessment was not viewed as an 'add on' at the end, but as a primary focus for the choice of content and teaching and learning approaches. In Harris and Bell's (1990) terms, assessment was not to be just something 'done to' learners, but also 'done with' and 'done by' learners.

Why did we use portfolios?

The development team set out to design a programme that could be used by all new staff with a teaching component to their role, not just lecturers. Therefore, both the content and assessment method would need to be flexible and adaptable. The team wished the programme to be accredited by the Staff and Educational Development Association (SEDA) and, therefore, a competence-based approach was used. (The programme is now SEDA accredited.) The programme was also validated as three Master's level modules, each module being worth fifteen M level credits.

The structure of the programme in ten sections also influenced the choice of assessment method, as the team wanted to assess each of the sections which represented key aspects of the teaching role. The development team decided to include self-, peer- and tutor-assessed components to enable participants on the programme to experience and gain confidence in their use, as well as needing to include both theoretical assignments and teaching practice assessments. The team needed to consider that staff would be undertaking this programme part-time and therefore, the assessment method should, as far as possible, use as evidence of achievement of the learning outcomes, work the participants were using in their day-to-day practice.

Finally, we were aware that some participants would also be required to undertake Training and Development Lead Body (TDLB) training and assessment qualifications, and we wanted an assessment method that would be congruent with that approach, and which would provide back-up evidence of achievement.

Portfolios seemed to be the most appropriate means to meet the requirements of this programme, with the added bonus that participants would, through experience, learn about their use as an assessment tool. The decision for its use was also based on a review of current literature. The development team identified a need to assess participants on this programme on their occupational competence as defined by Jessup in 1991.

> A person who is described as competent in an occupation or profession is considered to have a repertoire of skills, knowledge, and understanding which he or she can apply in a range of contexts and organisations.
>
> (Jessup 1991: 26)

A portfolio provides access to information about a participant's abilities across a range of qualities about what someone knows and can do. It also provides the participant with a learning resource for their future teaching.

Format of the portfolio

Participants complete a portfolio for each of the three modules that make up the postgraduate certificate. Three forms of evidence are included for each module:

Section	Self-assessed	Peer-assessed	Tutor-assessed
1. Students first-Starting to teach	Own personal learning agreement for the programme. (Formative)	(A) Student profile document. (Formative)	(B) 1 lesson or learning event plan and evaluation of the lesson. (Summative)
2. Planning		(C) A critical analysis of an existing programme or module. (Summative)	(D) An outline programme for a series of future lessons. (E.g. 3 or 4) (Formative)
3. Assessment TDLB D32 TDLB D33	(E) Evidence of having assessed/ marked either exam, coursework practical or work experience for a small group of students. (Summative)		(F) An assessment plan, a variety of assessment tools/ sources of evidence designed by the participant including a rationale for the methods chosen. (Summative)
4. Evaluation	(G) Evaluation of own student profile document as used so far. (Formative)		(H) Evaluation of a self-selected learning event. (Summative) (I) An evaluation strategy for one of the participant's own future learning events. (Formative)

Figure 10.1   Example of portfolio evidence of achievement

- written projects/reports/files
- teaching practice assessments
- example lesson plans

Figure 10.1 shows an example of what students are required to include.

Evaluation by participants

Three cohorts have completed the programme in the three-module format. Nearly all participants reported finding the portfolio format difficult initially. The first cohort experienced two main problems. One was timing, particularly for the inclusion of teaching practice assessments, as some participants had their teaching mainly in one part of the year. This was resolved for the later cohorts by requiring all the teaching practice assessments to be completed by the end of Module 3. Since participants received oral and written feedback at the end of each teaching practice assessment, making the pragmatic decision to attach them to the last module does not affect their educational experience. The second problem is getting the portfolios marked and returned to the participants quickly enough for them to make the most effective use of the extensive feedback. However, this is a logistical problem, created because the programme does not run on the university's normal academic timetable, therefore, delays have occurred waiting for the next assessment board. This is not entirely resolved.

Following the programme's first SEDA review in 1997, it was updated and redesigned as ten mini-modules each worth four credits at Master's level. This was done to align it with the university's revised credit scheme, and to make it easier for participants to study selected sections of the programme to meet their individual staff development needs. Successful completion of the programme will in the future give students advanced standing towards the MSc in Managing Learning Strategies being developed by the university's Centre for Complementary Learning. The assessment strategy has remained essentially unchanged, as it was designed in ten sections originally. The main change is the reordering of some sections and therefore the assessments, demonstrating the ability of this approach to withstand curricular change. A fourth cohort commenced the newly structured programme in October 1997. It is too early to evaluate these changes.

Advantages and disadvantages of portfolios

Measured against the ten-point manifesto for assessment designed by Brown *et al.* (1996) (Table 10.1), portfolios, as used on this programme, rate highly.

The key area that remains problematic is overassessment and as Phil Race (1996) has stated they '. . . take a lot of looking at!' Although I believe the

Table 10.1 An abridged assessment manifesto

- Assessment should be based on an understanding of how students learn
- Assessment should accommodate individual differences in students
- The purpose of assessment needs to be clearly explained
- Assessment needs to be valid
- Assessment instruments and processes need to be reliable and consistent
- All assessment forms should allow students to receive feedback on their learning and their performance
- Assessment should provide staff and students with opportunities to reflect on their practice and their learning
- Assessment should be an integral component of course design, and not something bolted on afterwards
- The amount of assessment should be appropriate
- Assessment criteria need to be understandable, explicit and public

---

(Modified from Brown *et al.* 1996)

assessment scheme still needs some revision, because assessment forms a key part of the learning experience and is not an 'add-on', evaluations have not emphasized overassessment as a problem. Marking the portfolios has also not proved too time consuming, once the markers became familiar with the format. The portfolios are criterion referenced with clear marking criteria for each assignment and are graded 'Pass', 'Refer' or 'Fail' only. The comments provide participants with information on how well or badly they performed. The use of this approach, coupled with the use of markers familiar with the programme, has led to high intermarker reliability. The only section where problems occurred with the initial cohort were when tutors marking a section had not been involved in either programme development or teaching. This difficulty was addressed by familiarizing the markers better with the aims and ethos of the programme.

To summarize our experience and learn from it, the key seems to be to have very clear portfolio guidelines for learners and markers (the more transparent the better), to make the scheme as simple as possible and to have staff preparation for this type of marking. The portfolio system for this programme has been fairly successful but it only has small student numbers (only between 12 and 15 students in a cohort) and uses a simple 'pass/fail' grading. The next task was to build on this experience and design a portfolio approach for use in the nursing and midwifery programmes in the Wolfson Institute of Health Sciences at Thames Valley University, which have large cohorts and require a percentage mark to be assigned both to theory and practice learning.

Portfolios for health sciences

Institutional changes

In 1994, Thames Valley University (TVU) gained the contracts for pre- and post-qualifying nursing and midwifery education from the Inner London Consortia resulting in North West Thames Regional Health Authority transferring the staff from Queen Charlotte's, Riverside and North West London Colleges of Health Studies to TVU, creating the Wolfson School of Health Sciences. (Renamed as the Wolfson Institute of Health Sciences in 1997.) The Schools of Nursing at Moorfields and the Royal Brompton Hospital also became part of the Wolfson, and in September 1995 the Berkshire College of Nursing and Midwifery joined TVU, after the university successfully bid for pre- and post-qualifying nursing and midwifery contracts from the Oxford and Anglia Region.

The Wolfson Institute now has approximately 300 staff and 3500 students, making it one of the largest providers of healthcare education in the UK. This rapid increase in size has produced a major problem in relation to practice (clinical) placements and assessment in the workplace. The Institute now uses over 900 different wards, departments, health centres and homes as practice placements. Assessment of practice is primarily carried out by NHS service staff, known as 'practice assessors', who are required by the professional body to undergo a programme of preparation for this role and be updated. Currently, the Institute's register of practice assessors contains approximately 2000 personnel. Systems of quality monitoring and staff development which just about functioned before the colleges of Nursing and Midwifery were amalgamated, now no longer work, requiring a rethinking and the development of new approaches.

In 1996–7 Thames Valley University restructured and introduced an innovative approach to higher education known as the New Learning Environment (NLE). One concept underpinning the NLE is 'learning through assessment' which is reflected in the revised process for all module development and reapproval.

> The process of module design commences with a statement of the learning outcomes to be achieved, followed by assessment information which clarifies how the achievement of these learning outcomes is demonstrated through the assessment. Learning outcomes, along with the associated assessment criteria, provide the means to enable an assessor to determine whether a student has met the module requirements.
> (TVU, NLE Learning through Assessment Working Group Report 1996)

The changes brought about by the introduction of the NLE has caused everyone to review their approaches to assessment and has led to a considerable expansion in the repertoire of assessment methods being used. Portfolios are one method which has been considered for wider application in higher education programmes, building on experience of their use in the university's further education programmes.

The problem

A new assessment strategy was developed as part of the Quality Enhancement Project designed to operationalize part of the Wolfson's 1996–2000 strategic plan. A task group was established to carry out an internal and external review of the current assessment situation and then to design a new scheme which would be generic to all Wolfson Institute programmes, would be based on the South East England Consortium for Credit Accumulation and Transfer (SEEC) academic level descriptors which the university was committed to implementing as part of the NLE, and would implement the English National Board (ENB) for Nursing, Midwifery and Health Visiting's assessment regulations requiring students to keep portfolios (ENB 1996). The greatest difficulties are with the practice assessment. Therefore, detailed below is an outline of the results of the review. Details of the theoretical review have not been included, as only two main issues were involved: creating a generic tool and implementing the SEEC level descriptors.

The problem is multifactoral. Firstly, the academic accreditation of pre- and post-registration programmes has led to a need to identify criteria to discriminate between assessment at different academic levels. Secondly, the amalgamation of colleges of Nursing and Midwifery and the resulting increase in size has led to increased problems preparing, and particularly updating, practice assessors. Thirdly, the move of Nursing and Midwifery education into higher education institutions which may be unfamiliar with professional programmes requiring assessment of both theoretical understandings and practice, and which consequently may have no systems for accrediting assessment of practice, has caused difficulties. Fourthly, the ENB 1996 'Regulations and Guidelines for the Approval of Institutions and Courses', particularly the revised assessment policy, requires assessment strategies to 'ensure that equal value and accreditation is given to assessment of the theory and practice' (ENB 1996: 5.7). They further require schemes of assessment of practice to 'include the collection of a range of information to serve as a basis for student/assessor discussion . . .' (ENB 1996: 5.13). In addition, the requirement of students to keep portfolios has led to the redesigning of assessment strategies.

All of these factors synthesized from the literature review and experience, must be reviewed against a background of concurrent, rapid change and reduction in resources in nursing and midwifery education, higher education and the NHS. From an analysis of all these factors, I believe the key elements are identifying whether schemes of assessment of practice are reliable and whether they can discriminate between academic levels. Evidence of this will be necessary, if a number of universities are to change their views about work-based learning and give equal value and accreditation with theory. Nursing and midwifery education are in a unique position, with their long history of assessment of practice, to provide a lead to the rest of higher education in the accreditation of work-based learning. However, I would put forward one caveat to this search for reliability. In discussions with some colleagues working in the field of educational research, the question arose that in the search for reliability, would validity be sacrificed? Therefore, in designing the scheme there is also the need to attain the right balance between validity and reliability.

The approach

The scheme has been designed so students develop a portfolio throughout their programme of study. This portfolio will include a practice and a theoretical profile and a learning contract for each module, plus an element of reflection on progress throughout the programme. The intention is to equip all students to understand how to create and use portfolios as life-long learning tools.

Generic theoretical and practice marking grids were developed for academic levels 1, 2, 3 and M, based on the SEEC level descriptors. Table 10.2

Table 10.2 Level 2 practice marking grid

Ability	Excellent (85%)	Very good (65%)	Good (55%)	Satisfactory (45%)	Unsatisfactory (>40%)
Psycho-motor Can perform complex skills consistently, with confidence and a degree of coordination and fluidity. Able to choose an appropriate response from repertoire of actions, and can evaluate own and others' performance.	Always has technical mastery of skills, performing smoothly, precisely and efficiently. Able to plan strategies and tactics and adapt effectively to unusual and unexpected situations.	Can always perform complex skills consistently, confidently and with a degree of fluidity. Able to choose from a repertoire of actions. Can evaluate own and others' performance.	Can always perform complex skills consistently, confidently and with a degree of fluidity. Usually able to choose from a repertoire of actions. Usually able to evaluate own and others' performance.	Usually able to perform complex skills consistently, confidently and with a degree of fluidity. Limited repertoire of actions to choose from. Usually able to evaluate own and others' performances, sometimes needs assistance evaluating others.	Rarely able to perform complex skills consistently, confidently and with a degree of fluidity. Very limited repertoire of actions to choose from. Rarely able to evaluate own or others' performances, without assistance.
Self-awareness, reflection on practice Is able to evaluate own strengths and weaknesses, can challenge received opinion and begins to develop own criteria and judgements.	Always confident in application of own criteria of judgement and in challenge of received opinions in action and can reflect on action.	Always recognizes own strengths and weaknesses against pre-set criteria. Begins to develop own criteria and judgement and challenge received opinion.	Usually recognizes own strengths and weaknesses against pre-set criteria. Begins to develop own criteria and sometimes challenges received opinion.	Usually recognizes own strengths and weaknesses against pre-set criteria. Begins to develop own criteria and judgements but does not yet challenge received opinion.	Needs assistance to recognize own strengths and weaknesses against pre-set criteria. Has not begun to develop own criteria and judgements or challenge received opinion.
Problem solving Can identify key elements of complex problems and choose appropriate	Always confident and flexible in identifying and defining complex	Can always identify key elements of complex problems and choose	Usually identifies key elements of complex problems and choose appropriate	Usually identifies key elements of complex problems. Sometimes needs	Rarely able to identify key elements of complex problems. Always

Table 10.2 (Cont'd)

Ability	Excellent (85%)	Very good (65%)	Good (55%)	Satisfactory (45%)	Unsatisfactory (>40%)
methods for their resolution in a considered manner.	problems and the application of appropriate knowledge and skills to their solution.	appropriate methods for their resolution in a considered manner.	methods for their resolution in a considered manner.	assistance to choose appropriate methods for their resolution in a considered manner.	needs assistance to choose appropriate methods for their resolution in a considered manner.
Communication and presentation Can communicate effectively in a format appropriate to the discipline and report practical procedures in a clear and concise manner with all relevant information in a variety of formats.	Can always debate and produce detailed and coherent project reports on practice issues, in a professional manner.	Always communicates effectively in an appropriate format/language in a clear and concise manner. Can use a variety of formats effectively.	Usually communicates effectively in an appropriate format/language in a clear and concise manner. Can use a variety of formats effectively.	Usually communicates effectively in an appropriate format/language in a clear and concise manner. Limited range of formats can be used effectively.	Rarely communicates effectively in an appropriate format/language in a clear and concise manner.
Interactive team work skills Can interact effectively within a professional team. Can recognize or support leadership or be proactive in leadership. Can negotiate in a professional context and manage conflict.	Can work with and within a team towards defined outcomes. Can take roles as recognized leader. Always able to negotiate and handle conflict. Can effectively motivate others.	Always interacts effectively within a professional team. Can recognize and support leadership or be proactive in leadership. Can negotiate in a professional context and manage conflict.	Usually interacts effectively within a professional team. Usually recognizes and supports leadership or be proactive in leadership. Usually able to negotiate in a professional context and manage conflict.	Usually interacts effectively within a professional team. Usually recognizes and support leadership but is not proactive in leadership. Sometimes needs assistance to negotiate in a professional context and manage conflict.	Rarely interacts effectively within a professional team. Cannot recognize and support leadership. Not able to negotiate in a professional context and manage conflict.

provides an example of the level 2 practice marking grid. Each learning outcome is broken down into psychomotor skills, problem-solving skills, and so on. Assessors are required only to grade students as 'satisfactory', 'very good', etc. for each of these skills. The module teachers then convert the grades into a percentage, and add the marks for each skill together to obtain an overall percentage mark for the practice component of the module. To accompany the profiles and learning contracts, a detailed 'Guideline for compiling a portfolio of learning and outcomes assessment' was written, which is included in the students' programme handbooks.

The Wolfson Institute of Health Sciences went for a generic approach to make student and staff (both teachers and NHS) preparation easier. Once people understand the generic process, preparation for individual programmes/modules will only need to be in relation to the specific criteria. The use of a generic tool makes it easier for teachers to support students and NHS staff in undertaking the practice assessment, as only one common format will be in use by all students in the area whether undertaking pre- or post-registration qualifications. Reliability will remain the most difficult aspect. Preparation of teachers to use the generic marking criteria is in progress, and preparation sessions for practice assessors are being carried out, but trying to update everyone is almost impossible in busy NHS hospital and community trusts.

The portfolio assessment scheme is now being used in Diploma and BSc (Hons) programmes in nursing and midwifery, which commences in autumn 1997, and will be used with other programmes starting in 1998. Two of the programmes use a problem-based learning approach and the others take a more traditional curriculum method. The Diploma in Nursing programme had an intake of 377 students in October 1997, 309 of whom undertook the adult branch, with another slightly smaller intake in April 1998. The question remains whether this assessment method will answer the problems outlined earlier in this chapter, especially reliability with these high student, and therefore, assessor numbers. Measured against the Brown *et al.* (1996) manifesto for assessment, it is only reliability that can be identified as a major question in the use of portfolios as an assessment method for these programmes.

References

Brown, S., Race, P. and Smith B. (1996) *500 Tips on Assessment.* London: Kogan Page.
ENB (1996) *Regulations and Guidelines for the Approval of Institutions and Courses.* London: English National Board for Nursing, Midwifery and Health Visiting.
Harris, D. and Bell, C. (1990) *Evaluating and Assessing for Learning.* London: Kogan Page.
Jessup, G. (1991) *Outcomes: NVQ's and the Emerging Model of Education and Training.* London: Falmer Press.
Race, P. (1996) 'The art of assessing: 2'. *New Academic,* 5(1), 3–6.

11

Group-based Assessment: An Evaluation of the Use of Assessed Tasks as a Method of Fostering Higher Quality Learning

Mike Heathfield

Introduction

The focus in this chapter is on a key element relevant to depth of learning, activity and interaction (Biggs and Telfer 1987), in the form of assessed group work. The majority of our course innovations were driven by changes in the nature of assessment and a more detailed exploration of the motivations behind this can be found elsewhere (Bloxham and Heathfield 1994). I am indebted to my colleague, Sue Bloxham, for her development and research on the induction course which forms the first section of this piece and is covered in more detail elsewhere (Bloxham 1997).

We have been involved in research into course development and innovation within our department since 1993. We are both tutors with responsibility for the professional training of youth and community workers within a higher education context. We have responsibility for two major courses: a three-year undergraduate programme which awards a BA in Community and Youth Studies (CYS), in which the professional training elements are contained within the first two years, and a postgraduate professional Certificate in Youth and Community Work taught over one year or five terms part-time. Over a number of years, both these courses have undergone considerable development brought about by our desire to maximize the opportunity for students to operate their learning at 'deep' levels (Ramsden 1992) and to produce more capable and employable professional youth and community workers.

Since 1994 we have continued to develop our approach to group work and there are a number of key reasons why this particular methodology has received such an investment within our professional courses, not least the previously mentioned link with the potential for deep learning. Group work, in its own right, is a taught subject on our courses; youth and community workers are trained in the skilled use of group work as a fundamental tool of their trade. For a practical professional course, it is particularly appropriate that students experience and practice their group-work skills in the real context of their own learning environment.

There were also some broader professional issues which encouraged our belief in group work as a fundamental tool. As noted in general discussions of professional education (Jarvis 1983), peer assessment is claimed to be an important signifier of professional practice. It also has pedagogical implications, in that despite our concern with the quality of individual learning on our courses, we accepted that all learning takes place in a social context (Jarvis 1987, 1992) and the development of a professional 'identity' is best generated in a shared, communal context. In the macro sense, the centrality of group work is also congruent with our structured attempts to work to counter the individualism which still seems such a significant part of the 'reflexive modernity' project of the millennium (Beck 1992).

Group work was not new to our teaching. However, a detailed investigation and investment into its effectiveness was. The anecdotal history from students was of difficult relationships and high stress levels whenever assessed group work was encountered and unfair grades as a result of the process. Assessed group work became a major structural feature of our redesigned courses in 1993 and our research findings into these changes were informative. All students had positive comments to make about their group work and the great potential for learning. However, it could easily become a negative experience through which the learning was considerably more painful:

> 'Pulling our hair out, pulling our hair out by the end of it. And the other two were pulling their hair out as well. It was dreadful. It was really, really dreadful. It was the most stressful thing I have been through on the whole course. Especially when one person at the end starts crying, you know, and starts saying that it's this problem that they have.'
>
> (Bloxham and Heathfield 1994: 186)

In response to these worries about group work, we identified two key problems to address: student preparation for group work and the appropriate and fair allocation of grades for group work-assessed items.

The first issue we decide to address was preparation for student group work, and this was done through the implementation of a new training and support course for all Year 1 students at the outset of the programme. This approach was part of a broader attempt to induct students into the specific culture of our courses and cover many of the issues pertinent to encouraging deep approaches to learning. The research of Eley (1992) adds to the case that there are many areas of intervention that can influence context-specific behaviour to encourage and indeed increase the use of deep approaches to learning. One of the newer areas under consideration is that of perception and how this may play a significant role in the actual learning strategy adopted (Entwistle and Tate 1990). Trigwell *et al.* (1994) have also introduced the notion that the intention of the lecturer may be significant in the actual encouragement of specific approaches to learning, regardless of the actual teaching style. In our Professional Support Course (CYS 123B) our intention was to lay the foundations for all students, including considerable preparation for their group-work tasks.

The second issue about the unfair allocation of grades for group work-assessed items, while considerably smaller in scale was, at times, no less stressful and problematic for both students and staff. It is also an issue which is still raised in validation processes where the validity and reliability of 'individual' degrees are questioned. We introduced a Group Assessment Sheet which was designed to allocate tutor grades to group-work items in a more open, negotiated and valid format. What follows is a discussion of the results of these two innovations specific to group work in our course design.

Group-work training and induction courses

Our previous research indicated that student support and preparedness for their new learning environment was significant in assisting them to make the most of this flexible context (Heathfield and Bloxham 1996). Gibbs *et al.* (1994) have suggested that study skills courses are unlikely to be taken very seriously or have much effect if they are seen as independent of the 'real' business of learning. Consequently, the newly validated Part 1 of our BA CYS degree included a half-unit course (CYS123B: Professional Support Course) which integrated the development of a range of learning skills into the wider subject matter of the other Year 1 units. For each student, the course involved an hour a week in a large group session followed by half an hour a week in a Professional Academic Tutorial (PAT) group of five students.

Our students were asked to complete an evaluation questionnaire which included a set of closed questions asking them to express their level of confidence in a range of skills covered in the course curriculum and a series of open-ended questions asking for feedback on the course methodology and the PAT group process. These result were compared with those of students in four other Part 1 groups: combined studies, geography, biological sciences and drama. All students were asked to identify their age, entry qualifications, degree scheme and Part 1 subjects. Questionnaires also included an opportunity for students to indicate what use they made of various learning resources. For all student groups, the questionnaire was administered after they had completed two full terms of their first-year programme. More specific methodological detail can be found in Bloxham (1997).

Our results indicate significant differences (at least $p \leq 0.05$) between the CYS123B group and all the other Part 1 groups in the survey in relation to confidence in the following learning skills:

- Using the computer catalogue
- Finding journal articles
- Using the CD ROM in the library
- Making and using a database
- Making and using a spreadsheet

- Using abstracts and Indexes
- Reserving library books
- Exam technique
- Wordprocessing
- Making oral presentations

The results did not indicate a significant difference in relation to the following learning skills:

- Using short loan
- Note-taking in lectures
- Distinguishing analysis and description in writing
- Identifying own learning needs
- Working in assessment teams

- Writing bibliographies
- Making notes from reading
- Writing essays
- Managing use of time
- Understanding how I learn best

Many of these skills are more frequently referred to as 'transferable skills'. The development of higher education interest in transferable skills is rooted in the notion that various personal and learning skills are vital, not only for effective functioning as a student, but also as essential preparation for the workplace, as specific subject knowledge becomes rapidly outdated (Gibbs *et al.* 1994). Such skills are considered to include communications skills, information skills, the ability to cooperate with others, record-keeping, and time and task management. Clearly, many of these skills have both a direct professional relevance to youth and community work and the broader employment field (Harvey and Knight 1996).

The Professional Support Course included an opportunity for students to review their transferable skills and concentrate on developing a number of them including, apart from those dealt with above, identifying their own learning needs, managing use of time and working in assessment teams. Consequently, it is somewhat disappointing that the student group demonstrated no significant confidence in these areas in relation to other students. This is particularly the case in relation to time-management and team assessments, as considerable emphasis was placed on them in the large group sessions and assignments. Our expectation was that CYS students would register considerable confidence in managing their assessed group-work projects; the survey results do not support this. There are a range of possible reasons for the failure to show significant differences:

1. Students are gaining experience and training in these areas in other courses. The content of the Part 1 courses included in this study did include a variety of transferable skills development such as working in teams, with or without a linked group assessment, and work on time management and organization.
2. In relation to team assessments, CYS123B students had been involved in four or five during the first two terms prior to this research. Consequently, they may have been much more aware of the complexities and possible frustrations of working effectively with others where a course

assessment was at stake. They were experienced enough not to be too confident about something which is difficult for pretty well everyone, throughout their working lives. Other courses had exposed students to fewer team assessments and therefore there was less chance of students having had bad experiences of team assessment when a lot was at stake. We may have been successful in helping students develop this skill by asking them to reflect on the process, develop strategies for improving and complete a reflective self-assessment of themselves as a team member. This development is not conceived by our students as significantly greater confidence.

3. It may be the case that conceptualizing time management as largely a skill is mistaken. Our experience suggests that time management is crucially linked to motivation which is demonstrably linked to academic success. The BA CYS degree is recruiting students with generally less successful educational histories and therefore poorer time management may be a characteristic of many of these students. This viewpoint may explain why the biology group with the highest average 'A' level scores had the strongest profile in relation to time management (but it may be something they do in biology). Do we need to work at improving our students' intrinsic and extrinsic motivation to do academic work? Many of our poorest time managers (in terms of their academic work) seem to manage their time very successfully when it comes to large and responsible student union commitments! Research elsewhere in the department has indicated that the wider range of learning activities associated with flexible learning is important in improving motivation and therefore we may be better off putting our energy into that rather than in working on time-management techniques, which may only be being used effectively by students who are already fairly good at managing their time.

Our students are constantly engaged in assessed groupwork and so our seeming inability to raise their confidence levels was disappointing. All staff have reported that less time is spent in dealing with conflict or crisis in groups and most group work now seems to be a positive experience for the majority of students, so there are indications that they are getting better practically at handling these complex group contexts, despite their lack of confidence. A second factor which may have had some influence in our attempt to minimize the potentially negative effects of assessed group work was our introduction of Group Assessment Sheets.

Group Assessment Sheets

Within our validation documents, we now had a maximum of 30 per cent of each unit which was assessed group work. Our use of group-assessed items in the past had indicated a problem with the final grade reflecting each individual's actual contribution to the piece of work. We had two primary concerns about the grading of assessed group work. Firstly, that weaker students were being carried by their group and receiving grades far beyond their individual capabilities. Secondly, more capable students were responsible for 'working' the group and producing the assessment item and this extra burden was not reflected in their final grade. The unfairness of every group member receiving the same final grade for the piece of work was self-evident to all concerned and resulted in some difficult conversations with students after the final grade had been awarded. Some considerable tutor time was spent dealing with deputations of students who were unhappy about their grade and wanted to discuss what went on in their group, after the grade had been awarded.

We decided that the assessment tool could also be used to drive the need for groups to engage in frank discussions about their group processes *during* the process rather than *after*. As tutors, we were not the most appropriate people to undertake this. Group members themselves were the only people who could arrive at a fair grade distribution. This student discussion needed to have some formal record that could then be used to ascertain the relative value of individual contributions to group work when a final grade had been allocated. We devised the Group Assessment Sheet to serve this purpose. The sheet was to become an integral part of every piece of group work and every assessed item had to be handed in with a signed Group Assessment Sheet, before marking could commence. In long-term group-work items, the sheet was to be used for monitoring purposes halfway through the process, so that students could build up a picture and discuss how their current patterns of working had the potential to influence their final grade. The Group Assessment Sheets measured contributions on five indicators:

- regular attendance at group meetings
- contribution of ideas for the task
- reading and researching material for the task
- organizing and analysing the material
- practical contribution to the end product.

Initially there was great resistance to the introduction of these forms, despite the general agreement about the unfair allocation of grades. One whole-year group (1992–3) on the professional undergraduate course refused to use them and felt that they destroyed the whole communal purpose of group work. With hindsight, this rejection was a reflection of our mismanagement of introducing a new working practice. Students needed to be brought into the process of solving the problem. The following cohort (1993–4) were given much more induction into the nature of group-work assessment and the Group Assessment Sheets were accepted as a standard part of their group-work processes rather than an additional, imposed assessment condition from tutors. These first pilot groups of students felt that the Group Assessment Sheet did not adequately reflect contributions to the group-work processes and that end-product factors dominated. In the light of these student suggestions, the Group Assessment Sheet was rewritten to add more factors measuring student contributions to the communal processes of group support. The indicators used on this newer version were (see Appendix):

- regular attendance at group meetings
- contribution of ideas for the task
- researching, analysing and preparing material for the task
- contribution to cooperative group process
- supporting and encouraging group members
- practical contribution to end product.

Currently, the sheets are well established as standard practice within the department for all group work-assessed items and the final grade allocation has become much less the focus of problems within group work. Indeed, in 1997, a small group of students formed to formulate new criteria to assist in the difficult grade negotiation section of the process (see Table 11.1). This development came out of a desire to encourage individual students to do considerable individual reflective work before the form is completed in the group, and to generate a process where actual grades were awarded as a

Table 11.1 Self-assessment for CYS123B students
Please award yourself a mark out of 20 for each category. Note the justification for your mark in the empty box. The criteria are designed to help you with your self-assessment.

Worth 20	*Worth 0*	*Justification for mark*	*Mark*
Regular attendance at group meetings Attended all meetings, stayed to agreed end, worked within timescale, active and attentive, prepared to be flexible about meeting times.	Missed several/most meetings, always or often late, left early, digressed, giggled, day dreamed or gossiped most of the time.		
Contribution of ideas for the task Thought about the topic in advance of the meeting, provided workable ideas which were taken up by the group, built on others' suggestions, and were prepared to test out your ideas on the group rather than keep quiet.	Didn't come prepared. Didn't contribute any ideas. You tended to reject others' ideas rather than build on them.		

Table 11.1   (Cont'd)

Worth 20	Worth 0	Justification for mark	Mark
Researching, analysing and preparing material for the task You did what you said you would do, you brought materials, did an equal share of the research and helped to analyse and evaluate the material.	You did no research. You didn't do what you promised to do. You didn't manage your workload. You didn't get involved with the task and allowed others to provide all the material.		
Contribution to cooperative group process Left personal differences outside the group, willing to review group progress and tackle conflict in the group, took on different roles as needed, kept group on track, willing and flexible but focused on the task.	Did not take initiative, waited to be told what to do. Always took the same role (leader, joker, etc.) regardless of circumstances, created conflict, and were not prepared to review group progress.		
Supporting and encouraging group members Keen to listen to others, encouraged participation, enabled a collaborative learning environment, sensitive to issues affecting group members, supported group members with special needs.	Sought only to complete the task, spoke over others and ignored their opinions, kept ideas and resources to yourself. Insensitive to individuals' needs and did not contribute to the learning process.		
Practical contribution to end product Willing to try doing new things. Not hogging the tasks, made a high level of contribution, took own initiative, was reliable and produced high standard work/ presentation.	Not willing to take on any task, did not take any responsibilities, were unreliable so others felt the need to keep checking up, and you made a limited, poor-quality contribution.		

positive contribution rather than the difficult feeling that one's grade was only increased by removing marks from a group colleague. This most recent refinement of both the tool and process has come solely from students themselves and they are articulate in their defence of this to students new to the process. Preparation and process issues now seem to dominate the agenda, which would seem much more productive and professionally appropriate. More significantly, students themselves have developed and refined the assessment tool in response to their own needs. This sits in stark contrast to the initial rejection in 1993 when we imposed the supposed 'improvement'.

The results

What is reported in this section are evaluative responses which have not been gathered in a systematic way. We have not conducted any specific research into the effect of the Group Assessment Sheets and so what is presented here are evaluative comments from the staff team. While this should be borne in mind, we do not feel it lessens the value of what is reported. Our expertise as tutors should also allow us to use our instincts to check the value of innovation.

Difficult conversations

Student groups working on assessed items now engage in difficult conversations about their group processes. This is now much harder to avoid and the group-work process has been given greater value by insisting that process issues are reflected in the final grade. We are reminded of the phrase 'competitive cooperation' which we think accurately pinpoints the inherently dichotomous nature of assessed group work. Whatever the exact nature of a group-work experience and the communal context of much learning, assessed group work structurally contributes to a range of individual degrees. Students are acutely aware of this, even when they understand and agree with the purposes and appropriateness of group work in their degree programme. The conflict between the communal group project and the individual degree classification is not one that will go away. The most recent student-initiated developments have attempted to minimize the competitive element of allocation.

The more significant element for us as trainers of professional youth and community workers is the balance struck between individual and group need. Group-work experiences and the skills gained in these contexts are professionally invaluable. The Group Assessment Sheet asks that students have frank conversations about their contributions to group work. This immediately pushes them into the difficult areas of group dynamics and professional identity, with some fairly complex negotiation skills being required.

We are asking students to engage in honest conversations of relative worth, ones which we studiously avoid among our own staff team! In this case, knowledge becomes the process through which students pass. Group-work skills become transposed into group-work knowledge through conscious acculturation (Blackler 1995).

Postgraduate differences
We have found that on our postgraduate course, both full-time and part-time, students are less likely to differentiate in their assessed group work. Although our postgraduate students also have to use Group Assessment Sheets on their course, they more frequently complete them in such a way as to ensure all group members receive the same final grade. Although this does happen on the undergraduate programme, it is much more frequent on the postgraduate course. There may be a number of reasons for this but one in particular may be significant. The postgraduate course is on a simple pass/ fail basis; however well someone does, it still can only result in a simple pass grade. Grade pressure may operate in a different way and students may be more willing to accept the grading implications of group work because, unless it affects a pass mark, there is no individual cost to their qualification.

Equal grades through debate rather than default
Even when a group feels they should all achieve the same grade, they have to complete the form and present a written case as to why their different contributions are equivalent. So individuals in groups can all gain the same grade but only if they indicate they have thoroughly discussed the reasons for this and presented the evidence to the tutor. This is helpful ideologically for those students who feel that one of the strengths of group work is the communal responsibility including the grade. The Group Assessment Sheet ensures that this is a conscious and overt decision rather than some covert structural result. Reflection on professional capabilities is thus integrated within the assessment profile.

Nominal differentiation
In most cases, the Group Assessment Sheet awards grades which vary little more than 5 per cent. It is not clear whether this is a result of the tool or student decisions when completing the grid. While obviously this may result in occasional differences in classification of results within one group, this small range seems to satisfy our need to ensure student marks are differentiated. We are not aware of any feedback from students about the unfairness of these results. The differences that result may be enough to satisfy their need for differentiation without causing the group dynamic problems that would surely result from more widely spread grades.

Picking off individuals
In a small number of cases, one particular group member has been significantly singled out by the group-assessment grid and the resultant grades show a dramatic differentiation. Frequently, this has been caused through

absence part way through the group process. It must also be noted that when an individual is picked off in this way, it results in much higher grades for the remaining group members. There are a whole range of issues in these contexts that require considerably more investigation. Are the resultant higher grades an adequate reflection of the additional burden carried by remaining group members, when one person fails to pull their weight or do they award a grade for an assessed item way beyond its academic worth? Are students less acceptable to the dominant order in any group more likely to be processed in this way; what part do race, gender and culture play in these decisions? In most of these cases, the disastrous grade of one group member is then reconsidered by the tutor in the light of the reasons for this result. If the absence was legitimate, then alternative means of assessment are provided for this student, the remaining group members retaining their higher grades as a reflection of the increased work burden they have encountered through no fault of their own. The later version of the Group Assessment Sheet may make a difference to this, but as yet we have not gathered enough evidence.

Conclusions

It is fairly clear that student access to library-based resources can be enhanced fairly cheaply and quickly using structured exercises and course assessment as the key lever. In reality these may be basic, technical skills and the same approach is not as effective when it comes to the more complex human interactions involved in group work. The challenges that assessed group work present are intricate, somewhat intangible and probably only resolved over longer periods of practice and reflection. We believe that our professional support course probably provides an appropriate awareness-raising context for the complexities of group work. In parallel with many other issues of awareness, this is only an important starting point; awareness and understanding do not necessarily lead to action, let alone confidence in an area. It is likely that this can best be encouraged through reflective experience. Group-work capability, a subset of transferable skills, may not be merely a matter of training; their acquisition may indeed be related to much broader cultural issues (Brown and Scase 1995). Practical experience over time and open reflection on this experience may prove to be more fruitful in maximizing the learning potential in group work.

Our Groupwork Assessment Sheet plays a vital part in encouraging this open dialogue and, although evidence here is anecdotal, it certainly contributes to this reflective experience. It would be helpful to research in detail the actual grade-differentiation results brought about by the use of the Group Assessment Sheets. However, the more interesting area for research would be around students' qualitative experiences of using these sheets and the negotiations that surround them. Indeed, the student-generated developments to the sheets indicate that students themselves are equally concerned with generating appropriate tools that do justice to the complexities of evaluating and assessing group work. We all appear to be concerned with finding appropriate ways to measure what we value, even in the complex domain of human interaction.

We feel that our Group Assessment Sheets have embedded group-work processes (and the discussion of these) into the actual process of the assessed task before a final grade can be achieved. This has to be advantageous for the quality of group work generally since parallels can be drawn with research on metacognitive awareness. What is less clear is whether the resultant final grades are any nearer to being an accurate and appropriate reflection of individual contribution to group-work assessment items. The general view among both staff and students is that the sheets do produce grades that acknowledge individual difference, however inaccurately, but that their greater benefit is in insisting that groups of students themselves take overt responsibility for their behaviour when working on group-assessment items. In this way, they contribute to the ongoing process of reflective practice and therefore add to the awareness that students have gained through their professional support course.

References

Beck, U. (1992) *Risk Society – Towards a New Modernity*. London: Sage.

Biggs, J.B. and Telfer, R. (1987) *The Process of Learning*. Englewood Cliffs, NJ: Prentice-Hall.

Blackler, F. (1995) 'Knowledge, knowledge work and organisations: an overview and Interpretation'. *Organisation Studies*, 16(6), 1021–46.

Bloxham, S. (1997) 'Integrating learning skills training: an evaluation' in C. Rust and G. Gibbs (eds) *Improving Student Learning – Improving Student Learning through Course Design*. Oxford: Oxford Centre for Staff and Learning Development.

Bloxham, S. and Heathfield, M. (1994) 'Marking changes: innovation in the design and assessment of a postgraduate Diploma in Youth and Community Work' in G. Gibbs (ed.) *Improving Student Learning – Theory and Practice*. Oxford: Oxford Centre for Staff Development.

Bloxham, S. and Heathfield, M. (1994) 'The unexpected outcomes of critical professional learning' in J. Tait and P. Knight (eds) *The Management of Independent Learning*. London: Kogan Page/SEDA.

Brown, P. and Scase, R. (1994) *Higher Education and Corporate Realities: Class, Culture and the Decline of Graduate Careers*. London: UCL Press.

Eley, M.G. (1992) 'Differential adoption of study approaches within individual students'. *Higher Education*, 23, 231–54.

Entwistle, N. and Tait, H. (1990) 'Approaches to learning evaluations of teaching and preferences for contrasting academic environments'. *Higher Education*, 19, 169–94.

Gibbs, G., Rust, C., Jenkins, A. and Jaques, D. (1994) *Developing Students' Transferable Skills*. Oxford: Oxford Centre for Staff Development.

Harvey, L. and Knight, P. (1996) *Transforming Higher Education*. Buckingham: SRHE and Open University Press.

Heathfield, M. and Bloxham, S. (1996) 'From theory to reality: research in practice and on action' in G. Gibbs (ed.) *Improving Student Learning: Using Research to Improve Student Learning.* Oxford: Oxford Centre for Staff Development.

Jarvis, P. (1983) *Professional Education.* London: Croom Helm.

Jarvis, P. (1987) *Adult Learning in the Social Context.* London: Croom Helm.

Jarvis, P. (1992) *Paradoxes of Learning.* San Francisco, CA: Jossey Bass.

Ramsden, P. (1992) *Learning to Teach in Higher Education.* London: Routledge.

Trigwell, K., Prosser, M. and Taylor, P. (1994) 'Qualitative differences in approaches to teaching first year university science'. *Higher Education,* 27, 75–84.

Appendix   Applied Social Sciences Department
Group assessment sheet for CYS123B students

This sheet is designed to divide a group mark between the members of a group, based on their contribution to the task.

You should start on the other side of this page with a self-assessment. Individually, students should award themselves a mark out of 20 for each of the six categories. The criteria are there to help you decide what you deserve. Please use the empty box to note the reasons why you feel your contribution was worth that mark. When you have all completed a self-assessment sheet, the group should have a meeting to discuss the self-assessments and agree each person's mark for each category. However, we think it is very difficult for all group members to make exactly the same level of contribution so the totals (*) for each student should not be the same unless you attach a short statement explaining why. Your group should submit the final group grid accompanied by each individual's self-assessment. .

Names of group members

Categories							
Regular attendance at group meetings							
Contribution of ideas for the task							
Researching, analysing and preparing material for the task							
Contribution to cooperative group process							
Supporting and encouraging group members							
Practical contribution to end product, e.g. writing, presenting, making materials, etc.							
Total for each student(*)							Total for group

Signatures of participating group members:_____

Each student's final mark is calculated by dividing their total mark (*) by N, and multiplying the answer by the group mark. N is found by dividing the total for the group by the number of students in the group. Therefore when the group total is 360 and there are four students in the group, $N = \dfrac{360}{90} = 4.$

Example: A group of four is awarded a joint mark of 60 per cent. Jane gets a peer-assessed score on the grid above of 94. Her final percentage mark is $\dfrac{94}{90} \times 60 = 63$ per cent.

12

Dimensions of Oral Assessment and Student Approaches to Learning

Gordon Joughin

Socrates: Now can we distinguish another kind of communication which is the legitimate brother of written speech, and see how it comes into being and how much better and more effective it is?
Phaedrus: What kind do you mean and how does it come about?
Socrates: I mean the kind that is written on the soul of the hearer together with understanding; that knows how to defend itself, and can distinguish between those it should address and those in whose presence it should be silent.
Phaedrus: You mean the living and animate speech of a man with knowledge, of which written speech might fairly be called a kind of shadow.

(Plato 1973 edition: 98)

Introduction

The dominant role of assessment in defining students' perceptions of courses and subjects is widely recognized (Rowntree 1987; Ramsden 1992; Knight 1995). It is equally well accepted that students' perceptions of the context of learning are a major determinant of their approaches to learning (Ramsden 1992; Marton and Säljö 1997; Ramsden 1997). Thus if assessment, from students' perspectives, tends to define the curriculum, the direct link between student approaches to learning and their perception of assessment is inescapable (Ramsden 1988). This link has been demonstrated repeatedly in a range of studies, beginning with Marton and Säljö's seminal work which indicated how changing the type of questions that students expected to be asked modified their approaches to learning (Marton and Säljö 1976), through to Entwistle and Entwistle's work describing students' intensive studying for final examinations (Entwistle and Entwistle 1997). Within these studies, several have examined the influence on approaches to learning of specific forms of assessment. Thus, for example, Scouller and Prosser (1994) considered students' experiences in studying for multiple-choice examinations; Tang (1991) explored approaches in relation to written assignments and examinations; and Thomas and Bain (1984) examined multiple-choice exams, short-answer exams and written assignments.

This chapter focuses on another specific form of assessment, namely oral assessment, and the ways in which this form of assessment may influence student approaches to learning. It is not concerned so much with whether oral assessment influences such approaches (the influence of context and assessment on student approaches to learning is so well established that we should expect any given form of assessment to exert its own particular influence on approaches). Rather, it will focus on why oral forms of assessment should be expected to influence approaches to learning by considering the particular qualities of oral assessment that might be expected to influence students' perceptions of their assessment and consequently the approaches they take in preparing for that assessment.

This chapter will: outline the qualities of oral assessment by suggesting six dimensions of oral assessment; suggest how these dimensions might be expected to influence students' approaches to studying; and describe students' perceptions of oral assessment in two disciplines and how these perceptions appear to be related to their approaches to studying.

Focusing as it does on student approaches to learning, this chapter is concerned with the use of oral assessment to measure cognitive learning rather than competence in oral skills themselves, such as language or general communication skills.

Dimensions of oral assessment

The dimensions of oral assessment discussed in this section were identified by analysing its treatment in the general literature on assessment in higher education (including Rowntree 1987; Habeshaw *et al.* 1993; Brown and Knight 1994; Banta *et al.* 1996; Nightingale *et al.* 1996) as well as an extensive range of analytical and descriptive literature on the use of oral assessment in specific disciplines, including medicine (e.g. Levine and McGuire 1970), geography (e.g. Hay 1994), economics (e.g. Moon 1988), law (e.g. Butler and Wiseman 1993) and architecture (e.g. Anthony 1991). The attributes of oral assessment noted in each piece of literature were listed individually, then categorized according to a common or underlying quality they were perceived to possess. Through this process, the six dimensions of oral assessment listed in Table 12.1 were identified. Each dimension of oral assessment covers a range of practices. For four of these dimensions ('interaction', 'authenticity', 'structure' and 'orality'), the range has the quality of a continuum. The dimensions of 'content' and 'assessor', however, are not continua but rather consist of more-or-less discrete categories. The nature and range of each dimension is considered below by defining each dimension

Table 12.1 Dimensions of oral assessment

Dimension	Range
1. Content	Knowledge and understanding; applied problem-solving ability; interpersonal competence; personal qualities
2. Interaction	Presentation vs. Dialogue
3. Authenticity	Contextualized vs. Decontextualized
4. Structure	Closed structure vs. Open structure
5. Assessors	Self-assessment; peer assessment; authority-based assessment
6. Orality	Purely oral vs. Orality as secondary

and noting the variability towards each pole in those dimensions that are more or less continuous (i.e. 2, 3, 4 and 6) and by discussing the discrete entities in the non-continuous dimensions (1 and 5).

These six dimensions do not encompass all of the issues associated with oral assessment, for example, reliability, costs and bias, though such issues and/or their resolution may be directly related to the dimensions. Reliability, for instance, can be increased by attention to structure (4) and the use of multiple assessors (5). However, the dimensions do constitute a basis for comprehensively describing this particular form of assessment, for recognizing the variety of ways in which it may be used and for analysing particular instances.

1. Content

'Content' is concerned with the object of assessment, what has been referred to as 'what one is looking for, or remarking upon, in the people one is assessing' (Rowntree 1987: 82). In the oral assessment literature, there is surprising agreement regarding what is tested by this form of assessment (Levine and McGuire 1970; Muzzin and Hart 1985; Raymond and Viswesvaran 1991; Glowacki and Steele 1992; Erhaut and Cole 1993; Habeshaw *et al.* 1993: 75). The learning which is assessed by oral means is usually classified into four categories, discussed below.

Knowledge and understanding
The terms 'knowledge' and 'understanding' are not used with any degree of consistency in educational literature. Sometimes they are used interchangeably and sometimes to denote clearly differentiated forms of learning. Here 'knowledge' is used in Bloom's sense to refer to the 'recall of specifics and universals, the recall of methods and processes, or the recall of a pattern, structure or setting' (Bloom 1956: 201) while 'understanding' refers to the comprehension of the underlying meaning of what is known (*Oxford English Dictionary*). 'Knowledge' is aligned to what has been described

as 'quantitative' or 'reproducing' conceptions of learning, while 'understanding' is aligned with 'qualitative' or 'transforming' conceptions of learning (Dahlgren 1984; Marton and Säljö 1997).

Applied problem-solving ability
The category of 'applied problem solving' has been variously described as 'the ability to think on one's feet' (Muzzin and Hart 1985: 73), 'the cognitive processes which constitute professional thinking' (Erhaut and Cole 1993: 10), 'the ability to think quickly and diagnose problems in novel situations' (Habeshaw *et al.* 1993: 75), 'clinical competence' (Solomon *et al.* 1990) and 'problem-solving skills, application skills, interpretive skills' (Glowacki and Steele 1992: 13).

Interpersonal competence
'Interpersonal competence' refers to a set of factors which Erhaut and Cole (1993: 10) describe as 'the personal skills, required for a professional approach to the conduct of one's work'. These typically include communication or interview skills, though it must be emphasized that it is not skills *per se* but rather skills exhibited in relation to a clinical situation or problem-solving exercise that are the focus of assessment in the oral examination.

Personal qualities
Oral examinations, particularly those designed for certification purposes to test candidates' suitability to enter a particular profession, are sometimes used to measure a candidate's intrapersonal qualities. Muzzin and Hart (1985: 72) cite a number of personal attributes that oral examinations have been claimed to measure, including personality, alertness, reactions to stress, appearance, confidence and self-awareness.

2. Interaction

'Interaction' refers to reciprocity between examiner and candidate, with each acting on, responding to, and being influenced by the other. Most non-oral forms of assessment involve the student responding to a task which is presented at the beginning of the assessment process: the examiner sets the task, the student responds and the response is then assessed by the examiner. In contrast to this, oral assessment creates the opportunity for a more complex set of interactions between examiner and student. It is this capacity that allows oral assessment to probe a student's understanding, widely recognized as one of the principal advantages of oral assessment (Brown and Knight 1994: 75).

At the 'presentation' pole of the interaction range, the oral assessment may resemble the written examination in that a task is set, the student responds, and this response is then assessed, with virtually no interaction occurring. The opposite end of this range is characterized by a high level of interaction between the examiner and student so that the assessment takes the form of a dialogue or conversation. Such interaction involves reciprocal statements by examiner and student in which each such statement includes a response to that made by the other participant. This interaction gives oral assessment an inherent unpredictability in which neither party knows in advance exactly what questions will be asked or what responses will be made.

Since the capacity for interaction appears to be one of the principal advantages of the oral assessment format, it is not surprising that most oral assessment includes a significant interactive component.

3. Authenticity

'Authenticity' refers to the extent to which the assessment replicates the context of professional practice or 'real life'. At the 'contextualized' pole, oral assessment is completely contextualized, being conducted in contexts of genuine professional practice. A common example is the clinical examination in Medicine when it involves genuine patients in hospital settings (see, for example: Solomon *et al.* 1990; Raymond and Viswesvaran 1991). At the opposite pole, assessment may be 'decontextualized' or remote from the situation of professional practice. The oral defence of a doctoral thesis, conducted in a classroom or public auditorium and focusing on ideas abstracted from their context, would exemplify this form.

4. Structure

The dimension of 'structure' refers to the extent to which assessment is based on a predetermined, organized body of questions or sequence of events. At the 'closed structure' pole, the assessment is tightly structured: the examiner asks a series of set questions in a given order, often following a carefully constructed set of protocols. The questions, the order in which they are asked and the manner in which they are posed, is not influenced by the student's behaviour (Van Wart 1974: 673; Moon 1988). At the 'open structure' pole, the assessment follows a loosely structured agenda. The student may be given considerable freedom regarding how they present their ideas (see, for example, Dressel 1991) or questions posed by the examiner may be dependent on the student's responses to previous questions, giving the examination the character of a free-flowing dialogue.

5. Assessors

The 'assessor' dimension concerns who judges the worth of the student's responses. Unlike written forms of assessment, the 'product' of oral assessment is relatively public and is accessible to whoever is present at the time of the assessment. Thus oral assessment lends itself to assessment by multiple examiners, including faculty-based panels, or, if the assessment is held in a class setting, by peers. The possibility of self-assessment is probably present in most assessment formats, including oral assessment.

6. Orality

'Orality' as a dimension of oral assessment refers to the extent to which the assessment is conducted orally, ranging from the exclusively oral format of, for example, the clinical examination in medicine, to assessment in which the oral component is secondary to another component, for example, the oral presentation of a written paper or the oral explanation and defence of a physical product such as an architectural design.

Dimensions of oral assessment, students' approaches to learning and the experience of oral assessment

At the beginning of this chapter, the undisputed relationship between students' perceptions of assessment and their approaches to learning was noted. In light of the dimensions of oral assessment, we are now able to consider how the particular qualities of oral assessment, as illuminated by these dimensions, might influence students' approaches to learning.

Deep approaches to learning are characterized primarily by the intention to understand, in contrast to the intention to simply cope with course demands which characterizes surface approaches, or the intention to achieve high grades which characterizes strategic approaches (Ramsden 1992; Entwistle 1997; Marton and Säljö 1997). In fulfilling this intention to understand, students adopting deep approaches to learning seek to transform rather than merely to reproduce what they are learning and consequently adopt strategies that include:

- relating ideas to previous knowledge and experience
- looking for patterns and underlying principles
- checking evidence and relating it to conclusions
- exercising logic and argument cautiously and critically
- becoming actively involved in course content.

(Entwistle 1997: 19)

Is there any reason to believe that oral forms of assessment might encourage deep approaches to learning, that is, that the dimensions of oral assessment might be associated with the intentions and strategies of deep approaches to learning? Tentative hypotheses could be proffered in relation to deep approaches to learning and each of the dimensions of oral assessment and a moderately complex research agenda developed on the basis of these hypotheses. Given the importance of assessment and the value of encouraging appropriate approaches to studying, such an agenda is recommended. The exploratory research described in the remainder of this chapter suggests that further research may well be justified.

Students' experience of oral assessment

A qualitative study involving a total of eight students (four in a certificate-level theology programme and four in an undergraduate law programme) has explored students' experiences of oral assessment and how they prepared for it. The theology students were studying a course in which assessment alternated between written papers marked by the programme coordinators and oral presentations (referred to as 'practicums') to their peers. The law students had opted to complete a viva before a panel of two lecturers as an alternative to a written paper. In both cases, the students were able to comment on the experience of oral assessment in itself as well as in comparison to written forms of assessment.

The students were asked to describe what the viva or practicum was like for them, what they thought was expected of them as they prepared for it and how they prepared for it. While the interviews generated information on a range of aspects of oral assessment, two dominant themes emerged: the students' intention to understand; and their perception of the personal nature of the assessment format, including an interesting sense of relationship to the spoken word.

On the intention to understand

Each student perceived a greater need to understand the material they were studying when preparing for oral rather than written forms of assessment. Seven of the students related this to an expectation that their understanding would be probed through questioning, whether by their peers (in theology) or by knowledgeable lecturers (in law), while the eighth student (law) referred to the need for knowledge to be better structured because the order in which questions would proceed could not be predicted.

> 'I really think . . . "Do I really understand what it is I've written and have I written it?" I mean I do that with a written assignment but I think there is more responsibility to really be clear about that when you know that somebody may in fact ask you a question on the spot.'
>
> (Theology student)

While all eight students saw a greater need to understand in the context of oral assessment, what is perhaps equally noteworthy is the degree of difference expressed by four of the students (three in theology, one in law). Not only was greater understanding required by the oral assessment (in written assessment they were prepared to express ideas which they knew they did not understand).

> 'In the written work I would just put it down and think "I really don't understand this anyway but I'll just quote from the book and put it in." I wouldn't do that in [the oral assessment] because I'd be worried someone would ask me, "Well what do you mean by that?" and "What do you think about it? Do you really agree with that?"'
>
> (Theology student)

> ... 'you think "I'll just read this book and I'll go there and do it like I do an assignment and just write some kind of bull, whether it relates to the topic or not." But [in the oral assessment] you know ... you're going to look a fool ... so you make sure you know what you are saying.'
>
> (Law student)

On students' sense of personal involvement

Three of the law students and all of the theology students described the oral assessment as more personal than their written assessment.

> 'In an exam you're just a number but the [viva's] personalized and you're in direct contact with the people who assess you.'
>
> (Law student)

> 'Yes, you prepare yourself better because you've got the added stress of like you're in front of someone. So because you know you've got to do that you try to make sure. You're not just sitting in an exam room anonymously.'
>
> (Law student)

> 'With a written assignment you submit that and you're just a number whereas when you're giving a presentation you're standing in front of ... other people ...
>
> (Theology student)

> 'It's directly associated, well it's directly associated with you.'
>
> (Theology student)

Three students expressed this involvement in terms of the different relationships that they experience in relation to the words that they speak and write:

> '... in a written assignment you can remain quite remote from what you write.'
>
> (Theology student)

> 'You've got to take ownership of the words that you speak.'
>
> (Theology student)

Conclusion

The intention to understand lies at the heart of the construct of deep approaches to learning. There is little doubt that the students in this study, having declared their intention to understand, would have engaged in the strategies which they believed would have promoted such understanding. In fact, most students detailed at least some aspects of their preparation that were directly aligned to the strategies noted by Entwistle. It is equally clear that, in forming the intention to understand, students were significantly influenced by their perception that the oral assessment format permitted the probing of their understanding through the direct interaction of student and assessor.

Along with the search for understanding, a sense of personal engagement equally lies at the heart of genuine learning. As Ramsden notes in his discussion of 'real' and 'imitation' subjects, 'the quality of our students' understanding is intimately related to the quality of their engagement with learning tasks' (Ramsden 1992: 39). It is clear that in the study reported here, the students experienced an unusually high degree of engagement and attributed this to the oral nature of the assessment, in particular to a sense of personal presence in the assessment task, to a sense of being 'seen' and to a heightened sense of relationship to their own spoken words.

In a quite different context, Walter Ong has concluded that

> for an oral culture learning or knowing means achieving close, empathetic, communal identification with the known . . . , 'getting with it'. Writing separates the knower from the known and thus sets up conditions for 'objectivity' in the sense of personal disengagement or distancing.
>
> (Ong 1982: 45–6)

Ong's words remind us of Plato's claim which opened this chapter.

To progress our understanding of oral assessment may require not merely an appreciation of the several dimensions of oral assessment and a willingness to listen carefully to the experiences of our students, but perhaps to engage in our explorations with an openness to related fields such as literary studies, and with an awareness of the richness of ideas to be found in the works of Plato, Ong and others. In doing so, of course, it is important to recognize the disparate voices in these fields, including, for example, Derrida's extended critique of Plato's prioritizing of the spoken over the written word (Derrida 1981).

One final word of caution should perhaps be made. Any form of assessment is located within a complex, multifaceted environment in which the form of assessment is but one aspect of assessment, and assessment is but one aspect of the total context of learning. A full appreciation of students' responses to oral assessment formats needs to be developed in relation to students' experiences, not only of all aspects of the assessment regime in a particular subject or course, but also of the broader context of learning in which they find themselves expressing their knowledge and understanding orally.

Acknowledgements

The author wishes to acknowledge the valuable contributions of Richard Bagnall and Paul Ramsden in suggesting the 'dimensions' approach and in discussing the emerging categories and examples.

References

Anthony, K.H. (1991) *Design Juries on Trial*. New York: Van Nostrand Reinhold.

Banta, T.W., Lund, J.P., Black, K.E. and Oblander, F.W. (1996) *Assessment in Practice: Putting Principles to Work on College Campuses*. San Francisco, CA: Jossey-Bass.

Bloom, B.S. (ed.) (1956) *Taxonomy of Educational Objectives: Cognitive Domain*. New York: McKay.

Brown, S. and Knight, P. (1994) *Assessing Learners in Higher Education*. London: Kogan Page.

Butler, D. and Wiseman, L. (1993) 'Viva the viva: oral examinations in Contract Law'. *Legal Education Review*, 4(2), 331–50.

Dahlgren, L. (1984) 'Outcomes of learning' in F. Marton, D. Hounsell and N. Entwistle (eds) *The Experience of Learning*. Edinburgh: Scottish Universities Press.

Derrida, J. (1981) *Dissemination*, trans. B. Johnson. London: Athlone Press.

Dressel, J.H. (1991) 'The Formal Oral Group Exam: Challenges and Possibilities – The Oral Exam and Critical Thinking', Paper presented at the Annual Meeting of the National Council of Teachers of English, Seattle, November 22027. (ERIC Document ED 347 527)

Entwistle, N. (1997) 'Contrasting perspectives on learning' in F. Marton, D. Hounsell and N. Entwistle (eds) *The Experience of Learning*, pp. 3–22. Edinburgh: Scottish Academic Press.

Entwistle, N. and Entwistle, A. (1997) 'Revision and the experience of understanding' in F. Marton, D. Hounsell and N. Entwistle (eds) *The Experience of Learning*, pp. 145–55. Edinburgh: Scottish Universities Press.

Erhaut, M. and Cole, G. (1993) 'Assessment of competence in higher level occupations'. *Competence and Assessment*, 21, 10–14.

Glowacki, M.L. and Steele, D.J. (1992) 'A Synthesis of the Research on Alternative Assessment Methods in Teacher Education', Paper presented at the Annual Meeting of the Mid-South Educational Research Association, Knoxville, Tennessee, 11–13 November, 1992 (ERIC Document ED 355 257).

Habeshaw, S., Gibbs, G. and Habeshaw, T. (1993) *53 Interesting Ways to Assess Your Students*. Bristol: Technical and Educational Services.

Hay, I. (1994) 'Justifying and applying oral presentations in geographical education'. *Journal of Geography in Higher Education*, 18(1), 43–55.

Knight, P. (1995) 'Introduction' in P. Knight (ed.) *Assessment for Learning in Higher Education*, pp. 13–23. London: Kogan Page/SEDA.

Levine, H.G. and McGuire, C.H. (1970) 'The validity and reliability of oral examinations in assessing cognitive skills in medicine'. *Journal of Educational Measurement*, 7(2), 63–74.

Marton, F. and Säljö, R. (1976) 'On qualitative differences in learning. Outcome and process'. *British Journal of Educational Psychology*, 46, 4–11.

Marton, F. and Säljö, R. (1997) 'Approaches to learning' in F. Marton, D. Hounsell and N. Entwhistle (eds) *The Experience of Learning*, pp. 39–58. Edinburgh: Scottish Universities Press.

Moon, R. (1988) 'Oral assessment in GSCE economics'. *Research Papers in Economics*, Number 14. London: Institute of Education, London University. (ERIC Document ED 307 199).

Muzzin, L.J. and Hart, L. (1985) 'Oral examinations' in V.R. Neufeld and G.R. Norman (eds) *Assessing Clinical Competence*, pp. 71–93. New York: Springer.

Nightingale, P., Wiata, I.T., Toohey, S., Ryan, G., Hughes, C. and Magin, D. (1996) *Assessing Learning in Universities*. Sydney: University of New South Wales Press.

Ong, W.J. (1982) *Orality and Literacy: The Technologizing of the Word*. London: Routledge.

Plato (1973) *Phaedrus and Letters VII and VIII*. London: Penguin.

Ramsden, P. (1988) 'Studying learning: improving teaching' in P. Ramsden (ed.) *Improving Learning: New Perspectives*, pp. 13–31. London: Kogan Page.

Ramsden, P. (1992) *Learning to Teach in Higher Education*. London: Routledge.

Ramsden, P. (1997) 'The context of learning in academic departments' in F. Marten, D. Hounsell and N. Entwhistle (eds) *The Experience of Learning* (2nd Edition). Edinburgh: Scottish Academic Press.

Raymond, M.R. and Viswesvaran, C. (1991) *Least-squares models to correct for rater effects in performance assessment*. ACT Research Report Series 91–8. Iowa: The American College Testing Program (ERIC Document ED 344 947).

Rowntree, D. (1987) *Assessing Students: How Shall We Know Them?* London: Kogan Page.

Scouller, K.M. and Prosser, M. (1994) 'Students' experiences in studying for multiple choice question examinations'. *Studies in Higher Education*, 19(3), 267–79.

Solomon, D.J., Reinhart, R.C., Bridgham, R.G., Munger, B.S. and Starnaman, S. (1990) 'Free-response formats for evaluating clinical judgment'. *Academic Medicine*, 65(9), 543–4.

Tang, K.C.C. (1991) Effects of Different Assessment Procedures on Tertiary Students' Approaches to Studying, unpublished PhD Thesis, University of Hong Kong.

Thomas, P.R. and Bain, J.D. (1984) 'Contextual dependence of learning approaches: the effects of assessment'. *Human Learning*, 3, 227–40.

Van Wart, A.D. (1974) 'A problem-solving oral examination for family medicine'. *Journal of Medical Education*, 49, 673–9.

Part 4

Towards Autonomous Assessment

Assessment is usually about one group of people (teachers) making judgements about the performance or work of another group of people (students). It is an exercise of power. Perhaps one of the most significant shifts in thinking about assessment is the recognition of the need to be mindful about how that power is exercised. If it is exercised in a way which inhibits the individual from making judgements about their own performance or if it is exercised in a way which lessens the person's sense of self-worth then it is unlikely that learners will develop the ability to think for themselves, or to develop confidence in their ability to learn and in their ability to evaluate what they learn and who continue to learn when their college days are over. This illustrates an important element in thinking about assessment practices. It suggests we have to look critically at who is doing the assessing and to what purpose and ask ourselves in what ways the exercise of power and authority is appropriate. Broadening the range of assessors including students themselves presents both a response and a challenge in this context.

Learning and assessment are traditionally seen as two quite distinct activities. The assumption has been that assessment follows learning. Assessment is something done to learners and to their learning. Students do some learning and then teachers do some assessing. Often the methods of teaching and learning are determined and decisions on the assessment strategy are made quite independently. In many forms of assessment, however, there is now the recognition that the method of assessment influences the learning in some way (Ramsden 1992).

> Students are often required to spend a great deal of time in completing major assessment tasks which culminate in a finished design, product or performance. The processes and stages of development undertaken to reach this end point are seen as producing powerful learning outcomes before final formal assessments are made.
>
> (Nightingale and Magin 1996: 173)

That students learn in and through completing an assessment task is increasingly being recognized. The development of self-assessment and peer assessment is allied to this realization. Students are required to learn by engaging in assessed tasks. Assessment is not peripheral to the course – a necessary evil to be endured. It is central to the whole course. Assessment, including reflection on their own work and that of their peers is the learning. This is an important way in which to conceptualize the process of assessment and its relation to learning. In many courses, assessment and learning are now being redesigned as an integrated activity.

The use of learner self-assessment and peer assessment is being driven on the one hand by educational considerations such as these. However, it is also being driven by the need for staff time to be most effectively used and a belief that new forms of self-assessment and peer assessment can achieve savings in staff time. In this context, it is important to understand the nature and variety of forms of self-assessment and peer assessment and to critically examine the motivations for their use. Chapter 13 by Angela Brew considers what are self-assessment and peer assessment and then asks why they are currently attracting so much interest. This discussion takes us beyond narrow considerations of assessment in higher education to broader cultural and intellectual shifts taking place. Self-assessment and peer assessment reside in a discourse where conventional notions of power and control are being challenged and they relate to a move away from dependence on judgements of others towards a greater reliance on an ability to decide for ourselves and present our achievements. This chapter thus provides a framework for understanding the broad range of self-assessment and peer assessment practices now in use and discusses how these contribute to sharing power and authority necessary for society's future citizens. It is followed by three chapters which present some examples of self-assessment and peer assessment where students are encouraged in various ways to develop the evaluative skills of the autonomous learner.

In Chapter 14, Shirley Jordan discusses a self-assessment and peer assessment exercise developed at Thames Valley University and derives some principles of general relevance from the experience. She suggests that any form of self-assessment and peer assessment should grow out of the stated aims and objectives of the course, so that students can clearly understand the rationale behind the use of these approaches.

Next Andy Lapham and Ray Webster in Chapter 15 describe the introduction of peer-assessed seminar presentations as a means of providing formative assessment and give an account of how the process has changed over time, as problems have been identified and processes refined.

Finally, Paul Roach in Chapter 16 concludes the section with an account of his own experience of introducing peer assessment as a relative novice, describing the pitfalls and benefits experienced during implementation and his proposals for improvement. Indubitably, self-assessment and peer assessment are approaches that are nowadays an integral element of higher education assessment, and this section explores the issues pragmatically, without glossing over the inevitable difficulties associated with them.

Thanks to Angela Brew for her very significant contribution to this section introduction.

13

Towards Autonomous Assessment: Using Self-Assessment and Peer Assessment

Angela Brew

Involving students in their own assessment is increasing and there are many different forms and varieties. Self-assessment and peer assessment are often talked of simultaneously in the literature of the field as if they were the same thing and pursuing the same goals. Not only are self-assessment and peer assessment not unitary ideas, there are some important differences between them which have significantly different consequences for the educative process and, in particular, for the ways in which and whether power and authority are shared, control is shifted and whether the student is led to develop the skills of independent, autonomous judgement. In view, therefore, of the growing importance of self-assessment and peer assessment, it is necessary to be able to discriminate between different types and approaches to avoid the confusion which exists because a single term has been used to refer to many practices, some of which are incompatible. There is a need to be clear about what aspects of self-assessment and peer assessment contribute to what kinds of learning.

What are self-assessment and peer assessment?

The defining characteristic of self-assessment has been expressed as:

> the involvement of students in identifying standards and/or criteria to apply to their work and making judgements about the extent to which they have met these criteria and standards.
>
> (Boud 1991: 5)

This reflects the two elements of any assessment process: the identification of standards related to specific criteria and the making of judgements based on them.

In a book examining many aspects of self-assessment, Boud (1995a) argues that the term 'self-assessment' is used to refer either to a process or to an activity. It is a practice in which to engage as well as a goal to which to aspire. The ability to critically assess one's own work may be a goal of higher education irrespective of whether or not self-assessment exercises as such are involved. Yet paradoxically, many courses in higher education have been designed in ways which inhibit the development of self-assessment skills. Boud makes a distinction between *informal* self-assessment which is a characteristic of all student learning and *formal* self-assessment where course-assessment tasks are structured in ways which involve students in the process.

There are a number of common practices which are allied to self-assessment, but where students are not normally expected to actively engage with or question the standards and criteria which are used. These are: *self-testing* where students check their performance against provided test items (for example, looking up answers in the back of a book), *self-rating* where students use a wide variety of personality, learning style, personal preference instruments to develop a profile of their strengths and weaknesses or, thirdly, *the use of reflective questions* (for example, in distance-learning materials where in-text questions prompt learners to reflect on what they have been reading).

There are clearly connections between reflection and self-assessment. Both involve focusing on learning and experience, but self-assessment is usually concerned with the making of judgements about specific aspects of achievement often in ways which are publicly defensible (e.g. to teachers), whereas reflection tends to be a more exploratory activity which might occur at any stage of learning and may not lead to a directly expressible outcome. All self-assessment involves reflection, but not all reflection leads to self-assessment.

A discussion of the ability of students to self-assess and whether they can indeed realistically engage in this process is central to the literature. Boud (1995a) suggests that students need to develop the skills of self-assessment as they progress through their course. What is clear is that self-assessment is increasingly being used in a variety of ways to assess skills, knowledge and competence. But the ability to self-assess effectively does not just happen on its own. Students need systematic practice in judging their own work and getting feedback on their ability to do so.

Peer assessment involves students making judgements about, or commenting upon, each other's work. Either individuals may comment on the work of other individuals or groups of their peers, or groups may comment on the work of individuals or groups. Sometimes the term 'collaborative assessment' is used when the peers' and sometimes self-assessment is combined with a teacher assessment (Heron 1988; Somervell 1993). 'Peer assessment' is the term used to refer to both peer marking and peer feedback. Although these may be combined, this is not necessarily the case. Peer marking can prove unpopular and disruptive, particularly in small, cohesive student groups (Boud *et al.* 1997). Peer feedback can, however, contribute to the cohesiveness of student groups and help them focus on learning.

Much of the literature on self-assessment and peer assessment is devoted to the issue of whether students' assessment is in line with teachers'. This obsession with comparing the marks given by each is perhaps surprising given the ease with which it is frequently assumed that two teachers would come up with the same mark (Warren Piper *et al.* 1996). In studies where the assessment of different teachers is compared and also in studies where teacher and student peer and or self-assessments are compared, it has generally been found that, provided criteria are discussed and agreed in advance, marks tend to be similar (Boud and Falchikov 1989). However, as Warren Piper and colleagues found, there is much confusion among examiners concerning what constitute criteria. Lapham and Webster in Chapter 15 present an example where students agreed the criteria but gave different weightings to different elements from their teachers who, for example, placed more emphasis on the length of the presentation as an indicator of depth of content.

Another dominant theme in the literature on peer assessment is with finding a way of assessing students' respective contributions to a group project. On the basis of a review of the literature, Conway *et al.* (1993) suggest a useful framework for conceptualizing the different ways this can be done and discuss the advantages and disadvantages of each method of dividing or weighting marks.

Falchikov suggests (1986, 1995) that peer assessment leads to a number of benefits in terms of the learning process; for example encouraging thinking, increasing learning and also increasing students' confidence. But other, more noble aims may be the motivating force behind the introduction of peer-assessment schemes. These have to do with the recognition that to assess is to have power over a person. Sharing the assessment with students may be, to some degree, in order to share the power of the teacher. It may be introduced with an intention to encourage students to take responsibility for their learning. Having power over each other, however, is reported to be unpopular by students (Falchikov 1986), so care has to be exercised in the way that peer assessment is introduced. In this respect, peer assessment, though often linked to self-assessment, is very different from it and involves additional processes and potential hazards which are not evident in self-assessment processes.

As mentioned earlier, the rationale for using peer assessment may derive from a desire to reduce the teacher's marking load, or for more pedagogical reasons, such as a belief in the ability of peer assessment to develop important skills needed when students graduate. (See Chapter 6.) When it is introduced with time saving as the major factor, it is rarely straightforwardly successful. Students can be suspicious if they believe they are being asked to do the job for which the teacher is paid. The way in which the proposed system of assessment is introduced to students, the need to get students 'on side,' the hazards of students taking a dislike to the process, concerns about whether students will realistically assess their peers, about whether they have sufficient knowledge or skill to do so, are all questions suggesting that care is needed if peer assessment is to be effectively implemented (Boud and Falchikov 1989). They all suggest that what is crucially important is attention to the context of the assessment and to relating what is being assessed and how it is to be assessed to that context. Introducing peer assessment in learning contexts where there is negotiation of learning outcomes and processes, or where students have practice at self-assessment is quite a different matter from introducing peer assessment in a traditionally taught and assessed course. On the other hand, in a context where collaborative peer learning is being encouraged, peer assessment can go against the ideal of collaboration (Boud *et al.* 1997).

Why is there so much interest in the use of self-assessment and peer assessment?

Whichever form of self-assessment or peer assessment is used, there are a number of factors which influence both the decision to use it, which form is used and its ultimate effectiveness. As mentioned above, changes in assessment practices are linked to questions of power and authority. Before discussing different varieties of self-assessment and peer assessment, it is important to look at this relationship in more detail. This will provide a basis for exploring the ways in which different forms of self-assessment and peer assessment can be used to develop autonomous independent learners.

In traditional teaching and learning, the authority to decide what counts as knowledge, what is important for students to know and therefore what it is important to assess resides with the academics. But this authority is now questioned. The student faced with an essay decides whether and what to search on the Internet. What she finds is idiosyncratic, untamed. How much of whatever she finds she then decides to use in the essay is her choice. Gone are the days of dependence on the texts chosen by the teacher. The student takes on the authority to decide what is, and is not, appropriate. Teaching her the skills of discrimination becomes crucially important. This can effectively be done through the formal use of self-assessment and peer assessment.

It is not just the presence of the Internet, however, which brings about a questioning of the authority of traditional knowledge. That knowledge is itself the subject of critical debate. It has become viewed as customary, if a little tongue in cheek, to talk about the 'half-life' of a fact. Knowledge is becoming fluid, viewed as a product of communication and interpretation. The emphasis on life-long learning, on developing the skills which students need for independent study, for discriminating good information from bad and for practice as a professional is now a priority. Preparing students for life-long learning implies a redefinition of the way in which we operate, for example, being explicit about how and where particular skills and attributes are to be taught and assessed, defining levels of competence and so on. This means changes to include the assessment of skills and attributes, not just knowledge. It also requires that students engage in the discussion and negotiation of their skills and competencies, learning to justify their ideas and giving helpful feedback to each other. Traditional forms of teacher assessment are limited in the extent to which students are able to develop sophisticated skills of discrimination and negotiation. Self-assessment and peer assessment are important arenas for the development of such skills.

We now know that knowledge is defined within a cultural context and gives expression to the interests of powerful groups (Lyotard 1993). There is now a recognition that higher education gives credence to certain kinds of knowledge, legitimating the power of dominant groups. We know that assessment enables the exercising of power by tutors over students. We know from research that assessment drives learning (Boud 1990). We know that students seek cues as to what will be examined. We know that they tend to focus on what is assessed at the expense of other non-assessed work. We know that students tend to be assessed on those matters on which it is easy to assess and that this emphasizes lower-level skills. We know that some students reject deep approaches to learning on the grounds that the assessment in their courses encourages them to learn to reproduce ideas in a 'surface' fashion. In this context, scepticism about traditional power relationships clearly points to the need to involve students in sharing power by assessing their own and each other's work. The many examples of self-assessment and peer assessment which are currently being tried are responses to this context.

Students are also increasingly exercising control over their study. There are many ways where the locus of control is shifting. For example, students may choose to pick up credits from different sources, they then determine the coherence of their degree programme and it is not controlled by their teachers. University students are increasingly influencing their own assessment as demonstrated in the growing numbers of appeals against grades and this relates to the questioning of authority. The lecturer's authority in lectures and classes is disappearing as students are becoming increasingly reluctant to sit quietly and to listen. I have heard, both in Australian and in UK universities, about problems of maintaining discipline in lectures. Authority is questioned, challenged at all levels. In this context, teaching and learning are becoming more resource-based, more varied and more flexible. This means freedom for students in choosing study programmes which suit their needs and interests, flexibility of place and times for study and supporting frameworks for this to happen, flexibility in assessment including assessment in a variety of modes: assessment in groups, or as individuals; computer-based assessment, involving a wider range of people in doing the assessment (for example, students themselves, their peers, employers, and so on).

The next generation of students increasingly view themselves as global citizens. They are well aware of the interconnectedness of world concerns. There is a constant flow of students from one country or institution to another, for example, American year-abroad students and European exchange students. Peer learning communities with counterparts on the other side of the world where each takes advantage of the local knowledge of the other suggest that peer learning is taking place on a global level. There is now recognition of the interconnectedness of issues and concerns and a shift away from viewing problems or knowledge as separate sets of entities and activities, towards viewing them holistically. Traditional ideas about assessment become increasingly irrelevant to this context. Increased trends towards involving students in their own and each other's assessment indicate a movement to more holistic conceptions of assessment. No longer can assessment be considered as merely the sum of its parts, all of which can be considered separately.

The impact of the total learning environment on students is increasingly being recognized. This means that we must inevitably look at the profile of assessment as students see it, from the point of view of the course, the total experience of the whole. This includes the experience of being judged by other people and the mismatches which occur when one teacher includes enlightened and innovative approaches in a subject. The effect of the interaction of this with their colleagues' assessment practices must be taken into account. It also means assessment must be related to practice. Assessment tasks must be 'authentic' in that they must relate to the actual tasks students will undertake in their professional practice and to the relationships of peer evaluation and feedback which exist in the workplace, as described in Chapter 6. All of this places self-assessment and peer assessment practices at the heart of learning.

How are we to understand the many approaches?

I have argued that self-assessment and peer assessment were important components of a greater recognition of the power dynamics of assessment and the ways in which assessment reinforces or challenges notions of control and authority. If self-assessment and peer assessment have such potentially significant effects on the development of what we understand by education in the future and if they have the potential to radically alter our notions of what students should be capable of, then we need to have some way of understanding the different approaches. In earlier publications (Brew 1995a, b), I developed a typology which could be used to understand the key variations in approach to self-assessment. This typology is productive in the analysis of both self-assessment and peer assessment practices and throws light on some major differences which can be observed. It is particularly useful in highlighting what different self-assessment and peer assessment practices are trying to achieve. This typology, which is based on Habermas' idea that knowledge is shaped by the needs and desires of human beings and that different kinds of knowledge give expression to different 'knowledge constitutive interests' (Habermas 1987), provides a framework for seeing the ways in which students can be encouraged to develop a range of skills and abilities across a full spectrum of self-assessment and peer assessment activities. In addition, it links to a broader theoretical framework about knowledge and it provides a basis for making evaluative judgements about the effectiveness of self-assessment and peer assessment practices. In the remainder of this chapter the typology is explained. To explain the typology, first, a brief explanation of Habermas' ideas is needed.

Examples of self-assessment and peer assessment can be seen to lie within one or other of the three knowledge interests which Habermas (1987) describes: the technical interest, the communicative interest and the emancipatory interest. Scientific knowledge is built up because humans have a desire to exercise control over their world. They attempt to exercise this control by seeing the world as separate objects which can be observed and measured and about which predictions can be made. Such knowledge has, what Habermas terms, a technical knowledge interest, 'interest in technical control over objectified processes' (Habermas 1987: 309). This interest is not confined to the sciences. It can be seen to be served whenever objectified statements are present. On the other hand, sometimes knowledge is more a question of interpretive understanding and objectivity is problematic. Habermas views this kind of knowledge as being constructed in a process of mutual negotiation and communication. Such knowledge has what he terms a practical or communicative knowledge interest which he says aims at action-oriented mutual understanding (Habermas 1987: 310). Finally, Habermas' third domain of knowledge pursues what he terms an emancipatory knowledge interest. He suggests knowledge includes a meta-level analysis where reflection is part of the process of building it up.

Taking this framework we can see that different knowledge interests are served by different learning and assessment tasks as demonstrated in Table 13.1. The knowledge interests are present whether what is being assessed is students' knowledge and understanding, academic, personal or transferable skills or whether they are assessing their own competency or learning outcomes (Brew 1995a). An ability to assess oneself and one's peers in each

Table 13.1 Typology of self-assessment and peer assessment practices

Interest	Knowledge and Understanding	Academic, personal and transferable skills	Competencies or learning outcomes and attributes
Technical knowledge interest			
Communicative knowledge interest			
Emancipatory knowledge interest			

of the knowledge interests and in each of the three areas (knowledge, skills and outcomes), is essential for the development of autonomous independent professional judgement.

Assessment of knowledge in the technical interest is, by and large, a question of checking what facts and ideas or how much information has been understood. Similarly, skills are viewed as objectified, that is to say, as being in a sense separate from the person who either demonstrates the skill or does not. In the technical interest dimension, in many cases, skills tend to be seen more or less independently of each other. The context in which they are developed is not considered particularly relevant in assessing them. Similarly, competencies or learning outcomes in the technical domain are viewed as separate objectified statements of expected performance. As far as self-assessment is concerned, we say that a technical knowledge interest is being served where students are engaged in checking their knowledge, skills, understanding or competency against a set of more or less objective statements, and for peer assessment, it is served where they check each other's. Indeed, in all of these cases, the simplest forms of self-assessment and peer assessment consist of a set of statements, the students' task being to assess how far they or their peers have achieved them. Students may alternatively check their own or their peers' answers against a model answer sheet, or against a pre-prepared set of criteria or competency statements. Self-assessment and peer assessment may be used together or separately in this way. Self-assessment and peer assessment in the technical knowledge interest can become quite complex as shown in the example of peer assessment of seminar presentations by Lapham and Webster (Chapter 15). However, in the technical knowledge interest dimension, control rests with tutors because they set the criteria which students then apply to their work. These forms of self-assessment and peer assessment are, in this respect, closest to traditional tutor-led assessment.

When the self-assessment or peer assessment involves elements of communication and interpretation, perhaps a negotiation of criteria, or discussion of the relationship of one element of the assessment to another, we may say that the practical or communicative knowledge interest is being served. From a communicative perspective, skills are viewed as part of a process of negotiation, the outcomes of some kind of dialogue or conversation. Transferable skills are likely to be integrated into academic study. They are viewed as part of a composite of skills within a broad capability in each person. Indeed, skills are more likely to be seen as integral to the process of acquiring knowledge. In this domain, competency is viewed as a professionally defined construct (compare this with the holistic notion of competencies described by Hager *et al.* 1994).

Examples of self-assessment or peer assessment within the communicative interest include students discussing what constitutes a 'good' answer and researching or negotiating criteria which they then apply to their own and/ or each other's work. For example, students in a class test situation outline an answer to a question. One student describes her answer and others add ideas to form a collective view of what is a good answer. Students then mark their own answers in relation to this. They then go on to the next question and so on to the end of the test (Pastol 1993). Either self-assessment or peer assessment may again be used in this domain or they may be used in conjunction with each other. There may be a negotiation of the assessment with their peers, agreement needing to be reached. An example of this is presented in Chapter 14. Students negotiate criteria and then evaluate their own performance. They then meet in groups to compare marks and discuss how they were obtained.

In the emancipatory perspective, meta-level skills including critical reflection may be developed through a change in teaching to strategies which encourage students to question assumptions. Where competencies are concerned, criticism of the competencies themselves is a characteristic of this mode. Competency statements are viewed as attempts to make relatively stable statements of learning outcomes which are to be questioned through the practice of self-assessment. In the emancipatory conception, skills, knowledge and understanding, competencies and learning outcomes are often difficult to separate. In this knowledge interest dimension, students reflect critically on their work and they also reflect on the processes and procedures used to assess it. They may be encouraged to critique the standards which are applied to it. Self-assessment approaches where students radically change perspective exemplifies this third knowledge interest. Students not only construct meaning for themselves, they also come to a critical understanding of the way in which that is done. Some of the emancipatory examples use reflective writing for learners to focus on a particular learning experience and to form judgements about it.

In the emancipatory domain, discussions which take place are not about whether the student has met a set of negotiated criteria. Here the criteria and students' understanding of them develop as they proceed. Students do not simply accept the standards or a set of given competencies. They engage in a critique of them and this informs their judgements about their work. This critique may take place on their own but may often take place with peers. In the example by Paul Roach presented in Chapter 16, students negotiate criteria which they then apply to their work. Following this, they re-examine the criteria. Learning comes about through an iterative process where the criteria inform the assessment and then the assessment informs the student's understanding of the criteria and so on.

An example of self-assessment in the emancipatory interest from computer science can be found in Edwards (1989). Students perform tasks, set up their own competency standards and assess themselves. They then justify these to their tutor and may change their assessment or the criteria in the light of these discussions. Other examples of self-assessment in the emancipatory area can be found in Boud (1992, 1995a), Cowan (1988), Kramp and Humphreys (1993) and Moore and Hunter (1993). The emancipatory domain constitutes the ultimate in autonomous assessment, for here the students are engaged in critiquing the standards. Peer assessment is intimately tied to some form of self-assessment in this domain, since going beyond standards and criteria to critique earlier criteria inevitably involves individuals in changing their whole ideas of what constitutes acceptable work and hence how their own work relates to it.

Conclusion

Nightingale *et al.* (1996) suggest three principles for assessment:

- 'the choice of assessment method should allow reasonable judgements to be made about the extent to which the student has achieved the aims, objectives or intended outcomes of the educational program';
- it 'should support learning and not undermine it';
- there should be consistency between the aims and expected outcomes of the program of study; the teaching methods [used] to help students achieve these [and] the ways in which the outcomes will be assessed'.

(Nightingale *et al.* 1996: 10)

These principles draw attention to the very real need to put the learning of students first in designing assessment activities. The growing number of inventive cases of self-assessment and peer assessment where this is happening is encouraging.

There are many organizational arrangements in universities to support traditional assessment strategies, for example, administrative divisions responsible for examinations, the structure of the year with its exam boards, assessment timetables, and so on. Occasionally, an attempt has been made to shift an organizational framework or to set up a new structure for assessment. However, the introduction of self-assessment and peer assessment is frequently at the lecturer or course level, with tutors and course leaders often battling with conventional attitudes and constrained by traditional structures and procedures. There is an urgent need to redesign and at the very least to question the organizational structures in which ignorance and malpractice with regard to assessment can flourish (Warren Piper *et al.* 1996). Yet one of the greatest challenges for all staff is to introduce realistic and relevant assessment within current resource constraints or in the face of traditional attitudes.

In many examples of self-assessment or peer assessment, there is a move away from an emphasis on marking as the main assessing activity to managing and organizing a complex process (Boud 1995a). One of the barriers to the development of new forms of assessment is the need to invest time in developing and carrying out these new procedures. This makes many innovations initially costly to implement. Innovators who have the development of students' autonomy in learning as their major motivation are frequently faced by a departmental requirement to match the time and resource demands of traditional assessment. In such calculations, the hidden organizational costs of the latter (costs of examination halls, invigilation, and so on) are rarely taken into account. Shifting these costs to departments may be a first step to encouraging them to think about alternatives.

However, in spite of these difficulties, the use of self-assessment and peer assessment is crucial in the development of learning which is genuinely related to the development of life-long learners. Assessment and learning must increasingly be viewed as one and the same activity; assessment must become an integral part of the learning process. Assessors have a responsibility to take account of the broad range of abilities, knowledge, skills and competencies which are required of graduates; and to balance the requirements of the discipline with students' need to be prepared for the future. Encouraging the development of the skills of self-assessment and peer assessment are important in this context. The typology which has been presented here shows how different forms of self-assessment and peer assessment progressively develop autonomous assessment, including the skills of critical self-evaluation and of listening to, and responding to, feedback and an ability to sensitively assess and give feedback on the work of others.

Assessors also have a responsibility to take account of what is known about student learning and assessment in an academic context and to 'confront the ways in which assessment tends to undermine learning' (Boud 1995b: 35). They have a responsibility to recognize that as Rowntree (1987) reminds us, the actions of assessors can profoundly affect the lives of others. This means there is a need to have a greater awareness of what is being assessed and the effects of that assessment on student learning and teaching. There is a need to have an awareness of the ways in which assessment contributes to inequity. Introducing self-assessment and peer assessment demands the development of such awareness.

When teachers share with their students the process of assessment – giving up control, sharing power and leading students to take on the authority to assess themselves – the professional judgement of both is enhanced. Assessment becomes not something done to students. It becomes an activity done with students. We may yet be a long way from this vision. However, self-assessment and peer assessment are now becoming firmly established and they challenge us to think afresh our fundamental assumptions about what it means to assess the work of another person.

References

Boud, D. (1990) 'Assessment and the promotion of academic values'. *Studies in Higher Education*, 15(1), 101–11.

Boud, D. (1991) *Implementing Student Self-Assessment*, HERDSA Green Guide, 2nd edn. Sydney: Higher Education Research and Development Society of Australasia.

Boud, D. (1992) 'The use of self assessment schedules in negotiated learning'. *Studies in Higher Education*, 17(2), 185–200.

Boud, D. (1995a) *Enhancing Learning Through Self-Assessment*. London: Kogan Page.

Boud, D. (1995b) 'Assessment and learning: contradictory or complementary?' in P. Knight (ed.) *Assessment for Learning in Higher Education*, pp. 35–48. London: Kogan Page.

Boud, D. and Falchikov, N. (1989) 'Quantitative studies of student self assessment in higher education: a critical analysis of findings'. *Higher Education*, 18(5), 529–49.

Boud, D., Anderson, G., Cohen, R. and Sampson, J. (1997) 'Developing assessment for peer learning'. *Research and Development in Higher Education*, 20, 117–25.

Brew, A. (1995a) 'What is the scope of self-assessment?' in D. Boud (ed.) *Enhancing Learning Through Self-Assessment*, pp. 48–62. London: Kogan Page.

Brew, A. (1995b) 'Self-assessment in a variety of domains' in D. Boud (ed.) *Enhancing Learning Through Self Assessment*, pp. 129–54. London: Kogan Page.

Conway, R., Kember, D., Sivan, A. and Wu, M. (1993) 'Peer assessment of an individual's contribution to a group project'. *Assessment and Evaluation in Higher Education*, 18(1), 45–56.

Cowan, J. (1988) 'Struggling with student self assessment' in D. Boud (ed.) *Developing Student Autonomy in Learning*, 2nd edn, pp. 192–210. London: Kogan Page.

Edwards, R.M. (1989) 'An experiment in student self assessment'. *British Journal of Educational Technology*, 20(1), 5–10.

Falchikov, N. (1986) 'Product comparisons and process benefits of collaborative peer group and self assessments'. *Assessment and Evaluation in Higher Education*, 11(1), 146–65.

Falchikov, N. (1995) 'Peer feedback marking: developing peer assessment'. *Innovations in Education and Training International*, 32(2), 175–87.

Habermas, J. (1987) *Knowledge and Human Interests*, trans. J. Shapiro. London: Polity Press. [First published in German in 1968 by Suhrkamp Verlag.]

Hager, P., Gonczi, A. and Athanasou, J. (1994) 'General issues about assessment of competence'. *Assessment and Evaluation in Higher Education*, 19(1), 3–16.

Heron, J. (1988) 'Assessment revisited' in D. Boud (ed.) *Developing Student Autonomy in Learning*, 2nd edn. London: Kogan Page.

Kramp, M.K. and Humphreys, W.L. (1993) 'Narrative, self assessment and the reflective learner'. *College Teaching*, 41(3), 83–8.

Lyotard J.-F. (1993) *The Postmodern Condition: A Report on Knowledge*, translated from the French by G. Bennington and B. Massumi. Minneapolis, MN: University of Minneapolis Press.

Moore, W.S. and Hunter, S. (1993) 'Beyond "mildly interesting facts": student self-evaluations and outcomes assessment' in J. MacGregor (ed.) *Student Self-Evaluation: Fostering Reflective Learning. New Directions for Teaching and Learning*, No. 56, pp. 65–82. San Francisco, CA: Jossey-Bass.

Nightingale, P. and Magin, D. (1996) 'Designing, creating and performing' in P. Nightingale, I. Te Wiata, S. Toohey, G. Ryan, C. Hughes and D. Magin (1996) *Assessing Learning in Higher Education*, pp. 163–201. Kensington, NSW: University of New South Wales Press.

Nightingale, P., Te Wiata, I., Toohey, S., Ryan, G., Hughes, C. and Magin, D. (1996) *Assessing Learning in Higher Education*. Kensington, NSW: University of New South Wales Press.

Pastol, G. (1993) 'Turning a test into a learning situation'. *Methomix* [occasional publication of the Teaching Methods Unit. Rondebosch: University of Cape Town.] 15(1), 3–4.

Ramsden, P. (1992) *Learning to Teach in Higher Education*. London: Routledge.

Rowntree, D. (1987) *Assessing Students: How Shall We Know Them?* 2nd edn. London: Kogan Page.

Somervell, H. (1993) 'Issues in assessment enterprise and higher education: the case for self peer and collaborative assessment'. *Assessment and Evaluation in Higher Education*, 18(3), 221–33.

Warren Piper, D., Nulty, D.D. and O'Grady, G. (1996) *Examination Practices and Procedures in Australian Universities: Summary Report.* Higher Education Division DEETYA Evaluations and Investigations Program. Canberra: Australian Government Publishing Service.

14

Self-Assessment and Peer Assessment

Shirley Jordan

Introduction

This chapter will discuss the self-assessment and peer-assessment exercise developed at Thames Valley University in response to the learning object-ives and learning methods of the module 'Ethnography for Advanced Lan-guage Learners'.[1] Although this is a highly specific context and a module which presented its own particular problems in terms of assessment (such as the issue of how we might measure cultural learning), there are never-theless principles of general relevance to be drawn from our experience.

The first of these principles is that any form of self-assessment or peer assessment should grow out of the stated aims and objectives of the course for which it is being used, and that students should therefore be able to see clearly the rationale for adopting it. In other words, it is unlikely to work very well if it is artificially grafted on as a time-saving device. I therefore begin by explaining briefly the nature of the course, its pedagogic methods and its objectives, before going on to discuss the form of assessment which was devised.

Background

'Ethnography for Advanced Language Learners' was designed to provide students of foreign languages with a framework for intensive, interactive cultural research during their period of residence abroad. It introduces them to ethnographic research methods (e.g. participant observation, con-ducting ethnographic conversations and interviews, recording and analysing naturally occurring events) and anthropological and sociolinguistic concepts, in order that they may better understand and account for cultural processes both in their own and in their target culture. The module takes place in the second year of their degree course, prior to their period of residence abroad, and provides students with the experience necessary to conduct fieldwork and write an ethnographic project on an aspect of the local culture of their host country. Assessment of skills acquired during the module thus continues throughout the remainder of their degree course, with assessment of the period-abroad project, and a final-year project-based viva which further tests the knowledge, the cultural awareness, and the linguistic and research skills they have gained. Although discussion of assessment here is confined to the module itself, it is important to highlight the cumulative acquisition of skills and knowledge, and to point out that the self-assessment and peer-assessment exercise was introduced partly in order to raise student awareness of this process.

There are two types of assessment on this semester-long module. Students must produce a 'home ethnographic project', which is a study of an aspect of their own culture, and a pilot for the longer and more challenging project written in the foreign language when they are abroad. This final assessment counts for 60 per cent of the total mark for the module. The remaining 40 per cent comes from two self- and peer-assessment exercises which may be defined as continuous assessment, and which are closely related to learning methods.

The ethnography sessions are rarely lecture-based, relying instead upon the accomplishment of weekly fieldwork assignments in data collection and analysis. The results of these are brought to the class, analysed in small groups and compared with selected, relevant literature from social anthropology or sociolinguistics. The module, then, is largely experiential. The students learn by doing independent fieldwork, and learn as much from each other in group work and the subsequent plenary sessions as they do from the tutors. If sessions are to be successful, they require a high level of commitment and active participation from all class members, and an ability and willingness to function successfully in groups.

Tutors felt it was particularly crucial that students remain actively analytical about their classroom contribution, about what they were learning and how, and that the best way of ensuring this was not to base assessment solely on the final written piece. Hence our introduction of self-assessment and peer assessment, although we embarked upon it with reservations, partly because there is little here which students can judge quantitatively. As opposed to their experience as language learners, they find that in ethnography, where they are negotiating cultural interpretations, there are no 'right' or 'wrong' answers; nor is there any single correct way to carry out fieldwork assignments. Everyone comes to the class with different data which is not handed in or marked by lecturers. It is compared with that of other students, but not in order to establish which data is 'best'. In addition, being an effective member of the class does not necessarily mean demonstrating understanding. It can mean asking useful questions, being, as one student put it, 'up-front' about not having understood something, or discussing problems encountered when fieldwork did not run smoothly. Students are often reluctant to engage with such issues in class, since they persist in identifying them with weakness.

Finally, as has been suggested, some of the module's key learning objectives involve the honing of skills which students will need when doing fieldwork abroad. These skills involve not only the more mechanical ones, such as note-taking and indexing, but also the more nebulous, such as being a good observer and a good listener, conducting non-directive interviews, being receptive and helping others to clarify their ideas, being flexible, showing initiative, demonstrating empathy, reserving judgement about cultural differences and analysing reflexively where one's cultural interpretations may be coming from (for example, how one's own gender, ethnicity, age or cultural background may be partially responsible for them). How can we assess those slippery objectives which we could place under the broad headings of 'cultural awareness', 'social interaction' and 'personal development'? It is patently inappropriate to arrive at a final evaluation of something like 'empathy' and give students a mark for it. What we can evaluate, however, is students' commitment and participation in every aspect of the course.

Learning to see ethnographically is a lengthy, cumulative process. No last-minute cramming from books or course notes can compensate for a lack of regular fieldwork experience, or a lack of presence in the classroom and contribution to discussions. The self-assessment and peer assessment we decided upon was therefore process-oriented rather than outcome- or product-oriented. Tutors felt that this mode of assessment would encourage students to take responsibility for their own learning – increasingly important since class contact hours had been cut since modularization, and the course effectively made shorter, necessitating a greater amount of independent learning. We felt that self-assessment would also encourage students to assess the extent of their effort and the quality of their output throughout the course (as opposed to, for example, one single assignment), to consider how effectively they were accomplishing group work and contributing to classroom debate, and to turn the ethnographic eye on themselves, examining critically and reflexively their own behaviour as members of an interdependent group.

Implementation

Our own conviction of the worth of such a method was one thing, but we were aware that convincing students of its worth may be quite another. Our first step, therefore, was to negotiate with the class an appropriate set of criteria and an acceptable procedure, rather than devising and imposing these ourselves. In this way, students were led to consider what it would take from each of them to make the weekly sessions useful and we could clearly demonstrate that they were to judge each other on criteria they themselves had negotiated. The self-assessment form therefore functioned a little like a learner contract.

Criteria chosen by students ranged from the basic quantitative elements which are easy to assess (such as frequency of attendance or completion of assignments and readings), to the qualitative (such as effective group work).

In the first class, a ten-minute slot was given over to initiating group work. Students discussed in small groups what contributions might be required from each individual to make group work effective, breaking down the component skills, abilities and contributions which might make for a successful session. Their ideas were then fed back to the class and a decision was made as to which of these should be included as criteria. In terms of the procedure adopted, students also had their say, and, perhaps unsurprisingly, chose to have staff involved as a 'control' to validate marks in assessment tutorials.

The results of this process of negotiation can be seen in the self-assessment and peer-assessment form (Appendix 1) with which students declared themselves satisfied. The form was divided into sections covering attendance and preparation, assignments, readings, group work and class discussion, and finally an overall assessment of student contribution.

Given the inevitable teething problems which arise when students are first called upon to assess themselves or their peers, we decided to conduct two assessment exercises, each worth 20 per cent of the module marks in the hope that any problems might be ironed out by the second round. The first took place half-way into the course (in week 6) and the second at the end. They involved a three-part process:

- Each group member assesses her/his performance against a set of criteria and completes a self-assessment form, giving herself/himself an overall mark. This is done individually.
- The peer-assessment group (of four students) then meets with the following aims: to compare marks and discuss how they were arrived at; to modify or endorse overall marks. Forms are then handed into the tutors.
- Finally, there is an assessment tutorial with the tutors and peer group present. Tutors further discuss and ratify marks or encourage moderation of any grossly misjudged marks. Students (and of course tutors) must be prepared to justify their suggested marks at this meeting.

The latter two stages involved the move from private to public assessment. They were by far the most interesting stages and also the stages in which conflict was most likely to arise. The most obvious source of conflict was due to students' unrealistic (usually inflated) perception of the value of their own contribution. Dickinson (1987) in an investigation of self-assessment in language learning, asks two important questions related to this: 'Can learners make reasonable assessments of their own learning?' and 'Will they make accurate assessments?' He assumes that they can make reasonable assessments, but asks whether they can be trusted to be honest, or whether they will succumb to the temptation to cheat. Cheating here was not really an issue (although students have been known to sign the names of their absent friends on the attendance register). We were faced instead with students' inability to judge themselves objectively and with their inability, or refusal, to judge their peers objectively, or even to judge them at all! We encountered an obvious lack of appreciation of what a mark such as 80 per cent (or in one case 95 per cent) signifies. Also common was an inability to distinguish between effort and quality of output. Some students felt that the effort needed to do all the readings and overcome shyness to carry out the fieldwork assignments should be enough to obtain a high Upper Second-Class or First-Class Honours degree. Comments recorded from the first assessment tutorial illustrate this difficulty:

'I feel I have put so much effort into this course, so my contribution is definitely above average.'

'I have at times sat up to the early hours of the morning reading texts over and over to help me understand the contents.'

'When I was in class and not sick I would contribute 100 per cent, sometimes a bit less.'

A further problem was that peer groups sometimes avoided engaging in debate and found it easier simply to endorse marks by signing everyone's form whatever the mark they had allocated themselves. When marks were modified, students tended to raise, but not to lower them, the rather unsurprising result being that assessment groups awarded each other marks in the same class (usually Upper Second) rather than attempting to differentiate between performances. For example, one group of students of very mixed ability and very different levels of commitment and contribution came out with 60, 60, 62 and 60 per cent.

In the first exercise, the marks for the whole cohort were as follows:

Moderation	First	Upper Second	Lower Second	Third	Fail
Before moderation	1	15	3	2	1
After moderation	0	11	7	3	1

Although they were set up informally, the first assessment tutorials were often difficult, even painful events. They required careful preparation and sensitive handling on the part of tutors, with discussion of problem cases beforehand. They were the control mechanism which prevented students from awarding each other 80 per cent across the board, but it was also crucial that students did not come away with the idea that we were in any case going to impose our own marks, which would have invalidated the exercise. There were particular tactics we used to encourage students to re-enter the debate about how their marks were arrived at, and persuade them to approach the exercise with appropriate reflexivity and objectivity. It helped, for example, to remind them of the following: that the self-assessment procedure was in itself a valuable ethnographic exercise in self-observation; that they were not being asked to be personally critical of anybody, but to be objective and that in terms of transferable skills, the process was a useful one (for example, going for promotion and proving they are worth it; doing jobs which involve evaluation of others; organizing team work, and so on).

For the second round of assessments, we decided to modify the form, and it is the second version which is shown here. It differs from our 'pilot' version in three significant ways: firstly, the form now comes along with a rationale, reminding students of what they are doing, why, and how to go about it. Secondly, under each heading, ample space is now left for comment and reflection. Students are also reminded of the type of questions they should be asking themselves (e.g. 'Did I prepare readings in advance of the class?' 'Did I prepare them so that I could comment on them in class?' 'Did I then react to questions in class quickly and meaningfully?'). Finally, there is also a brief explanation of the classification system (e.g. 40–49 per cent = poor, but a pass, whereas 70–80 per cent = excellent in every way, both the effort made and the quality of output).

The second exercise, conducted at the end of the module, ran far more smoothly than we had anticipated. Students were more confident about how to approach it. They felt more comfortable about engaging in open discussions of each other's performances, and commented usefully on the difficulties and responsibilities which they had experienced in the first exercise of being a student assessor. Tutors seldom needed to intervene, since students took control and were less passive. We found it unnecessary to modify any of the suggested marks, peer groups having determined at least their own classifications with what we felt was a high degree of accuracy. They were able to explain how these marks were arrived at through negotiation and demonstrated some maturity in analysing the differences in the performances of individuals between this and the previous exercise. They were also able to make some illuminating statements about the value of self-assessment:

'You've got to know how to judge yourself: it's a skill everyone has to learn.'

'It's good for everyone to think about their strengths and weaknesses.'

'If people had peers judge them more, there wouldn't be such a stigma about being personal.'

'It makes you work harder during the term because you know you've got to judge yourself. You're not accountable in the same way on other courses.'

'It is definitely worthwhile. It makes you think about what you've done in the course. It makes people like X realise how important things like attendance are.'

'It is to do with taking responsibility for yourself.'

Particularly gratifying here was the understanding that the ability to self-assess is in itself a skill – one which students will need to exercise continuously when doing fieldwork as well as in many other contexts. We were also pleased to find confirmation that this form of assessment helps to increase motivation throughout, and that having one assessment half-way through the course and one at the end allows self-monitoring in the interim, where deficiencies detected in the first round can be worked upon before the second. Students also seemed to appreciate the exercise as a valuable educational objective in its own right – a part of learning how to learn, and beneficial even when it is problematic.

Conclusion

We concluded that, although students clearly find self-assessment and peer assessment more personally challenging than conventional forms of assessment, it can be successful from their point of view, provided that the rationale for implementing it is clear, and that the criteria and process are at least in part student-generated.

From the staff perspective, the advantages are that students share the responsibility of assessment and remain aware throughout of precisely what is required of them. Since the peer-assessment groups are established in the early stages of the course, there is more of a team effort throughout. Students are more aware of each other's contributions to group work and are more democratic about sharing the opportunity to present the findings of the group in plenary sessions. In other words, the exercise helps to bring out the more reticent students and tones down those who tend to dominate.

The only disadvantage concerns the practicalities of organizing such an exercise outside class contact time, although this probably takes no more time than marking a batch of essays. It is also a refreshing alternative for staff, more challenging that the impersonal norm of taking in a piece of work and handing it back with a few comments. We have, I believe, had the pleasure of getting to know our ethnography students better than any other group owing to the methods of teaching and assessment adopted.

Note

1. The module 'Ethnography for Advanced Language Learners' is the result of a research and curriculum development project, 'Cultural Studies in Advanced Language Learning', funded by the Economic and Social Research Council for the period 1990–3. The project team was: Dr Ana Barro, Professor Michael Byram, Hanns Grimm, Dr Shirley Jordan, Celia Roberts, Professor Brian Street. Self-assessment and peer assessment were introduced by Hanns Grimm and Shirley Jordan in 1993.

Reference

Dickinson, L. (1987) *Self-Instruction in Language Learning*, p. 150. Cambridge: Cambridge University Press.

Appendix 1

ALS II ETHNOGRAPHY   SELF-ASSESSMENT GUIDELINES

To be handed in to the Course Office by [date]

Name:..

Please complete this form and comment in detail in all the spaces provided.

CONTRIBUTION TO THE COURSE: WHY SELF-ASSESSMENT?

The Ethnography course relies on the commitment and active participation of every member of the class for its success. We value all your ideas and perceptions; they are at the heart of the course. The self-assessment exercise described below reflects the nature of the course, which encourages you to examine critically some 'familiar' aspects of everyday life – including, in this case, your own behaviour as an ethnography student, a member of and contributor to an interdependent group.

You will be asked to complete two self-assessment forms during the course, and will be expected to discuss your own assessment with three other members of the class and have it validated by them.

40 per cent of the total course mark is an assessment of your own preparation and contribution to the effectiveness of the course. Consider how you have contributed to the course sessions. For each of the criteria listed below, comment on how you think you have performed. Note that what we are looking for is self-critical awareness, so do not exaggerate your strengths or your limitations.

When you have written-up your report, arrange to meet with the other three members of your assessment group and discuss in detail your own assessment of your contribution. Then, if necessary, modify your own assessment in the light of the discussion and get it endorsed by the other members of the group.

1   Attendance and preparation
1.1 Attendance record
     It is difficult to contribute if you are not actually there. So you need to think about your attendance record. Did you attend always/usually/rarely?

     ....

     ....

     ....

     ....

1.2 Assignments: fieldwork
     Did you (always/usually/rarely) do the assignments? Assess the quality of your work on the assignments. Did you take notes as suggested? Did you analyse your observations sufficiently and write them up coherently before the class? How much effort did you put into them?

....

....

....

....

1.3 Assignments: readings
Did you always read the texts in advance of the class? Did you prepare them in such a way that you could comment on them and react to questions in class quickly and meaningfully?

....

....

....

....

2   Group work and discussions in class
What contribution did you make to the discussions in groups/pairs?

2.1 Contribution to group discussion
Consider the quality of your contribution to the groups and class. To what extent did you contribute information and ideas?

....

....

....

....

2.2 Receptiveness to others
How receptive were you to the ideas of others? To what extent did you allow others to contribute and listen to what they had to say?

....

....

....

....

2.3 Effort and initiative
How much effort did you make? Were you just sitting there letting yourself be entertained by the others, or worse, encouraging others to go off at a tangent?

Did you take the initiative when you felt the discussion was going off course? Did you volunteer to report back from groups in the plenary sessions?

....

....

....

....

3   Class diaries
How often did you volunteer to do a class diary? How much effort did you make to provide us with useful feedback to improve the course?

....

....

....

....

4   Overall assessment of your contribution
How much effort have you put into it? How often did you ask questions if something wasn't clear to you? How much did you contribute to effective use of class time by responding quickly rather than waiting for someone else to do/say something? To what extent did you encourage others to contribute? Do you think the course was a better one for the contribution you made?
We are aware that many students invest a great deal of time on the readings and carry out assignments which they find personally challenging. Remember, however, that your overall mark does not only reflect the efforts you have made, but also the quality of your output.

....

....

....

....

5   Any other comments you would like to add?

....

....

....

....

6   Now give yourself an overall mark according to the following classification:

    70–80%   excellent in every way (effort made and quality of output)
    60–69%   very good, well above average
    50–59%   reasonably good, average
    40–49%   poor, but a pass
    30–39%   not good enough, a fail

7   Assessment group meeting
Allow about one hour for your meeting. Start with everybody reading everybody else's form. You might find it helpful initially to consider which class (e.g. 60s/50s) is appropriate for each individual. You can then refine this in your subsequent discussion. Both your own and the group's agreed mark should be on the form. Remember, we are not asking you to be personally critical, but to give careful and objective assessments of each other's contribution. Consider this an ethnographic exercise in personal and group reflexivity.

8   Your own suggested mark: .... %

Mark agreed by assessment group: .... %

Signed (1)   ....

Signed (2)   ....

Signed (3)   ....

Signed (4)   ....

Final mark agreed with tutors: .... %

9   Tutor comment:

15

Peer Assessment of Undergraduate Seminar Presentations: Motivations, Reflection and Future Directions

Andy Lapham and Ray Webster

Introduction

This chapter describes and discusses the introduction of peer-assessed seminar presentations as an element of the overall assessment on a level 3 (Year 3) module, part of the BSc (Hons) Information Management programme, at Thames Valley University. The module, Systems Analysis Methodologies, forms part of the compulsory element of the Business Information Technology pathway of the programme and is undertaken by approximately 60 students each academic year. The module builds on material introduced at levels 1 and 2, where students also experience group work and presentations. It considers some of the many issues in systems analysis today and how contemporary methodologies attempt to address those issues. Students are encouraged to form their own opinions on the latest developments in systems analysis, and are assessed on their critical abilities to compare and evaluate the different methodologies available to systems development professionals.

Previous module and assessment structure

In the years prior to the changes outlined in this chapter, learning on the module was supported by weekly one-hour key lectures from tutors, a variety of two-hour seminars including those presented by students and the availability of drop-in surgery sessions on a one-to-one basis with tutors.[1]

Assessment was through a three-hour end-of-module examination (50 per cent weighting), together with the submission of a written seminar paper

(25 per cent) and the presentation of that paper to a seminar of around 16 students (25 per cent). The report was expected to be no more than 2500 words long. The presentation took the form of a 20–25-minute talk, followed by the instigation of a relevant group activity as learning support for 10–15 minutes. Seminar titles were chosen by students from a list offered by tutors at the beginning of the module and were designed to support and broaden the syllabus areas covered by the lecture programme. Seminars were tutor observed and marked based on a standard marking schedule devised and modified over the three years that the module had operated. Informal peer feedback was sought for each presentation, based on an idea from Gibbs and Habeshaw (1989), although the presentation mark did not contribute to the grade.

Student evaluation of the module takes place towards the end of the semester, using a questionnaire designed to elicit open, discursive comments from students. Evaluation in previous years has shown that students see the module as relevant and important, in that it provides a backdrop for consolidating and contextualizing the learning that has previously taken place on other modules. Students generally feel that the seminar paper and presentation are demanding but useful. They also recognize the opportunities to practise transferable skills, in particular, those necessary for the preparation, presentation and communication of information to peers.

Motivation for changes

In response to student feedback and tutor experience, the structure and delivery of the module has been modified prior to each new delivery. Tutors felt it was time to consider something more than incremental change. National policy and institutional pressure for more cost-effective learning was driving up seminar group size, while at the same time increasing the demands on tutor time. As a consequence, the majority of the seminar input now came from assessed student presentations. It became apparent that either the structure of the module or the assessment method had to change.

Tutors felt that the existing method and mix of assessment were appropriate. The examination was felt to provide a reasonably effective means of measuring individual knowledge of the subject, but encouraged surface learning. The seminar paper encouraged deep learning and provided students with an opportunity to practise some of the skills identified by the Enterprise in Higher Education Initiative as being valuable to employers. This is a view shared with, for example, the MacFarlane Report on Teaching and Learning in an Expanding Higher Education System (Committee of Scottish University Principals 1992). It was felt that restructuring the delivery of the module to encourage students to take more responsibility for their own learning would free time for tutorial sessions to support the lecture programme. Previously, these had been integrated with the seminar sessions, but the increase in group sizes and the number of presentations had constrained this area. If the student seminar groups were to be charged with organizing and assessing their own presentations, it would enable a significant amount of tutor time to be shifted from passively observing and assessing student presentations to the active facilitation of tutorials while maintaining the benefits of the assessment method.

The new structure

The new structure of the module consisted of a weekly lecture programme as before: two-hour seminars used mainly for student-assessment presentations which the tutors largely did not attend; weekly one-hour tutorial sessions supporting the lecture programme where students were asked to prepare in advance questions and tasks for discussion at the tutorial; and, as before, the availability of the drop-in surgery sessions.

The peer-assessment process

First attempt – Cohort 1

On receiving the list of available paper titles, each student seminar group assumed the responsibility of allocating seminar topics. Seminars in the first four weeks consisted of exercises designed and run by tutors for the purpose of preparing for the task of assessment in addition to that of presentation. Topics covered included: the marking scheme to be used; marking standards in the overall context of the degree programme; and practice presentation and marking. The remaining seminars were organized by students, presented by students and assessed by students. Tutors did 'drop in' at times, particularly in the early stages of the process and were also available to sit in on a presentation if specifically requested to do so by the presenter, but they took no part in the seminar. Quality control over the process was implemented through the appointment of a student as administrator for each seminar, and the recording on audio tape of each presentation. The availability of this tape to tutors also facilitated a comparison of the presentation and the submitted paper at a later date.

Assessment was based on a marking scheme which had evolved from that used in previous years. The mark awarded for a presentation was calculated as the mean mark awarded by the group after the highest and lowest mark in the range were eliminated. Tutors maintained the right to adjust marks after listening to each tape recording and considering the range of marks given by the group members. The role of the student administrator was to assist the presenter by ensuring the smooth running of the seminar through the execution of various tasks. These included, among others, distribution of marking sheets, collection and operation of the tape recorder and the collation and handing in of the marking sheets and tape to the tutor. Each member of the group administered one seminar.

The mark allocation for the presentation was reduced to 20 per cent of the overall module mark and each seminar group was asked to devise criteria for the allocation of the remaining 5 per cent to individuals for their contribution to seminars. Students were asked to reflect on their own presentation by completing a marking sheet, which, while not counting in the marking process, was handed to tutors for comparative purposes. In addition to the normal student evaluation at the end of the module, all students were asked to complete a questionnaire aimed specifically at assessing their attitude to the peer-assessment process.

Amendments – Cohort 2

In light of student evaluation and feedback from presentations to colleagues, a number of changes were made for the next cohort of students. There was a general feeling that the exercise was asking too much of the students. They were being asked to assess the presentational skills of the presenter, the academic content of the presentation and the merits of innovative group activities. The recording of each session, with the tutors listening to each recording at a later date, was also considered too onerous and unnecessary in terms of quality control. Consequently, the major changes were:

- presentations would be assessed only on the form of the presentation and related skills
- the group activity was removed from the assessment
- the presentations would not be recorded.

The first two changes required alterations to the assessment sheet and the evaluation questionnaire to reflect these alterations. Once again, the first four weeks of the two-hour seminar sessions were devoted to developing a good understanding of the overall process. The initial short (5 minute) presentations by all students and the selected longer presentations were particularly useful for discussion and feedback.

Results from student questionnaire

The student evaluation questionnaire was designed to elicit their attitudes to the peer-assessment exercise. Ten questions asked students to rate various aspects of the exercise and, where applicable, to suggest improvements. These aspects were: preparation and training; the mark sheet; presentation as assessment; peer assessment as assessment; the tutors' right to change marks; and the use of audience involvement as part of the seminar presentation. A five-point scale was used for each question, five being strongly positive, one being strongly negative. In addition, students were asked two open questions eliciting perceived benefits and negative effects of the process to them as individuals and as a group.

The observations below are based on 34 returned questionnaires out of 55 from Cohort 1 and 52 returned questionnaires out of 56 from Cohort 2.

Quantitative data collected
Cohort 1 percentages are shown first unless indicated otherwise.

- Preparation and training. Both cohorts considered the preparation and training to be sufficient or better (88 and 85 per cent). A larger percentage of Cohort 2 (79 per cent) than Cohort 1 (59 per cent) found the training sessions fairly or very useful.
- Design of mark sheet. The design of the mark sheet was considered to be fairly or very helpful by both cohorts (58 and 69 per cent).
- Presentation as assessment. A consistent percentage (70 and 71 per cent) regarded the presentation to be a fairly or very appropriate form of assessment.
- Peer group assessment as assessment. The percentage considering this form of assessment to be inappropriate declined from 38 to 10 per cent.
- Tutors' ability to change peer mark. The number agreeing with this possibility declined from 64 to 40 per cent.

Qualitative data collected
Student perceptions of the benefits and negative effects of the peer-assessment exercise, as indicated by responses to the open questions, are given below. They were present in both cohorts except where indicated.

Benefits of the peer-assessment exercise

For the individual

- It provided valuable practice in presenting and assessing leading to increased confidence.
- Assessing other presentations helped reflect on characteristics of a good presentation.
- Doing the presentation gave students a better understanding of subject matter as assessing a presentation helped increase concentration (Cohort 1).
- It gave a sense of control and a say in the module.
- The absence of a tutor produced a more relaxing seminar (Cohort 2).

For the group

- It gave the group identity through a common cause and through discussions on the exercise outside the seminars.
- The experience developed group support for the individual.
- It improved the group's ability to work together.
- It improved attendance at seminars as group members felt a responsibility to attend (Cohort 1).
- It gave good experience of a range of views and approaches (Cohort 2).

Negative effects of the peer-assessment exercise

For the individual

- Prejudice, favouritism, friendships and ethnic division led to collaboration over marks and mark-fixing.
- It proved difficult to mark objectively.
- Students indicated a fear of marking inappropriately because of lack of knowledge of subject matter (Cohort 1).
- It was difficult to see past the form of the presentation, therefore more technical subjects sometimes were marked less well (Cohort 1).
- Students felt unable to grade fellow students with a Fail grade because of feared retaliation (Cohort 1).
- The lack of tutor presence tended to decrease the pressure to perform well (Cohort 2).

For the group

- Marks awarded became progressively lower through the semester as marking ability improved.
- Interest in the process, and therefore the appropriateness, of the marks tailed off towards the end of the semester, particularly after the Christmas vacation.
- A few group members did not take the process seriously, which led to a knock-on effect in the group.
- Collaboration and mark-fixing led to divisions in the group.

The concern over perceived bias and degeneration of group conduct was mentioned very frequently by Cohort 2. In total, 21 of the 27 who expressed concern referred to collaboration, bias or a lack of seriousness in approaching the exercise.

Other observations

Marks for individual contribution
Each of the four seminar groups in both cohorts decided that attendance would be the sole criterion for allocating up to 5 marks (5 per cent) for contribution to seminars.

Tutor adjustment of marks
In 14 cases of Cohort 1, marks were adjusted by tutors on the basis of the audio tape. In 12 of these cases, the marks were lowered, primarily because the length of presentation varied considerably from that required. The failure of peer assessors to recognize the importance of the length of a presentation appeared to be a major weakness in the marking process. This suggested that assessors concentrated on form and interest and failed to

consider that the content of a substantially shorter (up to 50 per cent) presentation would affect the depth of content.

Discussion

A primary motivation for changing the form of assessment was to try to maintain the prevailing assessment procedures in the face of increasing student numbers. In addition, it was felt that handing over control of part of the assessment process to the students would be beneficial. Some previous studies have indicated that student peer assessment can be a useful approach in maintaining quality in the prevailing environment of increasing group sizes and pressure to increase productivity (see, for example, Oldfield and MacAlpine 1995). One problem is that, while the mean marks given by different groups were often consistent with the tutors' mark, the range of marks awarded by the student group often showed a large variation. This is consistent with other findings (Hughes and Large 1993) and can also be the case when different tutors mark the same piece of work (Atkins *et al.* 1993). It remains a cause for concern, especially when the problem continues after a considerable amount of training and discussion.

One of the aims of the exercise was to allow the overall module structure and assessment procedures to remain relatively unchanged. The shifting of some of the responsibility for assessment to student groups allowed resources to be shifted to a lecture-based tutorial. With Cohort 1, a considerable amount of time went into listening to the presentation recordings and comparing the presentations to the reports. This led to the adjustment of some of the presentation marks. Ultimately, it was felt that this unnecessarily increased the demands on tutors' time. Consequently, tutors decided that the tape recording of the presentations as a quality-control measure would be dropped for Cohort 2. While there was some student concern over the possibility of bias in the student survey responses from Cohort 1, this increased significantly in the responses from Cohort 2. It is possible that the removal of some of the quality-control measures had a direct effect on student perceptions of their responsibilities in the new situation.

Stefani (1994) discusses some of the concerns of lecturers and tutors with regards to handing over more power and control of the assessment process to students, the major concern being the possibility of the marks awarded differing from those awarded by tutors. The effect of the changes for Cohort 2 indicates that there could be cause for concern here. This is certainly indicated in the student survey responses. On the other hand, there were several positive aspects to the students experience. Of the 45 out of 52 respondents who completed the personal benefits' section of the survey, the majority reported increased confidence and improved presentation and assessment skills.

Over both years, there was consistent feedback indicating that students felt the peer-assessment process helped groups to work together more effectively and helped individuals to understand the assessment process more fully. In the second year of the exercise, 79 per cent of the respondents felt that the training sessions were either fairly or very useful as against 59 per cent in the previous year. Similarly, 57 per cent of the respondents in the second year felt that peer assessment was a fairly or very appropriate form of assessment as against 38 per cent of Cohort 1. The percentage of respondents either disagreeing or strongly disagreeing with the idea that tutors should be able to change the peer assessed mark increased from 21 to 31 per cent.

Future directions

The general feeling of tutors and students is that the peer-assessment process used in this module has been successful in promoting student learning and making better use of tutor time. The process is continually developing and more detailed evaluation and analysis continues in order to inform developments for future cohorts. There is also potential for the development of a closely controlled study to examine the effects of the different modes of assessment and the different methods of quality control.

Note

1. Evaluation questionnaires and data collected from previous cohorts are available from either of the authors on request.

References

Atkins, M.J., Beattie, J. and Dockrell, W.B. (1993) *Assessment Issues in Higher Education.* London: Department of Employment.

CSUP (1992) *Teaching and Learning in an Expanding Higher Education System: Report of a working party of the Committee of Scottish University Principals.* Edinburgh: CSUP.

Gibbs, G. and Habeshaw, T. (1989) *Preparing to Teach.* Bristol: Technical and Educational Services.

Hughes, I.E. and Large, B.J. (1993) 'Staff and peer-group assessment of oral communication skills'. *Studies in Higher Education,* 18(3), 379–85.

Oldfield, K.A. and MacAlpine, J.M.K. (1995) 'Peer and self-assessment at tertiary level – an experiential report'. *Assessment and Evaluation in Higher Education,* 20(1), 125–32.

Stefani, L.A.J. (1994) 'Peer, self and tutor assessment: relative reliabilities'. *Studies in Higher Education,* 19(1), 69–75.

16

Using Peer Assessment and Self-Assessment for the First Time

Paul Roach

Introduction

The case study detailed in this chapter outlines the experiences I had in my first encounter with any form of assessment other than tutor-based. Despite assurances from colleagues that the outcome of the use of a combination of peer assessment and self-assessment is generally that the students end up with lower marks than a tutor would have awarded them, my expectation was that the reverse would be true. In the case described, my fears were realized, but further consideration of this outcome revealed much to me about my own attitudes towards assessment, and revealed flaws in my implementation of the assessment exercise, arising in particular from my use of peer assessment. In this account, I describe the assessment exercise and attempt to outline the flaws in implementation. I also offer proposals for an improved means of implementing it in the future.

As part of an introductory taught module on basic information technology and communication skills, students are to improve their skills in the presentation of information. One specific aim of the module is to give students experience of group presentations and to direct them towards good practices. The exercise is assessed to provide grades (Fail, Pass, Merit, Distinction) for certain Business and Technical Education Council (BTEC) common skills areas for the students (concerned with the presentation of information, working in teams, and oral and non-verbal communication). In the case described here, two classes were involved: 26 first-year Higher National Diploma (HND) Mathematics and Computing students, and 17 first-year HND Business Decision Analysis students.

In general, many of the students taking the module are not well motivated and make little effort in many parts of it, including the group presentations. Some means of involving them more in this important exercise was required. I attempted to make them feel that they had more control over the process by incorporating peer assessment and self-assessment into the overall assessment strategy. My original conception allowed for the moderation of these peer and self-assessments by tutor assessment where I felt necessary – that is, the final judgement would be mine. This attitude changed later, as will be described below.

An account of this exercise, along with an analysis of it, was offered as a module towards my own postgraduate Certificate in Educational Development.

Setting up the exercise

The chosen steps for the running of the exercise were designed to allow student control over the process and to ensure that reflection would be built in. The steps were as follows.

- Class construction of criteria and standards for assessment. Students in each of the classes were to suggest and formulate ideas for the eventual construction of assessment forms (involving students in the process of identifying criteria and standards was intended as a method of allowing students to learn more from the exercise, as others have suggested, e.g. Race 1991).
- Student selection of topics for the presentation and student self-selection of the groups which were to give the presentations.
- Group preparation of materials for the presentations.
- Group presentations and the peer assessment of them. During each group performance, the other students in the class were asked to fill in peer-assessment forms on the performance of the group as a whole and of the individual members of the group.
- Self-assessment. Immediately after giving the presentations, the students were to fill in self-assessment forms on their performance during the presentation and or delivery of the material.
- Individual reflection. The students were given a period in which to reflect on the experiences of the presentation and on the completed peer assessment and self-assessment forms.
- 'Post-mortem' group discussions. Each group was to meet with me, firstly to discuss the criteria and standards of the assessment, and secondly, through group discussion and consideration of the peer-assessment and self-assessment forms, the individual students were required to arrive at their own grades (Fail, Pass, Merit and Distinction) for each of the three common skills areas being assessed.

The students were informed of the above steps before the start of the exercise.

As a final note, rather than just foist the use of non-tutor assessment on the students, as something entirely separate from the rest of the taught module, I thought it best to integrate it into the taught module. As a means of familiarizing the students with the concept and execution of self-assessment through the use of forms, I chose a test (the Belbin test; Belbin 1981). This allowed the students to fill in assessment forms in accordance with their perceptions of aspects of their own characters and abilities, in a slightly humorous manner. The results of these tests were not to be shown to me. (It seemed inappropriate at such an early stage of the students' courses to attempt peer assessment; not having worked much with each other, they still had little knowledge of their classmates, and might rightly have felt such assessment to be uninformed and potentially undiplomatic! They would be better able to perform peer assessments further into the course, during the presentations themselves.)

Letting go of ownership

As described above, some control over the exercise was already to be given to the students in allowing them the choice of subject matter for the presentation and by involving them in identifying the criteria of assessment. However, it had not initially occurred to me that I might relinquish yet more of the ownership of the assessment exercise. When I considered documented case studies of peer and self assessment exercises (Boyd and Cowan 1985; Edwards 1989; Edwards 1991) and discussed these with colleagues, problems with my original scheme for the assessment became clear. That scheme relied on tutor assessment to moderate 'wayward' grades, invalidating any claims I might make of using true peer assessment and self-assessment. If I was to take this approach at all, I would have to embrace it whole-heartedly. With some trepidation, I removed all traces of tutor assessment from the exercise, and informed the students that they would have full control over the grades awarded for the presentations. (I did, however, keep my own notes on their performances, so that I would later be able privately to compare my marks with their marks, but these notes were not brought into any stage of the assessment process.)

It is worth noting the reactions of the students at that stage: only one student expressed alarm at having to take responsibility for assessment. Many others jokingly expressed the opinion that it offered the opportunity to award themselves and others high marks.

To further reinforce the students' perception of ownership of the exercise, I made it clear to them that they would retain the completed peer- and self-assessment forms relating to their work. At no time would they be under any obligation to give them, or even show them, to me. In fact I actively refused to look at them at any stage. In that way I hoped that they would believe that I had no intention of altering the grades they eventually were to award themselves.

The students' work

Before considering the award of grades and the outcomes of this exercise, I offer a little detail on the events of the exercise in order to highlight issues which are key to the outcomes.

Student discussions on criteria of assessment

In one lecture, I attempted to identify both good and bad practices for giving presentations, and in further tutorials I encouraged the students to put forward suggestions for criteria by which presentations might be judged. The students were initially reluctant to offer any criteria. It became necessary for me to point them towards some important areas, but the actual choice of specific criteria was left to them. This led to class discussions on which criteria were most appropriate, with the aim of laying down some idea of standards in each of the criteria. These standards were then loosely related to the Fail, Pass, Merit and Distinction grades which were eventually to be awarded. The students were free to choose any method of associating measures with these standards, but both classes seemed to favour the award of a numerical value in a fixed scale.

Lastly, I encouraged the students to consider who would be in the best position to judge the standards attained during their presentations in each of their chosen criteria. This was so that the criteria could be divided into separate assessment forms which I later produced in accordance with the students' choices. It is here that I guided the students most; I felt that three forms for the exercise (peer assessment of an individual's performance, peer assessment of a group and a self-assessment form for each member of a group) were required to adequately assess the common skills to be tested. The actual forms were produced by me, but were checked for approval by the students.

Student self-selection of groups and selection of topics

Attempting to organize students to choose their own topics and organize themselves into groups inevitably took far more time than would have been needed for me to perform both tasks for them. But I had hoped that this process would lead to the students working on areas that interested them, so increasing their motivation.

A great variety of topics were suggested (from 'racism' and 'rape' to 'the evils of chocolate' and 'a brief history of Manchester United') but when it came to deciding on the topic for presentation, most groups opted for 'safe' and uncontroversial topics. Despite this, the choice of some topics seemed to allow some of the group members to identify certain aspects of their own lifestyles which were of particular importance to them. This would seem to justify the decision to allow groups to choose their own topics. Pleasingly, of those who remained on the course, the majority demonstrated a great commitment at least by the deadline for presentation, and most a good deal earlier.

The presentations, the 'post-mortem' discussions and the award of grades

Most groups acquitted themselves well and put an unexpectedly large amount of effort into their presentations. Following the presentations, each group took all their assessment forms to consider (in their own time) the opinions of their peers. At pre-arranged times, each group came to a 'post-mortem' meeting with me at which their experiences and final self-assessed grades were discussed. The only condition I had set down for the final assessment to take place (that all the assessment forms were to be brought to the discussion), was met by all groups. These meetings were the first occasions on which I had any idea of the marks awarded on the self- and peer-assessment forms, and even then, as I had decided not to look at any of their forms, I knew only what the students chose to tell me, that is, the final grades they arrived at for themselves and any reasoning they offered on how they arrived at those grades.

I began each session by asking the group present to identify standards for the award of Fail, Pass, Merit and Distinction in each of three areas being tested by the presentations – oral and non-verbal communication, presenting information in a variety of forms, team work. This, I hoped, would constrain any tendency to be overgenerous in the remainder of the discussion.

All the students were very reluctant to award themselves marks and many wanted to hand me the forms so that I would come to a decision based on them – which I would not! But only one student expressed strongly negative views about the use of peer assessment and self-assessment. That student indicated a belief that the exercise would result in being awarded a lower mark than would have been awarded by me. (Unfortunately the student seemed unable or unwilling to articulate exactly why that should be the case.) All other students seemed willing to accept the framework of the assessment exercise.

An analysis of the marks the students awarded themselves, based largely on the opinions of their peers, is offered below.

The grades awarded

The marks the students awarded themselves were generally higher than I had expected them to be, and certainly higher than those I would have awarded. Figure 16.1 shows the percentages of students in the classes having

grade	Fail	Pass	Merit	Distinction
students' award	0%	12.90%	47.31%	39.78%
my award	2.15%	48.38%	26.88%	22.58%

Figure 16.1 Percentage award of grades awarded for the presentations by the students, and which would have been awarded for the presentations by me.

grade	Fail	Pass	Merit	Distinction
coursework	2.90%	55.07%	34.78%	7.25%

Figure 16.2 Percentage award of grades for other assessments by me.

awarded themselves grades of Fail, Pass, Merit and Distinction. It also shows the awards which I would have made, based on the notes I took during the presentations. It is worth noting that out of the 93 common skills grades awarded, in only two cases did the award differ by as much as two grade points from my own, only one was lower – by one grade point – and 40 did not differ at all. However, it is my conviction that the standard of work was generally higher than that produced for the other assignments of this taught module. Figure 16.2 shows the percentages of students attaining grades of Fail, Pass, Merit and Distinction in other entirely tutor-assessed assignments for the same taught module; my own assessment of the presentations, shown in Figure 16.1, makes clear the higher proportion of Merits and Distinctions than I awarded in these other assessments. This higher standard might be explained in part by the opportunity the students had to display some degree of individuality (owing to the student selection of topics). But I do not think that this alone is a sufficient explanation of the high marks.

My initial thought was that the cause of the problem I perceived was the use (or perhaps careless use) of the peer assessments of the presentations. Having deliberately avoided seeing any of the forms before these discussions, I had absolutely no idea of the sorts of marks the students had awarded each other. Some of the students told me that on their peer-assessment forms, marks of 7 out of 10 were common, and seemed to be awarded for what I had considered to be competent (if somewhat lack-lustre) performances. Seemingly, a good performance could expect many nines and even a few tens. Thus, despite a rough agreement at the start of each 'post-mortem' group discussion of what would constitute a Pass, Merit and Distinction, the high marks on the peer-assessment forms themselves were equated to high grades – that is, the forms were used to justify many apparently overgenerous final awards.

Although I am sure that the peer-assessment forms were used to justify high marks, this is not to say that the marks were necessarily undeserved. After further thought, it occurred to me that I might have made a mistake in appraising the assessment exercise by assuming that the grades awarded were to reflect only the perceived quality of the presentations. As the students were assessing their own performances, the grade awarded would reflect their perceptions of the value of their own experiences. These experiences include those of teamwork in which they were involved (and I most certainly was not). The view of this revised consideration is echoed in the following:

> [Higher marks] could be interpreted either as an indicator of successful learning or of slack marking.
>
> (Edwards 1989: 9)

If the intention of the exercise was for the students to learn from the experiences of preparing, giving and assessing the presentations, they may have more fairly assessed the work they put in and what they had gained than I was at first prepared to concede. Nevertheless, it still seems necessary for the use of peer assessment to be tightened up, as I discuss in the next section.

Lessons learnt and proposed changes

Problems occurred in the setting of standards and the use of somewhat artificial quantification of performances, producing peer assessments which could be used as justification for high self-assessments. So poor setting of standards and poor understanding of how numerical peer-assessment scores related to the quality of performances and grades led to misleading and oversimplified self-assessments in the reflection stage, even before the 'post-mortem' meetings.

Not having overseen a directly comparable exercise in students' presentations marked by tutor assessment, the exercise I performed had no 'control' with which to compare the standard of work. I was not able to ascertain any improvement in the quality of the work as a result of this means of assessment.

In order to use peer assessment and self-assessment for marking presentations in the future, a number of changes will have to be made:

- It will be necessary to ensure that the marks awarded in peer assessment accurately reflect performance.
- More care must be taken over constructing the rules for assessment. The idea of allowing students to construct the criteria for assessment still seems valid, but it would also be necessary to encourage the students to lay down clearer standards for the quality of the various aspects of assessment, i.e. clearer definitions of what would constitute a Pass, Merit and Distinction in each area. (Although this was done for each individual group prior to the award of marks, it was not done sufficiently rigorously prior to the peer assessment of the presentations.)
- Lastly, more follow-up exercises to continue the reflection stage would be helpful. It seems clear to me that the exercise will only be genuinely

worthwhile if more is done to integrate it into the taught module. In particular, there is a clear need to produce follow-up material which builds on the student's experiences of giving the presentations. (Part of this might be done by setting an assignment which requires students' experiences to be expressed in some way.)

The experience of using peer assessment and self-assessment has given me confidence that the approach is worthwhile. However, it is clear that the process of refinement and development has some way to go before I am fully satisfied with its implementation.

References

Belbin, R.M. (1981) *Management Teams: Why They Succeed or Fail.* London: Heinemann.

Boyd, H. and Cowan, J. (1985) 'A case for self-assessment based on recent studies of student learning'. *Assessment and Evaluation in Higher Education*, 10(3), 225–35.

Edwards, R. (1989) 'An experiment in student self-assessment'. *British Journal of Educational Technology*, 20(1), 5–10.

Edwards, R. and Sutton, A. (1991) 'A practical approach to student-centred learning'. *British Journal of Educational Technology*, 23(1), 4–20.

Race, P. (1991) 'Learning through assessing' in S. Brown and P. Dove (eds) *Self and Peer Assessment*, SCED Paper 63. Birmingham, Standing Conference on Educational Development.

Appendix: Sample student-devised assessment forms

There was a great deal of correspondence between the sets of forms arrived at by the two groups of students, and so only one set is presented here, but it is worth noting that the paths by which the criteria and standards were arrived at were very different for the two groups.

Assessing Group: _____

10 ——→ 1

Presenting Information
variety   sufficient ——— too few
OHP
   clarity   clear ——— unclear
   layout   good ——— bad
Blackboard
   clarity   clear ——— unclear
Handouts
   content   relevant ——— irrelevant
   layout   good ——— bad
Video
   content   relevant ——— irrelevant
   use   sufficient ——— too much

Content of Presentation
content   relevant ——— irrelevant
clarity   good ——— bad
pace   well paced ——— poorly paced
interest value   entertaining ——— dull

Teamwork
coordination   good ——— bad
workload   equal ——— unequal

Assessing Group:

5 4 3 2 1

Visual aids
variety   sufficient ☐☐☐☐☐ too few

OHP Transparencies
clarity   clear ☐☐☐☐☐ unclear
amount on slide   sufficient ☐☐☐☐☐ too much

Blackboard
clarity   clear ☐☐☐☐☐ unclear

Handouts
clarity   clear ☐☐☐☐☐ unclear
content   relevant ☐☐☐☐☐ irrelevant

Content of presentation
vocabulary   broad ☐☐☐☐☐ narrow
interesting   very ☐☐☐☐☐ dull
detail   relevant ☐☐☐☐☐ irrelevant
topic knowledge   sufficient ☐☐☐☐☐ insufficient

Teamwork
workload   equal ☐☐☐☐☐ unequal
coordination   good ☐☐☐☐☐ bad

Assessing an individual

Voice 10 ←→ 1

clarity of speech clear ——— unclear

intonation varied ——— monotonous

Non-verbal communication

gestures sufficient ——— too many

eye contact plenty ——— too much/little

Name: Group:

Assessing an individual

Voice

	5	4	3	2	1	
clarity	good	□	□	□	□	□ bad
volume	good	□	□	□	□	□ bad
intonation	good	□	□	□	□	□ bad

Non-verbal communication

| gestures | sufficient □□□□□ too many |
| eye contact | sufficient □□□□□ too many |

Name: Group:

Self-assessment

Name: Group:

Team Work

cooperation with   10 ←——→ 1
team   good ——— poor

Contribution

visual aids   a lot ——— nothing

eye contact   a lot ——— nothing

presentation   a lot ——— nothing

Self-assessment

Name: Group:

Team Work

                                5 4 3 2 1
workload   equal ☐☐☐☐☐ unequal

Individual Contribution

                              -2 -1 0 1 2
gathering   little ☐☐☐☐☐ a lot
information

the presentation   little ☐☐☐☐☐ a lot

preparation of   little ☐☐☐☐☐ a lot
visual aids

structuring   little ☐☐☐☐☐ a lot
the talk

Conclusion

Assessment does matter: it matters to students whose awards are defined by the outcomes of the assessment process; it matters to those who employ the graduates of degree and diploma programmes; and it matters to those who do assessing. Ensuring that assessment is fair, accurate and comprehensive – and yet manageable for those doing it – is a major challenge. It is a challenge which has been grappled with by many, as several of these chapters have recorded but one which, however, often has to be tackled in relative isolation. Despite the fact that there is a considerable body of international research about assessment and related issues, we experiment largely in ignorance of the way others have effected positive change, and we have limited opportunity to learn from the lessons of others.

Attending conferences is one way of finding out how others are tackling the challenges of changing curricula and changing contexts and of sharing good practice. A number of the chapters in this book arose from a conference held in April 1996 on 'Innovations in Student Assessment'. Attending that conference were over one hundred academics, many of whom had experience of trying to innovate – some more successfully than others. Internationally, there are many conferences and seminars for higher education teachers to develop their thinking about assessment, including in the UK the Northumbria Assessment conference organized annually by the University of Northumbria at Newcastle and events organized by the Staff and Educational Development Association (SEDA), Higher Education for Capability (HEC), the Society for Research into Higher Education (SRHE), the Oxford Centre for Staff and Learning Development (OCSLD) and the Open University. Events organized by the Higher Education Research and Development Society of Australia (HERDSA) and in the USA, the conferences of the American Association of Higher Education Professors, the American Assessment in Higher Education (AAHE) conference and Alverno College seminars, perform similar functions of enabling academics to think carefully about assessment issues, as do the myriad of other national and international conferences which focus on evaluation of student performance.

We can also learn a great deal from the literature in the field. In each country we have our own research literature on assessment (in the UK for example, the ASSHE Inventory (1996) provides a unique account of changing assessment practices in Scottish Higher Education) as well as there being innumerable texts which explore the practices and processes of assessment in higher education, both traditional and innovatory (see the References in each chapter of this volume). Nevertheless, we recognize that there is a need for further continuing research to enable us to continually improve and enhance assessment.

In the UK, as we wait to see the precise shape of the Institute of Learning and Teaching in Higher Education which has been given a remit for the development and accreditation of teachers in higher education, there are other network sources which can provide the advice and guidance. For example, the Higher Education Funding Council for England (HEFCE) established a Fund for the Development of Teaching and Learning in 1996 to stimulate developments in teaching and learning. A number of the projects which have been funded are concerned with computer-based software or other assessment systems. Others are associated with building a network (at national level within a single subject or significantly across several subjects) in order to identify and disseminate good assessment practice. There are projects concerned with the assessment of key transferable and employment-related skills, with peer assessment and the assessment of group work.

The longer-standing Teaching and Learning Technology Programme (TLTP) has funded a number of projects associated with innovative assessment methods, using information technologies to streamline assessment in ways that would have been inconceivable before multiple-choice and other forms of selected response assessments could be processed by computer. The art of computer-based assessment is still in its infancy, but new developments with optical character recognition enabling text to be scanned and 'read' by computers is likely to further change the ways in which we grade and evaluate student performance.

Those seeking to address the gap between their assessment strategies and the learning of their students do not have to embark upon the journey to measure innovation alone. However, academics need to ensure not only that they continuously evaluate the diverse traditional and novel methods by which they currently assess in order to ensure that they fit the bill, but also to ensure that the outcomes of such review are shared across the assessment community, to enable all to select and use appropriate instruments and strategies for assessment.

Reference

The ASSHE Inventory (1996) *Changing Assessment Practices in Scottish Higher Education*. The Centre for Teaching and Learning, Edinburgh University with the University and Colleges Staff Development Association (UCoSDA), Edinburgh.

Index

The Society for Research into Higher Education

The Society for Research into Higher Education exists to stimulate and coordinate research into all aspects of higher education. It aims to improve the quality of higher education through the encouragement of debate and publication on issues of policy, on the organization and management of higher education institutions, and on the curriculum and teaching methods.

The Society's income is derived from subscriptions, sales of its books and journals, conference fees and grants. It receives no subsidies, and is wholly independent. Its individual members include teachers, researchers, managers and students. Its corporate members are institutions of higher education, research institutes, professional, industrial and governmental bodies. Members are not only from the UK, but from elsewhere in Europe, from America, Canada and Australasia, and it regards its international work as among its most important activities.

Under the imprint *SRHE & Open University Press*, the Society is a specialist publisher of research, having over 70 titles in print. The Editorial Board of the Society's Imprint seeks authoritative research or study in the above fields. It offers competitive royalties, a highly recognizable format in both hardback and paperback and the worldwide reputation of the Open University Press.

The Society also publishes *Studies in Higher Education* (three times a year), which is mainly concerned with academic issues, *Higher Education Quarterly* (formerly *Universities Quarterly*), mainly concerned with policy issues, *Research into Higher Education Abstracts* (three times a year), and *SRHE News* (four times a year).

The Society holds a major annual conference in December, jointly with an institution of higher education. In 1995 the topic was 'The Changing University' at Heriot-Watt University in Edinburgh. In 1996 it was 'Working in Higher Education' at University of Wales, Cardiff and in 1997, 'Beyond the First Degree' at the University of Warwick. The 1998 conference was on the topic of globalization at the University of Lancaster.

The Society's committees, study groups and networks are run by the members. The networks at present include:

Access	Mentoring
Curriculum Development	Vocational Qualifications
Disability	Postgraduate Issues
Eastern European	Quality
Funding	Quantitative Studies
Legal Education	Student Development

Benefits to members

Individual

Individual members receive

- *SRHE News*, the Society's publications list, conference details and other material included in mailings.
- Greatly reduced rates for *Studies in Higher Education* and *Higher Education Quarterly*.
- A 35 per cent discount on all SRHE & Open University Press publications.
- Free copies of the Precedings – commissioned papers on the theme of the Annual Conference.
- Free copies of *Research into Higher Education Abstracts*.
- Reduced rates for the annual conference.
- Extensive contacts and scope for facilitating initiatives.
- Free copies of the *Register of Members' Research Interests*.
- Membership of the Society's networks.

Corporate

Corporate members receive:

- Benefits of individual members, plus.
- Free copies of *Studies in Higher Education*.
- Unlimited copies of the Society's publications at reduced rates.
- Reduced rates for the annual conference.
- The right to submit applications for the Society's research grants.
- The right to use the Society's facility for supplying statistical HESA data for purposes of research.

Membership details: SRHE, 3 Devonshire Street, London W1N 2BA, UK. Tel: 0171 637 2766. Fax: 0171 637 2781. email:srhe@mailbox.ulcc.ac.uk
World Wide Web:http:/ /www.srhe.ac.uk./srhe/
Catalogue: SRHE & Open University Press, Celtic Court, 22 Ballmoor, Buckingham MK18 1XW. Tel: 01280 823388. Fax: 01280 823233. email:enquiries@openup.co.uk